LESSONS AND LEGACIES II

LESSONS AND LEGACIES II

Teaching the Holocaust
in a Changing World

Edited and with an
Introduction by Donald G. Schilling

NORTHWESTERN   UNIVERSITY PRESS   EVANSTON,   ILLINOIS

Northwestern University Press
Evanston, Illinois 60208-4210

Printed in the United States of America

ISBN 0-8101-1562-X (cloth)
ISBN 0-8101-1563-8 (paper)

The paper used in this publication meets the minimum requirements of the
American National Standard for Information Sciences—Permanence of Paper for
Printed Library Materials, ANSI Z39.48-1984.

In memory of
Arthur D. Malkin, March 16, 1913–April 19, 1990
and
Perle S. Malkin, August 7, 1912–December 5, 1983
by their sons, Judd, Cary, and Robert Malkin

Contents

Acknowledgments

An earlier version of Michael Marrus's essay appeared in *Perspectives: American Historical Association Newsletter* 31, no. 5 (May/June 1993): 1, 6–12. A subsequent version of Christopher Browning's essay will be appearing in *The Holocaust and History: The Known, the Unknown, the Disputed, and the Re-Examined,* to be published by Indiana University Press in 1998. An earlier version of Judith Tydor Baumel's essay appeared in *Women: A Cultural Review* 7, no. 2 (Fall 1996): 114–24. An earlier version of Lawrence Baron's essay appeared in *Shofar: An Interdisciplinary Journal of Jewish Studies* 10, no. 2 (Winter 1992): 97–107.

Theodore Zev Weiss

Foreword

THIS IS THE SECOND VOLUME OF SCHOLARLY PAPERS THAT IS BEING published as an outgrowth of the Lessons and Legacies conferences that the Holocaust Educational Foundation sponsors in partnership with major centers of higher learning. As with its predecessor, Lessons and Legacies I, published in 1991, our partner is Northwestern University, and we are pleased to acknowledge the help of its academic officers, as well as the conference co-chairs, Professors Peter Hayes of Northwestern University and Christopher Browning of Pacific Lutheran University. These conferences sponsored by the foundation have become an ongoing tradition. The two Northwestern University conferences of 1990 and 1992 have now been followed by others at Dartmouth College in 1994 and Notre Dame University in 1996. Volumes from the latter two conferences are in preparation.

The success of the Lessons and Legacies conferences is only one of the areas in which the work of the Holocaust Educational Foundation has made gratifying strides in recent years. The number of colleges and universities teaching courses on the Holocaust with the foundation's help has grown from twenty at the beginning of this decade to over two hundred. Moreover, the foundation has established the biannual Summer Seminar Trip to Holocaust sites in Central and Eastern Europe, enabling, to date, some one hundred scholars who teach courses on the Holocaust to acquaint themselves on an immediate basis with the "topography of terror" that the Nazi regime established. Finally, by establishing the annual Summer Institute on Holocaust and Jewish Civilization held at Northwestern University, the foundation has begun a program of educating current and future college and university professors about the history, faith, and culture of the Jewish people who were targeted by Nazism for extinction. All of these efforts have brought us into ever more fulfilling contact with a growing "family" of decent and dedicated academicians who share our conviction that learning remains the best antidote to humanity's most inhumane impulses.

I want to take this opportunity to express my deep gratitude to the board members who have contributed so generously to the foundation's work and who made all this possible.

My personal thanks and appreciation to Professors Peter Hayes and Christopher Browning, and to all the scholars who participated and contributed so greatly to the success of the Lessons and Legacies conference.

Finally, as always, my strongest sense of gratitude is to my wife, Alice, and my children, Danny and Deborah, who have encouraged the work of the Foundation at every juncture, and replenished my energies at every step.

LESSONS AND LEGACIES II

Donald G. Schilling

Introduction

THE PHONE CALL WAS TOTALLY UNEXPECTED THAT MARCH MORNING in 1991. The voice, tired and unfamiliar, came directly to the point: "I'm Theodore Weiss of the Holocaust Educational Foundation and I'd like to talk with you about the possibility of offering a course on the Holocaust." A month later Theodore Weiss was in my office at Denison, telling me about the work of the foundation and how it would support my preparations to teach the course, should I be interested. Was I interested? As a historian of modern Europe with an emphasis on German history, I had included some material on the Holocaust in appropriate courses; the topic raised profound questions for me as a historian and a human being and invariably engaged my students—but to devote a whole semester to it seemed problematic, in four main ways.

The first problem was epistemological. Could the Holocaust be comprehended? A brief perusal of the issue suggested the difficulty. Almost a half-century before, Allied forces had confronted the horror of the Holocaust as they overran camps teeming with the human remnants of forced labor and mass destruction. The impact was shattering to soldiers in the midst of a brutal war's final phase, seeking to make sense of unimaginable barbarism. Many would share the judgment of American journalist Percy Knauth that "Buchenwald is beyond all comprehension. You just can't understand it, even when you've seen it."[1] The passage of time has seemingly not removed this problem. Arno Mayer, writing in 1988, asserts, "At bottom the Judeocide remains as incomprehensible to me today as five years ago, when I set out to study and rethink it,"[2] while Elie Wiesel, one of the most articulate and passionate commentators on the Holocaust, has consistently argued its unknowableness: "The Holocaust? The ultimate event, the ultimate mystery, never to be comprehended or transmitted."[3] When I read his statement that "facts, on which historians base their research, are only facts, whereas survivors reveal the truth," my unease grew.[4] How could I presume to attempt to bring comprehension to students for whom the Holocaust is part of the remote past? I could deal with the Holocaust superficially in a broader survey course where the expectations for understanding were minimal, but in a course wholly devoted to it the problem could not be skirted.

Second, I worried about the emotional costs of teaching the Holocaust. Searing, raw, profoundly disturbing, Holocaust literature is among the most affecting material I have ever encountered. Reading it has aroused in me frustration, anger, despair, and sadness that could not be erased by testimony of courage, sacrifice, and the resilience of the human spirit. Serious study of the Holocaust had the potential to destroy faith in God and humanity. How could I cope with the demands of facing this subject on a regular basis? If I were not torn apart by this material, would I gradually become indifferent to it? I could not lightly brush aside the warning of Philip Hallie: "My study of evil incarnate had become a prison whose bars were my bitterness toward the violent, and whose walls were my horrified indifference to slow murder. Between the bars and the walls I revolved like a madman. Reading about the damned I was damned myself, as damned as the murderers, and as damned as their victims."[5]

Third, had my training as a German historian prepared me adequately for teaching the Holocaust? Although I was well versed in the nature of Nazism, the Nazi state, and basic elements of anti-Jewish policy, I knew less of the history of the Jewish community in Europe, especially Eastern Europe, or that of other victim groups. Further, while the course could legitimately be set in a historical framework, the subject seemed to demand an interdisciplinary approach. Some of the best materials were literary, not historical. Important issues required the insights of the psychologist, the theologian, and the philosopher. In teaching the Holocaust I would quickly find myself operating outside my areas of expertise.

Fourth, given the magnitude and sensitivity of the subject, I questioned whether I had the aptitudes and skills necessary to make the course worthy of it. Again, Wiesel has starkly framed the issue:

"I don't think a university can teach history without including the Holocaust, but how can you grade papers on that? It is still a sacred area for me. When it is taught, it shouldn't be 101 Holocaust. It should be a life-changing experience."[6] Why should I set myself up for failure to realize the potential of this course, I asked myself, when I had many others to teach that did not carry such daunting expectations?

I had good reasons, then, for saying no to Zev Weiss; and yet, in the end, that was not the answer I gave. He applied no pressure—just offered to help prepare me for the task—but his very persona and his obvious commitment to Holocaust education moved me to take the first step in what has become a journey of unparalleled personal and academic significance for me. In taking this journey I have joined many others (over two hundred fifty teachers sponsored by the Holocaust Educational Foundation alone) who have also come to offer courses on the Holocaust. I suspect that many of them, like me, have found only partial answers to the problems posed above and have learned to live with paradox.[7] It is true that aspects of the Holocaust remain incomprehensible, requiring humility of all who wrestle with its troubling questions. However, I am at least partially reassured by Peter Hayes's eloquent introduction to the first volume of *Lessons and Legacies,* where he advances four cogent arguments "for challenging the incomprehensibility of the Holocaust,"[8] and by Michael Marrus's compelling claim in this volume that "Holocaust history has become one of the most sophisticated and methodologically self-conscious fields of historical study."

There is no doubt that teaching the Holocaust involves an emotional cost—against which I partially protect myself by offering the course every other year—but there are also the compensating rewards of gaining, if painfully, greater self-knowledge and of having a major impact on students, for some even life-changing. No other course I teach inspires end-of-semester comments such as these:

> This is the most interesting, most intense course that I've taken at Denison. A student can't just slip through this course without having his/her personal morality system defined, questioned, and redefined.

> The course was excellent. I have learned so much, and it has really helped to increase my awareness of certain issues—the morality of human behavior in the Holocaust, the nature of man, etc.

The Holocaust course was a powerful journey into the past and into our own minds and hearts.

As teachers and scholars, we are probably best equipped to address the third problem, that of insufficient background knowledge. If nothing else, we are trained to learn. In addition to our own reading and research, the opportunities provided by the Holocaust Educational Foundation—the Lessons and Legacies conferences, travel seminars in Eastern and Central Europe, and the Institute on the Holocaust and Jewish Civilization at Northwestern University—go a long way toward filling the gaps and making us more effective teachers.

The second Lessons and Legacies conference, held in Northbrook, Illinois, and sponsored by Northwestern University and the Holocaust Educational Foundation, in the fall of 1992, was especially important in this regard, for it explicitly addressed the formidable tasks of teaching the Holocaust. In the scheduled presentations and in animated conversations, conference participants engaged issues from the theoretical to the practical that confronted them as committed Holocaust educators. This volume grew out of that event. Those who pore over these pages will find much to nourish the scholar and teacher of the Holocaust.

These revised conference papers are grouped into three sections: "Issues," "Resources," and "Applications." In their totality these essays not only speak directly to the four concerns that kept me from teaching a Holocaust course for most of my career; they also illustrate the reciprocal relationship between excellent teaching and scholarship.

In part I, "Issues," the lead essay by Michael Marrus emphasizes the growing maturity of Holocaust studies as a field. Some scholars oppose this process of change, fearing that the subject will lose its power and uniqueness. Marrus, however, argues that in historians' pursuit of the normal activities of definition, the framing of questions, historiographical debate, the use of evidence, and comparative analysis, Holocaust history has become "a remarkably complex, advanced field of historical inquiry and needs no other reason than that to command the close attention of scholars and students." Granting Marrus's essential point, it is still the case, as Gerhard Weinberg incisively makes clear in the following chapter, that scholars and teachers of the Holocaust can have their vision limited by the blinders imposed by the field. Weinberg exposes "the fairly common tendency to write, talk, and teach about the Holocaust and about World War II as separate and only barely related events," and by contrast illustrates the benefits of looking "at the war and at the Holocaust in . . . interconnected ways." The three remaining essays in this section are narrower in compass, but each raises vital issues and provides essential information for the teacher of the Holocaust. Those by Christopher Browning and Allan Fenigstein address the difficult issue of explaining the perpetrators' behavior, a subject that recently received fresh attention thanks to the best-selling but much-criticized book *Hitler's Willing Executioners: Ordinary Germans and the Holocaust,* by Daniel Jonah Goldhagen. The ongoing debate between Browning and Goldhagen over whether the killers on the ground were essentially motivated by "a unique and particular German antisemitism," a position Goldhagen espouses and Browning rejects, is strikingly illustrated by Browning's lucid essay here. Approaching the question as a social psychologist, Fenigstein challenges the explanatory value of constructs that focus on the perpetrators as individuals (such as Adorno's "authoritarian personality" or Milgram's "situational influences"). He instead suggests that social identity theory, as framed by Henri Tajfel, is best able to account for their behavior, since it analyzes "the actions of individuals *qua* group members." In addition to examining in detail various psychological paradigms, Fenigstein engages the work of both Browning and Goldhagen by bringing together theory and empirical evidence. In the last essay in part I, Dina Porat explores a vital but much-neglected subject: processes of decision-making within Jewish communities during the Holocaust. After considering four illuminating cases, she concludes that despite the unprecedented nature of those years' events, "decisions were made on the basis of factors that had guided decision-making during former, relatively quiet periods."

Given the broad, interdisciplinary nature of the Holocaust as a field of study, many teachers will benefit from the selections in part II of this volume, most of which combine analysis of resources in a particular area with discussion of their classroom use. Judith Tydor Baumel opens the section with a rich historiographical study analyzing the work on gender and the family written in the half-century since the war. She not only identifies and explains the patterns of publication in this area but also provides an extensive set of references in her notes. If Baumel examines survivor literature through the frame of gender, Dan Laor uses the frame of the survivor in Israel to explore the contributions to Holocaust literature of four seminal figures: Abba Kovner, Ka.Tzetnik, Aharon Appelfeld, and Dan Pagis. In so doing he provides the background, including the Israeli context, and the critical commentary essential for anyone using these authors' work. While victims and perpetrators have long been central to the study of the Holocaust, it is only recently that scholars have paid significant attention to bystanders or rescuers. Lawrence Baron's critical review of the psychosocial research on rescuers, with emphasis on their motivation, introduces the growing body of literature in this field, with suggestions on how to use it in a Holocaust course. Similarly, Judith Doneson offers her judgments about a number of films that might be screened in Holocaust courses. These follow her consideration of the problems of representing the Holocaust on film and her provocative reading of *Europa, Europa,* which she employs as a case study to remind educators who use film that "they must be informed not only about the history of the Holocaust, about stereotypes and images, but also about the language of film."

While the writers in parts I and II make connections between content and teaching, their primary focus is on content. In part III the emphasis is on teaching. In the first of these selections, two educators with substantial experience discuss their Holocaust course and the implications of teaching in this field. While many Holocaust educators ground their courses in a particular discipline, Marshall Lee and Michael Steele examine the benefits of an interdisciplinary course, rooted in both history and literature. The interplay of historical and literary texts and materials is subtly explored, but Lee and Steele also discuss, with sensitivity and insight, the affective aspects of the students' encounter with the Holocaust. This is rugged terrain, and they honestly confront the rewards and liabilities of moving into it. In the volume's concluding chapter, the setting for education moves from the classroom to the public arena as the goal of enlightenment is linked with those of commemoration and memorialization. Reuven Hammer, who has been at the forefront of developing ways to commemorate the Holocaust, persuasively argues that commemoration is "a legitimate part of Holocaust studies." Through his richly informed discussion of its purposes and methods, Hammer establishes the context for a more profound understanding of Holocaust commemoration. Appropriately, he reminds us that the scholar's work is not limited to the classroom but "is of central importance to the process of the commemoration of the Holocaust." These two final selections affirm that for committed educators there are many ways to teach the Holocaust effectively, and each will have its particular challenges.

For decades following 1945, the task of Holocaust education fell essentially on the shoulders of survivors. There were few institutional structures or formal courses through which to carry out the work. Now as the generation of survivors, of necessity, passes on this responsibility, growing numbers of other people and institutions have committed themselves to Holocaust education. This is encouraging, but the formidable task should not be underestimated. We cannot speak with the survivor's voice of experience, and yet we must face denial and indifference, as well as the subtler dangers accompanying success and institutionalization. If, however, as we hope, these essays are indicative of the health of the field, then we have grounds for optimism about our ability to teach the Holocaust in a changing world.

I. I · S · S · U · E · S

Michael R. Marrus

Good History and Teaching the Holocaust

THE OTHER DAY I PICKED UP A BOOK THAT WAS WAITING FOR ME AT the University of Toronto Library's interlibrary loan desk. My interlibrary request was *Voluntary Hostages of the S.S.,* by Drago Arsenijevic, a well-written, journalistic account of the rescue activity of the International Red Cross during the last phases of the Holocaust. The work rests upon solid research, and while it is a bit too uncritical for my taste, I think it provides a worthwhile look at a neglected subject: the last phase of the ordeal of European Jewry. It is a good book. But the cover, at least of the volume I received, is appalling. It is blood red, with black letters, framed in gold. Emblazoned on the front is a stylized Nazi eagle, grasping in its claws a black disk, ringed in gold, on which shines forth a large, golden swastika.[1]

It may well be that this ghastly Nazi motif comes not from Arsenijevic's Swiss publisher but rather from an overly imaginative worker in some library bindery, who turned a benign paperback into an offensively covered hardback. Or it may be that this is just a publisher's egregious lapse of taste and judgment. What I want to consider for just a moment, however, is not the source of the cover design but rather my experience on picking up the book. For this is a good starting point for my reflections on university teaching of the Holocaust, a theme that may have wider implications for us all.

I think the librarian who handed me the book was suspicious. "Clearly it's no accident we don't have books like this in *our* collection," I imagined her thinking. "Who is this fellow," she might have continued, "and what is he doing with this stuff anyway?" I turned the book over quickly and left the office. At the periodicals desk, where I had another transaction, another librarian commented on what clearly appeared to be a Nazi tract, which now bore the green interlibrary loan flag. "We keep those books in a special section," she told me in a low voice, without any preliminary discussion. "And it's a good thing, too, because otherwise the students would *take* them—as has certainly happened in the past." Now it was my turn to be suspicious. Just what did she mean by saying students *take* such books? Were these Jewish students objecting to the presence of Nazi works in the collection, or to their classification as nonfiction? (We have had such protests at the University of Toronto, I might add.) Or were these Nazi sympathizers, "liberating" works of their own canon from the liberal-bourgeois, Jewish-dominated university? And which side was the librarian criticizing? Not having the patience to pursue this issue, and preoccupied with my hunt for periodicals, I pressed on without seeking any answers.

The point I draw from this story is that the topic of this essay, university teaching of the Holocaust, is not quite a "normal" one, for even book jackets can raise disturbing questions, set people on edge, and (almost certainly unnecessarily) put them on guard against each other. Researching and teaching the Holocaust is not quite like researching and teaching anything else. And yet for all of that, I have argued that Holocaust history is on a path of "normalization," that it is gradually entering the mainstream of historical understanding.[2] Particularly over the past two decades, when the historical literature has grown substantially, an entire new field has been created—one in which historians of other fields will immediately feel at home with the sources, methodology, and investigatory agendas with which specialists in the subject spend their time. So in what concrete ways does Holocaust history still stand out, and has this had any effect on the kind of scholarship students encounter?

I want to suggest that Holocaust history remains special in a way that is not commonly discussed. For a variety of reasons, among them the fact that this is an emotionally charged topic, Holocaust history has become one of the most sophisticated and methodologically self-conscious fields of historical study. The questions historians put to it tend to be broad rather than narrow, and require the making of distinctions that are frequently avoided in other fields of study. Far from having to apologize for cutting corners, for making concessions to the nearness of the event, or for deferring to nonprofessional considerations, Holocaust history has become exemplary in the demands that it makes upon researchers, teachers, and students alike. And the results are impressive, not only for those who seek historical understanding of the destruction of the European Jews but for plenty of curious onlookers from other historical fields as well. Quite apart from the moral imperatives that are usually advanced for inclusion in the curriculum, these particular qualities constitute additional reasons to champion the study of the Holocaust.

Let me begin with definitions—the troublesome intellectual distinctions that preoccupy so many other disciplines but which historians seem to evade or treat perfunctorily on the way to what they do best, formulating descriptions. Definitions stalk Holocaust history, and in many cases they are essential prerequisites for study. Without them, one could hardly begin. To start, what do we mean by "Holocaust"? Does the term itself obscure, by virtue of its etymological origins?[3] Are we better served by "Shoah," as Claude Lanzman and many others insist, or "Judeocide," as Arno Mayer argues, or a variant of *"le génocide des Juifs,"* as French scholars prefer? Does "the Holocaust" include the persecution and massacre of other groups beside Jews, as Simon Wiesenthal, among others, has suggested? And when does it begin? In 1933, with the coming to power of Nazism? In 1938, as was said at the fiftieth anniversary of the *Kristallnacht* riots in Germany? In 1941, with the beginning of mass killings in the Soviet Union? In 1942, with the Wannsee Conference and the functioning of death camps in Poland? Answers to such questions rest on definitions, and these depend in turn on a careful sifting of the evidence and a coherent assessment of it. The process of definition itself, spurred by the urgency many feel to press one case or the other, helps to clarify historical argument.

    Another example of how Holocaust historians are forced to define is the much-discussed issue of Jewish resistance. Jews first defined "resistance" during the events themselves, when the mainly young, mainly Bundist or Zionist youth who championed armed uprisings in the ghettos of Poland and the Soviet Union charged that their fellow Jews were going to their deaths "like sheep to the slaughter." In the view of these youthful zealots, there was only one honorable response to the Nazis for people in their position: violent attack upon their oppressors, notwithstanding the terrible consequences to themselves and their fellow Jews. In practical terms, the Jewish revolt that they urged was to be suicidal—and even worse, in the eyes of many, it would trigger an immediate, furious retaliation against other Jews who had managed, against all odds, to survive to that point. But the activists' eyes were on history, on people like ourselves. "What will posterity say about us if we go to our death without any attempt at resistance?" some of the earliest organizers of revolt in the Warsaw ghetto asked an elder of the Jewish Council. "The Jews of the world, the succeeding generations, will be ashamed of us; they will believe that we . . . were meek, devoid of any sense of honor, and this will depress them. We want to act in a manner which will serve them as an example and a testament of valor."[4]

Raul Hilberg, the dean of Holocaust historians, argued strenuously in his 1961 *Destruction of the European Jews* that traditional patterns of Jewish life militated against this kind of response, and indeed conditioned Jews to comply with their murderers. The Jews' "reaction pattern," he wrote, was "characterized by almost complete lack of resistance." Its relative insignificance was demonstrated in terms of German casualties: "It is doubtful that the Germans and their collaborators lost more than a few hundred men, dead and wounded, in the course of the destruction process. The number of men who dropped out because of disease, nervous breakdowns, or court martial proceedings was probably greater. The Jewish resistance effort could not seriously impede or retard the progress of destructive operations. The Germans brushed that resistance aside as a minor obstacle, and in the totality of the destruction process it was of no consequence."[5] Three decades later, Hilberg qualified his views somewhat. In *Perpetrators, Victims, Bystanders,* he acknowledges the heroic disposition of a small number of youthful resisters who took up arms against crushing odds. But importantly, he considers them among the "unadjusted," those who refused to conform to the general pattern of "accommodation" to the Nazis and their demands.[6] Resistance, in his perspective—what Hilberg defines as "pitting oneself against the oppressor"—remains the resistance of the young idealists who challenged the Warsaw Jewish Council.[7]

Another approach is to consider as "resistance" all of those efforts, as Israeli historian Yehuda Bauer puts it, to keep "body and soul together" under circumstances of unimaginable privation and brutalization.[8] Such efforts include smuggling, ministering to the weak and the ill, cultural organization, and a tenacious commitment to communal values. Historians who have looked closely at the experience of Jews facing Nazi persecution, at ghetto life, or even at the camps in which Jews met their end, have testified to a considerable range of such activity, often of the most heroic kind. Those for whom the concept of resistance extends to such behavior emphasize the Nazis' intention to humiliate the Jews, to extinguish their spirit as well as their lives. Resistance, to them, includes any and all efforts to oppose the Nazis by maintaining Jewish dignity and social cohesion. From this perspective, Warsaw resisters must include not only Mordechai Aneliewicz, the fiery young Zionist leader of the armed ghetto uprising, but also the gentle physician Janusz Korczak, who sheltered two hundred children in his orphanage and in the end, refusing a proffered exemption from the deportations of the summer of 1942 for himself, led a dignified procession of his little charges to the *Umschlagplatz* and their doom. As one witness later testified: "Bare-headed, with a leather belt around his coat, with tall boots [Korczak] bent, held the youngest child by the hand, and went on ahead."[9]

Definition here is crucial, and points the way to alternative visions. Roger Gottlieb's careful examination of approaches to resistance during the Holocaust suggests that there is more at stake in this discussion than the determination of which actions qualify as resistance and which do not. At issue in the final analysis is how we look at certain Jewish behavior, how we evaluate and ultimately understand it in historical perspective. Gottlieb himself takes the wider view of resistance, arguing that such acts are "motivated by the intention to thwart, limit, or end the exercise of power of the oppressor group over the oppressed."[10] With this definition, attention centers not only on the character of Nazi persecution but also on Jewish perceptions of the assault against them, and hence their own intentions in responding as they did—frequently, to thwart, limit, and so on. Starting with a philosophical meditation on resistance, Gottlieb is led to a close investigation of the historical record.

Without entering into the substance, I want to point out how in this case an obviously emotionally charged debate has refined rather than obscured understanding. There is much at stake in the controversy over Jewish resistance. For some Jews, there remains a pool of anger at the apparent ease with which the Nazis carried out their plans, and a related anger at the failure of Jewish leadership to motivate or organize a violent response. Their instinct is to accuse, both

Jews and Nazis, albeit in radically different ways; in practice, they minimize the extent of Jewish resistance. For others, there is an urge to relate the Jews' capacity for self-assertion, taken in much of our culture as a validation of communal worth. Their tendency is to accent both the incidence and significance of resistance activity. Given the intensity of research on the Jewish victims now available, writers on both sides of the resistance debate have been forced back upon definitions as a way of justifying the inclusion or exclusion of certain material—with the ultimate effect, I believe, that their history has been clarified considerably. The two sides do not agree in the end; but for outsiders to the debate, and for students who first encounter it, the differences over Jewish resistance are far clearer than they would have been otherwise.

I have also said that questions put forth in Holocaust history tend to become broader rather than narrower as specialists press alternative points of view on students of the subject. For example, take the exploration of the origins of the Final Solution itself. There exists a well-known debate between the so-called intentionalists and functionalists: between those who see the decision to murder the Jews of Europe as deriving from a long-nurtured plan for their physical annihilation, worked out by Hitler himself and launched at the propitious moment, and those who see the Nazis' policy as evolving gradually, radicalizing within the context of a Hitler-inspired antisemitism and the changing circumstances of war, particularly the early evolution of the German campaign against the Soviet Union.[11]

Without engaging the substance of this issue, and simply by way of illustration, I want to stress the way this debate quickly takes one to one of the most difficult historiographical issues of the Third Reich: the question of how Nazi government and society actually worked. Holocaust historians on both sides have been forced to explore the nature of Hitlerian politics—the role of the Führer and his antisemitic obsession—and at the same time to assess how, both in general terms and in particular with respect to the murder of Jews, personal and ideological obsessions were translated into policy, and then actually carried out.

There are weaknesses on both sides of the intentionalist–functionalist controversy over origins. Because of Hitler's notorious disinclination to put his orders in writing, as well as the Nazis' reluc-

tance to air publicly their murderous anti-Jewish objectives, intentionalists lack a "smoking gun"—plain-speaking, written orders or
directions from the Führer to murder Jews. At the same time, because of the sometimes chaotic processes of decision-making in the
Third Reich, functionalists are unable to reconstruct precisely the
timing and circumstances of the transition to Europe-wide mass
murder. Because our sources are inadequate, partisans of one hypothesis or the other have been constantly on the lookout for a crucial, missing document or for new evidence of the radicalization of
the Third Reich under the impact of Operation Barbarossa, the German attack on the Soviet Union in June 1941.

Most students of the subject, I believe, have tired of the sharply
opposed points of view and have hesitated to opt entirely for one
side or the other. But they can hardly abandon interest in the origins
of the Final Solution, one of the most troubling historical questions
a historian can pose. So what they have done is to broaden the perspective. Ian Kershaw points in the direction many have taken, seeking understanding through a more extensive examination of how
Nazi Germany operated: "Hitler's 'intention' was certainly a fundamental factor in the process of radicalization in anti-Jewish policy
which culminated in extermination," he writes; "but even more important to an explanation of the Holocaust is the nature of 'charis-
matic' rule in the Third Reich and the way it functioned in sustaining the momentum of escalating radicalization around 'heroic'
chimeric goals while corroding and fragmenting the structure of
government. This was the essential framework within which Hitler's
lunacy could be turned into practical politics." [12]

On the other side of the debate is Richard Breitman, who in his
recent study of Heinrich Himmler, the "architect of genocide," sees
Hitler making "a fundamental decision to exterminate the Jews" as
early as March 1941, far earlier than most historians on the subject
would accept. [13] But much of Breitman's book illustrates the effect
on Jewish policy of a more general question: how decisions of any
kind were reached in the Third Reich. The most valuable part of
his book describes the intense rivalry between Himmler and other
paladins of the Third Reich: the SA (*Sturmabteilung*) leadership (particularly at the time of *Kristallnacht*), General Johannes
Blaskowitz and the army during the Polish campaign and later, Hans
Frank during 1940–41 over policies in Poland, Alfred Rosenberg

and his Ministry for Occupied Eastern Territories, and various *Gauleiter* who governed in the East. An issue crucial to Holocaust history, once again, is illuminated as the perspective broadens, and as matters not directly related to Nazi Jewish policy are taken into account.

The same point could be made about other aspects of the debate over the origins of the Final Solution. Historians have challenged us to understand the Nazis' assault against Jews as it relates to many important and quite different perspectives. As Robert Koehl and Martin Broszat each pointed out some time ago, and as Christopher Browning has demonstrated more recently, the timing of the Nazis' decisions about the Jews in Eastern Europe was crucially tied to the development of Nazi occupation in Poland.[14] Andreas Hillgruber, Jürgen Förster, and others stressed for many years the connection with Operation Barbarossa.[15] Closely related to this is the systematic killing by the *Einsatzgruppen* in the early phase of that campaign. Here, too, there is disagreement: about how vague or specific the planning process was with respect to Jews, about whether men alone or all Jews were targeted for murder at the beginning, about the widening frenzy of murder during the course of the summer of 1941, and about whether these murders represent a clear turning to Europe-wide killing.[16] But the connection with Barbarossa and the accompanying radicalization of the Third Reich is now widely accepted. And finally, there is the challenge of relating the Nazis' attack on Jews to their policy toward other victimized groups in the Third Reich. In their study of the Nazi racial state, Michael Burleigh and Wolfgang Wipperman assemble a considerable body of literature linking the Nazis' attack on Jews and the attempted construction of a vast racial utopia, in which persecution extended to all kinds of "racially impure" or "undesirable" elements.[17] None of this broadening of perspective, I might add, necessarily detracts from the uniqueness of the Nazis' objectives for Jews. It does, however, put the Final Solution in a context that makes it easier to understand.[18]

Public opinion is another theme that Holocaust historiography seemingly addresses on a much more sophisticated level than do many other fields of history. Some questions are obvious. What did people in various countries think about Jews? About the Germans? How powerful was wartime antisemitism? What did people know about the Holocaust? On each of these, research has been extensive and controversy continues. Because the emotional fallout from such questions can be intense, historians who have turned their minds to them have refined the object of study considerably. There is widespread agreement that terms have to be carefully defined, that both Nazi sources and memoirs must be used with great care and with due allowance for their respective biases, that we have a lot to learn about how public opinion actually works, and that the process of "knowing" about an unprecedented historical event is much more complex than meets the eye.

Consider antisemitism. Nothing could be easier, one might think, than to demonstrate its salience in Germany before and during the Hitler era, and hence its relevance to the Holocaust. Yet for more than a decade historians have been putting such generalizations to the test, with results that sometimes go against the grain of conventional wisdom. Some writers still assume the existence of "a profoundly anti-Semitic, hallucinatory image of [Jews]" that was rampant in German society and that largely explains the willingness of so many Germans not only to look the other way but actually themselves to murder Jews.[19] Yet these voices are a distinct minority. Most historians, I think, are aware of how perilous such generalizations are. Problems arise the moment one makes comparisons. For the pre-Hitler period, it is difficult to make the case that Germany was the antisemitic country par excellence—something implied in at least some writing on the subject. On the contrary, to the general observer, the level of anti-Jewish feeling in Eastern Europe, particularly Poland, Hungary, and Romania, seems unquestionably higher.[20] Going back a generation to discuss the 1890s, George Mosse used to point out how, excluding the tsarist empire, it was France rather than Germany that seemed to be heading for a bloody reckoning with Jews.[21] Investigations of interwar antisemitism in various West European countries, and in North America for that matter, show levels in many respects comparable to those in Germany before Hitler. One also can point to well-documented, widespread popular antisemitism in Canada and the United States during the war.[22] Such studies are a reminder of how careful one must be in generalizing on the subject. At the very least, historians must try to ascertain the *intensity* of anti-Jewish opinion, must distinguish between social snobbery, prejudice, and the kind of pathological, murderous Jew-hatred one associates with Hitler and the Nazis.[23] Comparative history, the subject of periodic admonition on the part of historians of other subjects, has in this case sharpened critical appreciation and forced historians to put the entire question of anti-semitism into broader perspective.

Comparative history imposes itself as well on questions about the variable incidence of the Holocaust. These are sometimes burning questions, posed at the very end of the war by those seeking to condemn or defend collaborationist governments, and sometimes put today in the form of anguished explorations of what "might have been." Why were proportionally fewer Jews deported from France than from Belgium or the Netherlands, as some Vichy collaborators protested at their postwar trials? Did some forms of collaboration provide a screen of protection, as Lucjan Dobroszycki has suggested?[24] "Could the Jews of Hungary have been saved?" historian István Deák boldly asks in a review of Randolph Braham's important book on the subject.[25] From the start, those who pose such questions have needed a comparative perspective, and have sought explanations for the remarkable differences between the countries of occupied Europe.

Several writers have proposed models or frameworks for analysis. The uninitiated may be surprised at the range of variables, which have prompted at least one specialist in this problem, sociologist Helen Fein, to tabulate them for a computer-assisted analysis.[26] Needless to say, difficulties abound, familiar enough to practitioners of quantitative history. There is the problem of isolating and quantifying diverse characteristics that we sometimes amalgamate in some conception of "national character": religious traditions, forms of government, social organization, and so on. Most difficult of all, German policy must also be taken into account. For, notwithstanding their obsessive concern to murder as many Jews as they could find, the Nazis had entirely different priorities when it came, for example, to the few hundred Jews of Finland and the nearly nine hundred thousand Jews of Hungary.

A final illustration of the refinements of Holocaust history is the matter of what was known about the massacre of European Jews at the time. Here, Holocaust historians from the start faced seemingly contradictory evidence. Some firsthand testimony suggests that very early on, victims and bystanders penetrated the ruse by which the Nazis attempted to deceive people about the Final Solution. Reports of the Polish Home Army or the Jewish Bund, newspaper articles, and the eloquent testimony of eyewitnesses all tell us that information about the killings seeped out of Eastern Europe, and that those who wanted to know, "knew." Yet on the other hand, there is abundant, persuasive, and sometimes equally compelling evidence of reasons for the reverse: distraction, a refusal to believe the "unbelievable," the acceptance of false rumors, continued belief in the story that Jews were being deported to work camps, hope against hope, indifference, and so forth. With this issue, vitally important to those who pursue the emotionally salient issues of resistance and rescue, Holocaust historians find themselves plunged almost immediately into a reflection on the value of sources, on how information is transmitted, how facts register upon the mind, and how mind and memory can play tricks on people in different circumstances.

These considerations, vital in a sense for all historical testimony and relevant to all fields of historical inquiry, have come to the surface more quickly with Holocaust history than with any other field I know. Several books have been written about the subject—for example, the works of Walter Laqueur, Martin Gilbert, and Deborah Lipstadt—and there have been numerous studies treating particular situations and aspects of the problem.[27] Once again, one cannot say that all this work has produced agreement; differences persist. Even after an intense critical review of the sources, historians will tilt one way or another on the question of what was known, by whom, when. But they will do so, I think, with a degree of critical awareness of the problems associated with the issue of knowledge that is very high. I have the impression that other fields of historical study could benefit from this kind of critical consciousness.

Therein my conclusion. Holocaust history is a remarkably complex, advanced field of historical inquiry and needs no other reason than that to command the close attention of scholars and students. I have avoided reference to the more familiar admonitions that it be studied for reasons of social policy—that study of the Holocaust imparts lessons about the dangers of antisemitism or intolerance, that it is a basis for good citizenship, and that it contributes to the fight against racism. I do not quarrel with these views, which have their place in shaping primary or secondary school exposure and may also be relevant to Holocaust studies at the university level. But I am not sure about them, and would point out some dissenting opinions.

To some, the "lessons" of the Holocaust are so simple as to be banal, hardly warranting an elaborate investigation. The late I. F. Stone once summed it up: "The lesson of the Holocaust," he said, "is that if you treat people like things it can end up in the gas chambers." From this viewpoint, there is no need for an elaborate academic enterprise, for the "lesson" is the moral equivalent of common sense. Alternatively, the lessons may be, as some religious people believe, beyond our understanding altogether. As they have it, no amount of secular study will get to the bottom of the matter, and vital truths about the massacre of European Jewry will always elude those who presume to understand.[28] Different again is the view of many who feel there has been "too much" preoccupation with the Holocaust. It has been suggested that Holocaust studies have risen in popularity as part of a wider vogue of "oppression studies" in a "politically correct" curriculum. Through the study of the Holocaust, it is said, Jewish students are able to participate in "a vast and murky cult of victimhood" that permeates the culture of many on the academic Left.[29] In a related view, Jewish studies specialist Lionel Kochan has worried that students may actually draw the "wrong" lessons from Holocaust study: not only a morbid view of the Jews as victims, but also stimulation of the imagination of those who seek to renew this and other victimizations.

As a professional historian, I confess to having always been skeptical about the so-called "lessons" of history, which seem continually to elude historians even when they are operating at their peak. Individuals may claim from time to time that they have discovered such lessons, or admonish people to heed them, but invariably other historians within earshot divide among themselves like angry parliamentarians and are unable to agree. And so I conclude that if good history revealed commonly agreed-upon, useful lessons, we would have extracted and put them to use a long time ago.

What we *can* say, I think, is that good history deepens and extends our appreciation of human reality, and that in a very general sense its study can make us more mature, wiser, more "experienced" observers of the human scene. Historians are far more likely to agree on what is good history than on the conclusions of particular historical works. The key, I think, is "good" history—accounts of the past that challenge received wisdom by deepening understanding, that stand up to intense critical inquiry, pose challenging questions, and reach plausible answers, firmly grounded in evidence. This has always been the challenge to historians of the Holocaust, who attempt to explain events most of us have difficulty even imagining. What I argue here is that they have succeeded remarkably well.

Gerhard L. Weinberg

The Holocaust and World War II:
A Dilemma in Teaching

THERE EXISTS A FAIRLY COMMON TENDENCY TO WRITE, TALK, AND
teach about the Holocaust and about World War II as separate and
only barely related events. Many books that deal with the war cover
only military and diplomatic issues; if they allude to the Holocaust
at all, it is as a sort of addendum or afterthought. You will look in
vain in the table of contents or even the index of H. P. Willmott's
book *The Great Crusade: A New Complete History of the Second World
War* for entries under "Holocaust" or "Jews."[1] Other such books
may have a short reference or a section added at the end, but as a
general rule the whole issue is either omitted or shifted to the side-
lines.

Works on the Holocaust often do something similar. There may
be references to the bystanders, the German campaign in the East,
and the destruction or liberation of killing centers and camps in the
last stages of the war in Europe, but the authors obviously have little
interest in and familiarity with the war as a whole. Such preposterous
inversions of the chronology as Sebastian Haffner's and Arno Mayer's each attributing the decision to kill Europe's Jews to the German
defeat on the eastern front in the winter of 1941–42 when it had
actually been made months before, at a time when the Germans
were certain they had won, can only be explained by ignorance
about both the war and the Holocaust.[2]

Certainly those in charge of both the war and the Holocaust on
the German side had no doubts on the connection themselves. No
one needed to explain to them that the overwhelming majority of
the Jews they killed had come into their reach only because of the

war. We know today that the figure was at least 95 percent; had the Germans won (as they certainly expected) the percentage would have been even higher. The special racial character of the war in German eyes can be seen quite easily in two characteristic and deliberate misdatings. When Hitler issued his notorious written authorization for what was euphemistically called a "euthanasia" program in October 1939, that document was backdated to September 1, 1939, not only to mislead the public if the document ever did come to light (it was not supposed to) but because that was the way those in charge saw the program: as tied to the beginning of the war. Similarly, Hitler himself repeatedly misdated in public his January 30, 1939 threat that the Jews of Europe would be exterminated in any new war to the same date, September 1, 1939. It is worth noting that this misdating, designed to associate the killing of Jews with the war, was not only broadcast on German radio and printed with the wrong date in German newspapers of the time; it was also repeated in print in the volumes of Hitler's speeches published at his orders during the war by Philipp Bouhler in a series entitled *Der Grossdeutsche Freiheitskampf,* "Greater Germany's War for Freedom."[3]

It is similarly no coincidence that the Nazis' plans for the campaign in the Soviet Union included the creation of killing squads, the *Einsatzgruppen,* and that those preparations were greatly affected by the experiences the Germans had already gained in the campaign in and occupation of Poland. An even more striking illustration of the connections those who ran the killing program saw between it and the war may be found in an aspect of the famous Wannsee Protocol that is all too often ignored by people who discuss it without carefully studying the text. Included in the geographical list of Jewish communities to be deported for killing were not only those of areas under German control, such as Poland and Denmark, and those of Germany's allies and satellites, such as Finland, Italy, and Croatia, but also those of England, which had not yet been invaded, and such neutrals as Sweden, Spain, Ireland, and Switzerland.[4] One may contrast the extensive discussion at that conference of what to do about the *Mischlinge,* those of mixed Jewish and non-Jewish parentage, with the lack of discussion of those Jewish communities that were then out of the reach of German power. The people at the meeting took it for granted that the progress of the war they expected Germany to win would automatically solve that problem. Invading England was evidently considered easier than figuring out what to do with *Mischlinge!*

Let me mention one more example of this type. When the Germans took over Denmark in April 1940, they were able to take control of the bulk of the existing administration and utilize it for their own purposes in the war. As part of the price for this, the Jews of Denmark were to be left alone for the time being. As just mentioned in connection with the Wannsee conference, these Jews were scheduled to be killed; but as long as the government of Denmark was left with some power over local affairs, there was simply no chance for the Germans to extricate the country's Jews for deportation: the Danes would not stand for it. In August 1943 the Germans decided to take over the administration of Denmark themselves, displacing the existing Danish government. This action was supposedly aimed at ensuring internal security in the face of a rising tide of Danish strikes and other forms of resistance. But the Germans' first major action was guaranteed to have the opposite effect, to heighten rather than lower the level of resistance to German rule: they immediately began preparations to deport Danish Jews to the killing centers in occupied Poland. The rescue of Denmark's Jews by evacuation to Sweden is well known, but the wartime context of that drama is generally overlooked.

How come this connection between the war and the Holocaust, so obvious to those who ran both, has not been equally a part of the discussion and teaching of the two topics? Let me make a few suggestions. In the first place, outside the Axis there was a reluctance to believe what was becoming increasingly obvious by 1942, and thereafter to credit it fully even when the accounts could no longer be denied. Furthermore, during the war there was concern in Allied countries that stressing the connection would reinforce at home the effectiveness of German propaganda that this was a war caused by the Jews and fought for their benefit. In the postwar years, the subject of the killing of Jews somehow seemed less inspiring to historians than the great battles, strategy conferences, and related developments that were and often still are seen as the proper foci for a study of war. Also, people were reluctant to confront how little had been done to help the victims and naturally focused on the accomplishment of military victory over the Axis powers.

If this was true in the victorious countries, what about the defeated? In East Germany, the postwar years saw a complete denial that antisemitism was a real element in a real ideology, not just a propaganda tool of the fascists to gain support. In West Germany there was a flood of memoirs whose authors deliberately concealed their knowledge of, and frequently their complicity in, the process of mass killing.[5] It became a staple of much literature from West Germany that the army had kept its hands clean and that whatever awful things had happened were a sort of incidental affair of the SS. The uproar occasioned by some of the works issued by the Institute for Contemporary History in Munich and the German Military History Research Office in Freiburg, when these have taken a more honest line, shows how strongly the early apologias still influence popular memory.[6]

Postwar scholarship in the West outside the German Federal Republic also took routes that obscured rather than illuminated the connections between the fighting and the Holocaust. The endless fascination over the internal squabbling and jurisdictional disputes of the Nazi system, revealed in the enormous volume of records that increasingly became available for research, deluded scholars into confusing the size of the paper trail with the significance of what they were tracking. Emphasizing the anarchic aspects of National Socialist rule, scholars overlooked the vast degree of consensus; writers failed to see that a society that had held together to the bitter end in spite of enormous blows and all sorts of internal bickering must have had some elements of cohesion—among them, perhaps, a grim determination to carry forward the racial war and an awareness of horrendous crimes committed in that pursuit.

The arguments between those scholars who came to be referred to as "functionalists" and "intentionalists" tended to ignore that the Germans had expected to win, not lose, the war, and that therefore the leaders of the Third Reich always assumed they would have decades, even centuries, to carry out their plans. When seen in that light, a number of issues look different. Time and again, the German government postponed steps in the racial transformation that was a major purpose of the war in order to appease unanticipatedly strong domestic opposition, but always with the clear intent of resuming them after victory. The change in the so-called euthanasia program in August 1941 clearly belongs in this context. So does the rescinding of orders to take crucifixes out of the schools. In a few instances, smaller portions of the killing program were also deliberately postponed, a dramatic example being the deferral of the deportation of Jewish men living in mixed marriages after their non-Jewish wives rioted in the streets of Berlin in February 1943. I have already mentioned the temporary postponement of the deportation of Denmark's Jews; Germany's either easing the pressure for deportation or practically ignoring for the moment Jewish communities in allies and satellites such as Finland and Bulgaria should be seen in the same framework. What could be done only at unacceptable cost immediately would be simple once victory had been won.

But what those debating the functionalist–intentionalist issue have not, in my judgment, given sufficient attention is the extent to which in this one case, that of the Holocaust, the practical considerations of conducting the war were subordinated to the perceived needs of the killing program. Whether the choice was to transport Jews east to be shot instead of using the trains to ship winter clothing to German soldiers in Russia in late 1941, or to kill thousands of Jewish workers in defense plants and repair shops during 1943 instead of keeping them working to meet the growing needs of the desperately embattled German armed forces, time and again the killing program took priority over all else. Those in charge saw the priorities in a way that scholarly discussions have not fully engaged.

If we turn the issues around for a moment, we can quickly recognize the converse problem in accounts of the Holocaust. These authors generally assume the course of the war as somehow predetermined, and in particular indicate no comprehension of the Holocaust as a German program to kill not only the Jews of Europe but those of the whole globe, if they could get their hands on them. Hitler's promise to the Grand Mufti of Jerusalem on November 28, 1941, to get rid of not just European Jews but also those of Palestine and all other Jews living outside Europe—those living among *"außereuropäische Völker"*—has been too easily disregarded.[7] Let me pursue this matter further. Books that discuss the deportation of the Jews of Rhodes do not, as far as I know, ever call attention to the fact that these Jews were technically living in Asia, not Europe. The point here is that from the perspective of those who ran the German war effort and the German killing program, the Jewish population of the globe as a whole was the target. The museum the Nazis were planning in Prague was to be one for "an extinct race"; the many Jewish congregations that today possess Torah scrolls from the collection intended for that museum often do not grasp that their *own* survival was at stake during the war. The victory of the Allies saved about two-thirds of the world's Jews from murder by the Germans—by no means as far-fetched a possibility as may appear in retrospect.

Consider another part of the same conversation between Hitler and Haj Amin el-Husseini. Hitler told the Grand Mufti that Germany's only interest in Palestine was the killing of the Jewish population there; the phrase attributed to him by the interpreter, Paul Schmidt, is *"die Vernichtung des im arabischen Raum unter der Protektion der britischen Macht lebenden Judentums,"* "the destruction of the Jews living in Arab space under the protection of British power."[8] We do not need to consider at this point whether in fact German aims in the Middle East extended *beyond* the killing of the Jewish community in Palestine; it most certainly included that as a minimum.

On two occasions the Germans came very close to being able to carry out this portion of their program: in the late spring of 1941 and in the summer of 1942. Today we also know that the British plans for evacuating the Palestine Mandate provided for the evacuation of only the non-Jewish population,[9] so a German advance would have meant the death of the Jewish community there—and thus surely no Jewish state in an area entirely devoid of Jews, even if the Allies had still eventually won the war. Under these circumstances, President Roosevelt's decision of April 1941 to declare the Red Sea open to American shipping so that the British in Egypt could be reinforced,[10] and his decision after the surrender of Tobruk in June 1942 to strip an American armored division of its tanks so as to send them to Egypt, must both be seen as prerequisites for the survival of Jews in Palestine and for the eventual establishment of the State of Israel.[11] But you will not find them discussed in this way in accounts of the Holocaust.

Similarly, in connection with the campaign in North Africa and its critical significance for the survival of the Jewish community of Palestine, one does not find in discussions of the Holocaust anything about the role of Muslim soldiers in the defense of that community. The largest volunteer army of World War II was the Indian army; of that army of two and a half million, over six hundred thousand were Muslims.[12] Thousands of them fought in the North African campaign, and fully 65 percent of the Indian soldiers engaged there were Muslims.[13] Whether known to scholars of the Holocaust or not, these facts were most certainly known to the leaders of Great Britain's war effort: Churchill and his chief military aide, General Ismay, had served in India themselves, and the British commander in the area for much of the war, Field Marshal Sir Claude Auchinleck, had come up through the Indian army. If the subject is not discussed at length in the archives, it is because at the time no one needed to be told the obvious; but for that very reason it has generally escaped the notice of historians.

I am not suggesting that Muslims joined the Indian army and fought against the Germans and Italians in Africa to protect Jews; rather I wish to emphasize that, just as certain developments in the war proved catastrophic for Jews without that being the main purpose, many actions turned out to have major beneficial effects for Jewish survival even though that, too, had not been the intent. What I am trying to clarify is the extent to which developments in the military and diplomatic course of the war and in the Holocaust intersected with each other, and how a failure to take these intersections into account reduces our ability to understand either.

What is needed in our teaching of both subjects is a sense of their connectedness. Ironically, one of the historians who made a beginning of this was a German, Andreas Hillgruber. Originally published in 1972 in the quarterly of the Munich Institute for Contemporary History, his article pointing to the Final Solution and Germany's attempt to seize an empire in Eastern Europe as the central focus of the racial-ideological program of National Socialism is a major attempt to integrate the history of the war and the Holocaust at a critical juncture.[14] An important pointer in the right direction, Hillgruber's article has been followed by the works of a fine German historian who is often thought of, and who thought of himself, as in an opposite camp from Hillgruber, Eberhard Jäckel. Jäckel's books on Hitler's ideology and rule effectively combine analysis of ideology with discussion of military and foreign policy, exactly the sort of combination that is needed.[15]

World War II in Europe must be presented by teachers as a war that was initiated for the purpose of vast conquest of space within which there was to be a massive demographic change: people displaced, people killed, people settled. The war cannot be understood without reference to that purpose. This was clear to the initiators; it has to be clear to students. When students ask, for example, as they frequently do, why the Germans did not recruit the peoples of the Soviet Union to fight on their side against a Soviet leadership so many of them hated, they need to understand that had the German leaders wanted to help the Soviet people, they would never have invaded in the first place. It was precisely to enslave, displace, or exterminate the peoples of the Soviet Union that Germany invaded the country, and from the German point of view it made no sense to arm those whom they intended to treat in this fashion.

If at the time these connections were so obvious to the Germans, why were they not understood by most leaders and peoples on the Allied side? There is a twofold answer we can give our students. In the first place, the whole concept of the genocide seemed unbelievable. A state, it was assumed, might wish to conquer more territory to acquire resources, power, workers, or prestige, but the very notion of killing large portions of the population to settle one's supposedly excess urban population on new farmland seemed too bizarre to credit. And a good case can be made that in the event of a German victory, the Germans themselves might have found such a program far more complicated to implement than their leaders appear to have realized. It is indeed difficult to visualize millions of Germans from Berlin, Hamburg, Cologne, Munich, and other cities signing on to move to farm villages in the central and southern Ukraine to start over as farmers on the fertile but hardly scenic plains. Many German generals looked forward to acquiring huge estates, *Rittergüter,* in the East, but in their eyes these were to come with a proper allotment of indigenous peasant serfs, not transplanted German farmers.[16] The early stages of German leaders' implementation of their radical projects for a world demographic revolution were, therefore, not recognized for what they were.

A second reason the Allies did not fully perceive the nature of the war was a fundamental difference in their views of National Socialism. The western powers saw Nazism as a particularly evil and ruthless form of German aggression, the result of wrong turns taken by bad leaders. This view could, and eventually, but very slowly, did evolve into the beginning of a realization of what was actually going on in German-controlled Europe. For the Soviet Union, however, National Socialism was merely a tool of monopoly capitalism, which utilized antisemitism to capture support inside Germany when the real aim of those who ran the country lay in seizing the markets and investments of other capitalist powers. This interpretation—which explains both Stalin's unwillingness to believe that Germany would attack the Soviet Union and the refusal of the Soviet Union and its satellites after the war to acknowledge anything special in the anti-semitism of the Nazi regime—prevented any understanding of the true nature of the war or of the Holocaust, then or later.

The most important single effect of this incomprehension of the war while it was under way is that practically no efforts were made to rescue the Jewish—or any other—victims of the Nazis. On the other hand, the exertions called forth by the obvious threat of German military power forced the unnatural allies of East and West to stick together and turn the tide of war, thereby rescuing about two-thirds of the world's Jews from the fate the Germans intended for them—but without any recognition that this was what they were doing.

When we look at the years of war and Holocaust in light of their connections, however, we can begin to see new aspects to the functions of the German armed forces. A major role of the German army fighting on the eastern front—and for most of the war this was most of the army—was to ensure continued German control of the killing centers in the East so that these could keep functioning. A major role of the German navy—and for most of the war this was the submarine force—was to do exactly the same thing, but in the West. Keeping the Allies from disrupting the continued implementation of the Final Solution was a central, not an incidental, purpose of German military operations. It was entirely appropriate that the crews of German U-boats were issued footwear partly made of human hair gathered in the killing centers and that they were rewarded with watches stolen from Jewish victims.[17]

The turn of the tide in the war, especially in 1943, then also needs to be seen in a framework that connects it to the Holocaust. On the one hand, the halting of German expansion restricted the area the intended global program could reach; those whom the Germans had not gotten to by the summer of 1943 were unlikely to be threatened thereafter. On the other hand, this same process also made it possible for the Germans to intensify the persecution in those areas that they did control, as I have already alluded to in the case of the island of Rhodes. The collapse of Italy opened up to German deportation and killing operations Jews hitherto shielded by Italian refusal to take part in them—a refusal that had temporarily protected many Jews not only within Italy but also in Italian-controlled portions of France, Yugoslavia, and Greece.[18] Furthermore, the turning of the war against the Germans can be seen as endangering Jews living in the territories of Germany's other partners. The projects to occupy Hungary and Romania, on which the Germans began to work in the fall of 1943, resulted from defeats, not victories, at the front.[19] Only that against Hungary was carried out successfully—with horrendous implications for Hungary's large Jewish population—while that against Romania was first postponed and then botched; but here, too, the history of war and Holocaust intersect fatefully.

Another area of the war often examined in complete isolation from its related Holocaust aspect is the behavior of the neutrals. Here we can see something of a parallel in several neutral states' blockade and refugee policies. The European neutrals—Sweden, Spain, Switzerland, Portugal, and Turkey—followed an essentially identical pattern. I do not suggest there were no significant individual and even national exceptions to this pattern, but the pattern is itself surely worthy of note. In the first half of the war, these countries tended to conform to German demands, which ranged from allowing German troops to travel across them to providing the German war machine with critical raw materials, and to generally refuse to allow Jewish refugees to enter. In the latter part of the war, as the neutrals could see the Allies winning and Germany's opportunities for violent retaliation lessening, they tended to shift on both subjects: they became more resistant to German demands, especially for raw materials and direct military aid, and more willing to assist victims of German persecution, including Jews. The year of major change in both fields of policy was 1943. While exceptions to the general trend can be identified both before and after that year, the striking thing is the extent to which the European neutrals followed similar policies regardless of their form of government.

Major geographic characteristics of the war also intersected with the Holocaust. The most important of these, by far, was related to the significant difference in the political configurations of the two world wars: the different timing in the alliance structure on the Allied side. In World War I, the Russians pulled out of the war near the end, leaving the western powers to face Germany by themselves, but doing so at a time when Germany was already too exhausted to drive the western powers off the continent. In World War II, the Soviet Union sided with Germany in the *initial* phase, assisting the Germans, then at the height of their relative strength, to drive the western powers off of Europe in the North, West, and Southeast. The effect of this, of course, was to leave the Soviets facing the Germans by themselves in the East, not as a result of evil plotting by others but because of Stalin's stupidity. More basically, the German victories that the Soviet Union had facilitated left the eastern and western major powers of the anti-Hitler coalition in fundamentally different positions vis-à-vis their Axis enemies. Britain and the United States had excellent defensive positions: it was exceedingly difficult for Germany to get at them. But they were in a very difficult situation for offensive operations. The same bodies of water that separated them from Germany might hinder them from turning their own offensive power against the Germans. The situation of the Soviet Union was exactly the reverse. Stalin's policies had placed the Soviet Union in an extraordinarily vulnerable defensive position. Germany could very easily bring its power to bear directly on the USSR, assisted in this by the absence of continental enemies and the presence of Finland and Romania as its own allies on the flanks of the attack, both factors again the product of prior Soviet policies. But conversely, the Soviet Union, once it had succeeded in halting the German advance, was in the superior position for offensive operations: it could send its forces into Central Europe across the same land route used by the German invaders.

What has all this to do with the Holocaust? A great deal. Because the overwhelming majority of Europe's Jewish population was located in Eastern Europe, the main part of the Final Solution, not surprisingly, took place in Eastern Europe. The Germans first took the killers to the victims and then, beginning in the winter of 1941–42, established facilities and procedures for bringing the victims to the killers, both of them in Eastern Europe, primarily occupied Poland. Since the Soviet leadership never recognized any special characteristic in the program to kill Europe's Jews, that program proceeded in what was from the German perspective the best, and from the victims' perspective the worst, possible location: with little prospect of interference from the nearby Soviets, as the Germans saw it; little likelihood of any special help, as the victims saw it.

This geographic situation also meant that the killing centers in Eastern Europe, which retreating Germans would either destroy or evacuate, were in areas that would be overrun by the Red Army, while the camps that would eventually be liberated by the western Allies were of a less grisly type, however terrible. One cannot overlook the role of this differentiation between East and West in facilitating those postwar claims that the Holocaust never happened and that pictures and documents emanating from the eastern part of Europe can be dismissed as fabrications.

When we consider the war and the Holocaust in such joint perspectives, we can also do a better job of integrating into the general picture those aspects of the great conflict that are, in fact, related to both. I have already mentioned the so-called euthanasia program. That massive racial project not only provided the precedent for defining, collecting, and killing in a new type of installation a specific group of people, and gave the Germans practice in mass killing and the disposal of vast numbers of corpses; it also created a body of individuals who had become accustomed, as volunteers or willing participants, to killing on a steady, day-by-day, week-by-week basis, from breakfast to lunch break and then to dinnertime. It is no coincidence that so many of the techniques and individuals first involved in the euthanasia program were transferred to the program for killing Jews. It is also not surprising that eventually those individuals acquired a great vested interest in the extension of such programs to additional categories of people; after all, their promotions and decorations, and their exemptions from the far more dangerous task of fighting at the front, depended on a continuing supply of victims.

With that in mind, it may be easier to place certain otherwise confusing developments into the broader picture of the war and the Holocaust. The persistence of the German bureaucratic apparatus and the killers in trying to locate additional victims in 1943, 1944, and 1945 must be seen, I believe, not simply as a product of the high priority assigned the killing program by Nazi leaders and the inertia of any bureaucratic apparatus, but also as a reflection of the vested interest those involved in the killing had developed in its continuation. The increasing shift, especially obvious during 1943, toward the systematic killing of Gypsies, the Sinti and Roma, can be better understood as a part of both the racial reordering of Europe and the search for victims by the killers.[20] The extensive experimentation in certain camps aimed at finding means of mass sterilization must also, in my judgment, be seen in this context.

Since the Europe of a German-dominated future was to have no Jews and no Gypsies in it, then for whom would the mass sterilization procedures have been destined, had they been developed? Here, it seems to me, we come back to the general reordering of Europe's population that the Nazis intended. If the Slavic peoples of Eastern and Southeastern Europe were to be displaced by German settlers, here was a mechanism by which the Slavs' labor might be utilized for a while even as their future as peoples was being terminated in stages. Fortunately, the German doctors failed in their search and Germany lost the war, but any revolution stopped short in its tracks can be understood only in view of the destination toward which those tracks pointed. And as long as the war lasted, the Germans, or at least a large portion of their leadership and many in the governing apparatus, still looked toward a victory that they expected Hitler's secret weapons or a split in the alliance against them to bring. In the meantime, they would go on killing.

When we look at the war and at the Holocaust in these interconnected ways, we may also find additional insights that could help our students understand the end of the war and the world after 1945. At the end of World War I, the peacemakers at Paris had attempted to rearrange Europe on the basis of the national principle. The thrust of their efforts had been to make the boundaries fit the peoples. They were neither always successful nor consistent in this process, but on the whole, they tried harder and succeeded better in this than anyone before or since. Germany, as is well known, did not like their settlement at all. During World War II, Germany's fundamental approach was the exact opposite: it preferred to draw the boundaries first and then push the people around to fit the boundaries. This fact may assist students in understanding the post–World War II arrangements. The Allies applied to the Germans the new procedure the latter had originated; that is, by having about twelve million Germans moved to fit the new boundaries, they created the largest migration of people in a short period that we know of. Though by far the largest, it was by no means the only such movement of people in the last stages of the war and the immediate postwar period. On the whole, the process can be seen as less humane but in some ways more lasting than the one applied in 1919.

Let us turn to the impact of war and Holocaust on subsequent developments in the Middle East. The success of the Allies in keeping the Germans out of the Palestine Mandate meant that at the end of the war a small but substantial Jewish community remained there. Its presence suggested a logical goal for those Jews who had survived the Holocaust in Europe, including those who tried to return to their homes but quickly discovered, especially in Poland, the violent objections of the local population. This growing Jewish community also provided the basis for the establishment of a Jewish state within the territory of the former mandate.

Two further interrelated aspects of war and Holocaust strongly influenced the development of Israel as a state, both at the beginning and into our own day. In the first place, the fact that the leadership of the Palestinian Arabs had sided with the Axis meant, in effect, that despite whatever *other* Arab leaders might say or do, in pretense or in reality, on behalf of Palestine's Arab population, that population was effectively excluded from any significant role in the Allied-dominated debates of the immediate postwar years. In particular, although Great Britain continued to favor the Arab cause and did what it could to strengthen those elements in the Arab world, especially in Jordan, that supported its own remnant imperial position, the Grand Mufti of Jerusalem was hardly a credible spokesman to the victors. And Britain's position was to be weakened by the tides of nationalism within India, which deprived Britain of much of its motivation for holding on in the Middle East at all, and particularly within such Arab states as Iraq and Egypt.

The other major impact of wartime developments on the "Palestine question," as it was then called, lay in its meaning for the future State of Israel. The prewar partition scheme of the Peel Commission had been abandoned because of the approaching war with Germany, which made the British government reluctant to antagonize the Arabs and unable to spare the troops needed to enforce partition in Palestine. Already during the war, however, the British cabinet was discussing new partition schemes for the postwar era, with some sort of Jewish state to emerge from the ruins of Britain's position in the Middle East.

What the Holocaust proper did was to reduce tremendously the major reservoir from which Jewish immigrants had come to Palestine in the last decades of Ottoman rule and during the Mandate period. The overwhelming majority of immigrants had come from Eastern Europe, whether pre-1914 Russia or interwar Poland. It was precisely in these areas that the German killing program had been most extensive and most comprehensive. Survivors struggled to get to Israel, legally or illegally, but the reservoir had shrunk drastically. The early demographic shift in Israel toward a Sephardic majority was a by-product of the destruction of a great part of the population of East European Jews from which the Jewish community in Palestine could draw. That shift would have implications for subsequent internal Israeli politics, a subject I do not want to get into but which cannot be viewed without reference to its origins in the slaughter of potential immigrants during World War II.

Those who teach the Holocaust, either as a part of some subject that is defined more broadly chronologically or thematically or as a subject by itself, I believe, need to pay close attention to the origins, nature, and course of World War II. The launching of the systematic killing of Jews, the limits placed on that process, and the way parts of it continued into the last days of the fighting can be understood only in the context of the war and its military and political development. The converse is also true: the Second World War must be set in its racialist context. The war was fought because some people wanted to turn the demographic map of Europe and the world upside-down, saw the killing of Jews as a major facet of that enterprise, and moved forward toward that goal with a consistency of will and purpose as astonishing in retrospect as it appeared incomprehensible to contemporaries.

Christopher R. Browning

Ordinary Germans or Ordinary Men?
Another Look at the Perpetrators

IN 1989, WHEN I HAD THE PRIVILEGE OF ADDRESSING THE INITIAL CON-
ference on Lessons and Legacies of the Holocaust, I spoke for the
first time in public about my research into Reserve Police Battalion
101 and its role in the Final Solution in Poland. At that time I analyzed one crucial event in the history of the battalion, namely its
initiation into mass murder at the Polish village of Jozefow. Subsequently, I completed my study and published it under the title *Ordinary Men*. In general the book has been quite well received, but it
has not been without its critics. While these critics have accepted the
narrative presentation in the book that reveals the mode of operation
and degree of choice within the battalion, they have objected to my
portrayal of the perpetrators, particularly their motives and mindset,
and the conclusions that I draw—the crux of which is summed up
in the title *Ordinary Men*. As the writer of one friendly but critical
letter suggested: "Might not a preferable title . . . possibly have been
Ordinary Germans?"

The argument of my critics for German singularity rests above
all upon their assertion of a unique and particular German antisemitism. The letter writer just cited argued that "cultural conditioning"
shaped "specifically German behavioral modes." He went on to hypothesize that "even many decidedly non-Nazi Germans . . . were so
accustomed to the thought that Jews are less human than Germans
that they were capable of mass murder." Non-Germans in the same
situation as the men of Reserve Police Battalion 101, he implies,
would have behaved quite differently.

Daniel Goldhagen, my severest critic, puts the matter more
pointedly. The "Germans' singular and deeply rooted, racist anti-

semitism" was not "a common social psychological phenomenon" that can be analyzed in terms of "mere" negative racial stereotypes, as I had so "tepidly" done. "The men of Reserve Police Battalion 101 were not ordinary 'men,' but ordinary members of an extraordinary culture, the culture of Nazi Germany, which was possessed of a hallucinatory, lethal view of the Jews." Thus ordinary Germans were "believers in the justice of the murder of the Jews." In their "inflamed imaginations," Goldhagen writes, Jewish "destruction was a redemptive act."[1]

The issue raised here is an important—indeed central—question that is posed to virtually anyone teaching the Holocaust. I would like to approach this issue along two lines of inquiry. First, what has the bulk of recent scholarship concluded about the nature, intensity, and alleged singularity of antisemitism within the German population at large? And second, what is known about *non*-German killing units that might, through comparison, shed light on the issue of "specifically German behavioral modes"? In this case, by virtue of recently accessible documents from the former Soviet archives, I shall be looking at rural police units in Belorussia and the Ukraine that were recruited and trained by the Order Police (*Ordnungspolizei*).

Let us turn to the first line of inquiry, namely the nature and intensity of antisemitism within German society under the Nazis. As late as 1975, Lucy Dawidowicz argued that

> generations of anti-Semitism had prepared the Germans to accept Hitler as their redeemer. . . . Of the conglomerate social, economic, and political appeals that the NSDAP directed at the German people, its racial doctrine was the most attractive. . . . Out of the whole corpus of racial teachings, the anti-Jewish doctrine had the greatest dynamic potency. . . . The insecurities of post–World War I Germany and the anxieties they produced provided an emotional milieu in which irrationality and hysteria became routine and illusions became transformed into delusions. The delusional disorder assumed mass proportions. . . . In modern Germany the mass psychosis of anti-Semitism deranged a whole people.[2]

A large number of other scholars, however, have not shared this view.[3] Three in particular—Ian Kershaw, Otto Dov Kulka, and David Bankier—have devoted a significant portion of their scholarly

lives to examining German popular attitudes toward National Socialism, antisemitism, and the Holocaust.[4] Despite their differences
of emphasis, tone, and interpretation, the degree of their consensus
on the basic issues is impressive.

While Kulka and Bankier do not pick up the story until 1933,
Kershaw argues that in the pre-*Machtergreifung* era, antisemitism
was not a major factor in attracting support for Hitler and the Nazis.
He cites Peter Merkl's study of the "old fighters," in which only
about one-seventh of Merkl's sample considered antisemitism their
most salient concern and even fewer were classified by Merkl as
"strong ideological antisemites."[5] Moreover, in the electoral break-
through phase of 1929–33, and indeed up to 1939, Hitler rarely
spoke in public about the Jewish question; this reticence stands in
stark contrast to his speeches of the early 1920s, in which his obsession with and hatred of the Jews was vented openly and repeatedly.[6]
Kershaw concludes that "antisemitism cannot . . . be allocated a de-
cisive role in bringing Hitler to power, though . . . it did not do anything to hinder his rapidly growing popularity."[7]

For the 1933–39 period, all three historians characterize the
German popular response to antisemitism by two dichotomies. The
first is a distinction between a minority of party activists, for whom
antisemitism was an urgent priority, and the bulk of the German
population, for whom it was not. Party activists clamored and
pressed, often in violent and rowdy ways, for intensified persecution.
The antisemitic measures of the regime, though often criticized as
too mild by the radicals, served an integrating function within Hitler's movement; they helped to keep the momentum and enthusiasm
of the party activists alive. And despite Hitler's pragmatic caution
in public, most of these radicals correctly sensed he was with them
in spirit.

The second dichotomy concerns the reaction of the general population to the antisemitic clamor of the movement and the antisemitic measures of the regime. The vast majority accepted the *legal*
measures of the regime, which ended emancipation and drove Jews
from public positions in 1933, socially ostracized the Jews in 1935,
and finally completed the expropriation of their property in 1938–
39. But the same majority was critical of the hooliganistic *violence*
of party radicals aimed at the same German Jews whose legal persecution they approved. To the boycott of 1933, the vandalistic out-

breaks of 1935, and above all the *Kristallnacht* pogrom of November 1938, the German population reacted negatively. Bankier and Kulka emphasize the pragmatic concerns behind this negative response: destruction of property, foreign policy complications, damage to Germany's image, and general lawlessness offensive to societal notions of decorum. Kershaw thinks their discounting of virtually any moral dimension to be "a far too sweeping generalization."[8] Nonetheless, all three agree that a gulf had opened up between the Jewish minority and the general population. The latter, while not mobilized around strident and violent antisemitism, was increasingly "apathetic," "passive," and "indifferent" to the fate of the former.[9] Antisemitic measures—if carried out in an orderly and legal manner—were widely accepted, in part because such measures held out the hope of curbing the violence most Germans found so distasteful, but also in part because most Germans ultimately agreed with the goal of limiting and even ending the role of Jews in German society.

For the war years, the records upon which Kulka, Bankier, and Kershaw base their studies become sparser and more ambiguous and the differences in interpretation correspondingly greater. Kulka and Bankier deduce a more specific awareness of the Final Solution among the German people than does Kershaw.[10] Kershaw and Bankier advocate a more critical and less literal reading of the Security Service (*Sicherheitsdienst* or SD) reports than does Kulka.[11] For Kershaw, a general "retreat into the private sphere" was the basis for widespread indifference toward Nazi Jewish policy. Kulka sees a greater internalization of Nazi antisemitism among the population at large, particularly concerning the acceptance of a solution to the Jewish question through some unspecified kind of "elimination," and he thus prefers the term "passive complicity" or "objective complicity" over "indifference."[12] Bankier emphasizes a sense of guilt and shame among Germans, widespread denial and repression, and a growing fear about the consequences of impending defeat and commensurate rejection of the regime's antisemitic propaganda.[13] But these historiographical differences are matters of nuance, degree, and word choice. Fundamentally, the three scholars agree far more than they differ.

Above all, they accept that the fanatical antisemitism of the party "true believers" was not identical to the antisemitic attitudes of the population at large, and that the antisemitic priorities and genocidal commitment of the regime were not shared by ordinary Germans. Kershaw concludes that while "the depersonalization of the Jew had been the real success story of Nazi propaganda and policy," nonetheless "the 'Jewish question' was of no more than minimal interest to the vast majority of Germans during the war years. . . . Popular opinion, largely indifferent and infused with a latent anti-Jewish feeling . . . provided the climate within which spiralling Nazi aggression towards the Jews could take place unchallenged. But it did not provoke the radicalisation in the first place." [14] He sums up his position in the memorable phrase: "The road to Auschwitz was built by hatred, but paved with indifference." [15]

Despite his subsequent critique of Kershaw, Kulka's conclusions are strikingly similar. Surveying the Security Service reports, he states that "during the war period the unquestionably dominant feature was the almost total absence of any reference to the existence, persecution, and extermination of the Jews—a kind of national conspiracy of silence." The few reactions that were noted are "characterized by a striking abysmal indifference to the fate of the Jews as human beings. It seems that here, the 'Jewish Question' and the entire process of its 'solution' in the Third Reich reached the point of almost total depersonalization." [16] "What is known is that the composite picture that the regime obtained from popular opinion reports pointed toward the general passivity of the population in the face of the persecution of the Jews." While the Jewish question "might not have been high on the list of priorities for the population at large . . . there were sufficient numbers who chose to give the regime the freedom of action to push for a radical 'Final Solution.'" [17]

Bankier notes the "deep-seated anti-Jewish feelings" in German society but likewise concludes that "on the whole the public did not assign antisemitism the same importance as the Nazis did. . . . The policy of deportations and mass murder succeeded because the public displayed moral insensibility to the Jews' fate." But he goes beyond moral insensibility and passivity to argue for a growing schism between the people and the regime. "From 1941 onwards, the failure of Nazi promises to materialize drove a wedge between the population and the regime. . . . Declining hopes of victory and spiralling presentiments of a bitter end issued in a move to distance themselves from propaganda in general and from the Jewish issue in particular." Concludes Bankier: "Ordinary Germans knew how to distinguish between an acceptable discrimination . . . and the unacceptable horror of genocide. . . . The more the news of mass murder filtered through, the less the public wanted to be involved in the final solution of the Jewish question." [18]

The general conclusions of Kershaw, Kulka, and Bankier—based on years of research and a wide array of empirical evidence—stand in stark contrast to the Dawidowicz/Goldhagen image of the entire German population "deranged" by a delusional mass psychosis and a "hallucinatory, lethal view of the Jews." If "ordinary Germans" shared the same "latent," "traditional," or even "deep-seated" antisemitism that was widespread in European society but not the "fanatical" or "radical" antisemitism of Hitler, the Nazi leadership, and the party "true believers," then the behavior of the "ordinary Germans" of Reserve Police Battalion 101 cannot be explained by a singular German antisemitism that made them different from other "ordinary men."

My characterization of the depersonalizing and dehumanizing antisemitism of the men of Reserve Police Battalion 101, which Goldhagen finds too "tepid," places them in the mainstream of German society, as described by Kershaw, Kulka, and Bankier, but distinct from ideologically driven Nazi leadership. The implications of my study are that the existence of widespread negative racial stereotyping in a society—in no way unique to Germany—can provide fanatical regimes not only the freedom of action to pursue genocide (as both Kershaw and Kulka conclude) but also an ample supply of executioners.

In regard to the centrality of antisemitic motivation, moreover, it should be noted that German executioners were capable of killing millions of *non*-Jews targeted by the Nazi regime. Beginning in 1939, systematic and large-scale mass murder was initiated against the German handicapped and the Polish intelligentsia. Over three million Soviet prisoners of war perished from hunger, exposure, disease, and outright execution—two-thirds of them in the first nine months after the launching of Operation Barbarossa but before the death camps of Operation Reinhard had even opened. Tens of thousands of non-Jews in Nazi-occupied Europe fell victim to horrendous reprisal measures. And finally, the Nazi regime included Gypsies in their genocidal assault. Clearly something more than singular German antisemitism is needed to explain perpetrator behavior when the regime could find executioners to murder millions of non-Jewish victims.

Let us now follow a second approach to this issue as well, by examining non-German units in the Ukraine and Belorussia that carried out killing actions quite similar to those performed by Reserve Police Battalion 101.[19] Thus I will not be looking at those elements that carried out the initial murderous pogroms in the summer of 1941, often under German instigation, and were then frequently formed into full-time auxiliaries of the *Einsatzgruppen* for the large-scale systematic massacres that soon followed. The zealous followers of Jonas Klimaitis in Lithuania or Viktors Arajs in Latvia, who eagerly rushed to help the invading Germans kill communists and Jews, are not appropriate counterparts of Reserve Police Battalion 101 for the purposes of cross-cultural comparison.

Instead I would like to examine the rural police units in Belorussia and the Ukraine, which did not really take shape until 1942. They then participated in the "second wave" of killing on Soviet territory. Like the members of Reserve Police Battalion 101 in Poland, these policemen provided the essential workforce for the "mopping-up" killings of Jews in small towns and villages and for the "Jew hunts" that relentlessly tracked down escapees.

On July 16, 1941, Hitler made known his desire for accelerated pacification in the occupied Soviet territories. They were to be turned into a "Garden of Eden" from which Germany would never withdraw.[20] Nine days later, on July 25, Himmler gave orders for the formation of units to be designated as *Schutzmannschaften*. Kurt Daluege, head of the Order Police, issued guidelines on July 31 stipulating what form these *Schutzmannschaften* were to take. A card file of all recruited *Schutzmänner* was to be sent to the Security Police for political screening, though formation of the units was not to be held up in the meantime. The men were to wear a distinctive armband over old Russian army uniforms shorn of their insignia. For the most part, they were to be equipped with clubs, but in special circumstances they might be given rifles or pistols. Trainers and initial officers were to come from either the Security Police or Order Police. Future officers and noncommissioned officers would be carefully selected from among the new recruits.[21] During his inspection tour of the Baltic in late July, Himmler spoke about the immediate creation of police formations of Estonians, Latvians, Lithuanians, and Ukrainians to be used outside their home areas.[22]

While Himmler concerned himself primarily with the formation of battalion-sized police formations, the behind-the-front security divisions and the local *Feldkommandanturen* and *Ortskommandanturen* of the military administration found themselves confronted with the need to create smaller units of local police as well, for what the Germans called *Einzeldienst,* or precinct service. As early as July 11, 1941, the chief of staff of the Rear Army Area Ukraine had approved the formation of Ukrainian police to maintain order and provide protection within the Ukrainian communities.[23] As one *Wehrmacht* officer subsequently explained: "The vast tasks of the German security forces in the rear army areas require an extensive recruitment of reliable portions of the population to provide help of all kinds."[24]

German army officers of the military administration toured the outlying small towns and villages in their occupation zones and appointed mayors, who in turn helped recruit local police units.[25] One *Ortskommandantur* noted that the local population was very hesitant to provide manpower to the German-appointed mayors until after the fall of Kiev in mid-September.[26] As an enticement, each mayor was to offer ten rubles per day to each volunteer, as well as free rations to his wife and children. If sufficient volunteers were not forthcoming, the *Ortskommandantur* was to contact the nearest prisoner-of-war camp concerning the release of Ukrainian prisoners for police service.[27]

The local police units lacked uniformity as well as uniforms. They were variously called "auxiliary police" (*Hilfspolizei*), "order service" (*Ordnungsdienst*), "citizens' guard" (*Bürgerwehr*), and "militia" (*Miliz*). The army freely conceded, indeed desired, that the personnel should be checked by the Security Service.[28] However, in most places there was no Security Police (Sipo) or Security Service (SD) available to train and supervise these units.[29] Training was therefore undertaken by the *Ortskommandanturen,*[30] the military police,[31] or in much of the Ukraine by a special detachment of Order Police under a Lieutenant Hardt from Police Battalion 311.[32]

Initially only a minority of these local police were armed, and only then for special assignments and with limited ammunition (10 rounds per man).[33] In Uman the *Ortskommandantur* provided weapons for only 20 of 139 Ukrainian police.[34] In Dnepropetrovsk, arms were given to 100 of 400.[35] In Novi Saporoshje, 50 guns were provided for 126 police.[36] These local police were to be used for numerous tasks: guard duty, patrol, and price and market controls, as well as "guarding Jews" (*Judenüberwachung*) and "special tasks" (*Sonderaufgaben*). In the larger cities where the *Einsatzgruppen* were organizing large massacres, the Ukrainian police were involved. As one *Ortskommandant* reported in mid-October 1941: "At the moment a police action against the remaining Jews in Krivoy-Rog is in progress, during which the entire Ukrainian auxiliary police is being put to work. Krivoy-Rog shall become free of Jews."[37] In contrast to the Baltic, however, such participation in *Einsatzgruppen* mass killings during 1941 seems to have been less widespread in the Ukraine.[38] Other employment of the Ukrainian police was apparently much more mundane. Their use as "errand boys" (*Laufbursche*) and private servants in the military was apparently so common that it had to be explicitly forbidden.[39]

When large portions of the Ukraine were switched from military to civil administration in mid-November 1941, the army prepared to transfer its plethora of local Ukrainian police units to the Order Police. The Rear Army Area South insisted, however, that this transfer not take place until these units were militarily dispensable.[40] The transfer of the local Ukrainian police to the Order Police and their renaming as *Schutzmannschaften* generally occurred in December 1941 and January 1942.[41] Kurt Daluege, head of the Order Police, reported a phenomenal increase in the *Schutzmannschaften* over the next year: from 30,000 in December 1941 to 300,000 in December 1942.[42] The initial figure may well not have included numerous police still under army jurisdiction, but the growth of the *Schutzmannschaften* was still significant. What must be kept in mind, quite simply, is that the vast majority of the 300,000 *Schutzmänner* in December 1942 had been in German service for less than a year. They had not yet become policemen during, much less been personally involved in, the "first wave" of killing in 1941.

The Order Police were vastly outnumbered by the *Schutzmannschaften* they recruited, trained, and supervised. This was particularly the case for the German and Ukrainian police scattered throughout the occupied territories in precinct service. For instance, in the *Generalbezirk* (district) of Nikolayev in the Ukraine, 271 German *Schutzpolizei* (city police) supervised 700 Ukrainian police at the urban precinct level as well as three *Schutzmannschaften* battalions totaling about fifteen hundred men. In the rural areas, 410 German gendarmes supervised 4,946 Ukrainian *Schutzmänner.* The overall ratio was more than ten to one. In the neighboring district of Kiev, the ratio was nearly twelve to one.[43] Approximately two-thirds of the German police, moreover, were not career police but middle-aged reservists conscripted after 1939.[44] As Lieutenant Deuerlein, the commander of the gendarmerie outside Brest-Litovsk, complained, 14 of his 22 German police were reserves who had had only four weeks of training with weapons and themselves were in need of basic weapons training. Such was the manpower with which he was to train and supervise his 287 *Schutzmänner*—surely a case of the one-eyed leading the blind.[45]

Recruiting and training remained ongoing problems. The Order Police's calls for new recruits were issued in the press, over the radio, on placards, and through flyers.[46] In addition to the pay and family rations, there was one further inducement, which proved to be the most effective in attracting recruits: the immediate families of *Schutzmänner* were to be exempt from deportation to forced labor in Germany.[47] Lieutenant Deuerlein outside Brest-Litovsk reported: "Whenever the natives are supposed to be sent to Germany for labor, the rush for employment in the *Schutzmannschaft* is greater."[48] Nevertheless, he concluded, recruitment went very slowly, and those who did volunteer were "not always good human material."[49]

Initially, squad leaders of *Schutzmannschaften* were to be instructed through a translator by a German trainer and would in turn instruct their own squads.[50] The results were apparently unsatisfactory, and special training schools for the *Schutzmannschaft* noncommissioned officers were created; failure to attend meant loss of rank.[51] The inadequate training of the *Schutzmannschaften* nonetheless continued to be a major concern.[52]

Indoctrination was also intensified as part of the training process. Initially the Order Police in Berlin ordered "political nurturing" (*politische Betreuung*) in the form of "politically enlightening instruction," but not an "ideological education" (*weltanschauliche Schulung*). The initial intent was to familiarize the *Schutzmänner* with Germany and its people.[53] Once the schools for noncommissioned officers were established, a regular course of indoctrination was included alongside the usual lessons in drill and weaponry. The focus was primarily upon the identity of Jews and Bolsheviks and the salvation of the European peoples by Hitler and Germany from this "Asiatic" threat. The conclusion was brutal and blunt: "The Jew must be destroyed" (*Der Jude muss vernichtet werden*).[54]

In summary, the precinct-level Ukrainian police were first organized by the military administration in 1941. They were vastly expanded under the Order Police in 1942, whom they outnumbered by at least a ten-to-one ratio. Attempts at training and indoctrination were intensified, but the German Order Police were never fully satisfied with the results. The local police joined for numerous reasons, including pay, food for their families, release from prisoner-of-war camps, and a family exemption from deportation to forced labor in Germany. Although the Germans had difficulty recruiting as many Ukrainian police as they wanted, nonetheless the Ukrainian police numbered in the tens of thousands and constituted a major manpower source for the "second wave" of the Final Solution that swept through the Ukraine in 1942.

There is a lack of documentation from the precinct level on the day-to-day participation of the Ukrainian auxiliary police in the mass murder of Jews. From neighboring Belorussia, however, several series of police reports exist, from which we can see that the local *Schutzmänner* and their supervising German gendarmes performed precisely the same duties as Reserve Police Battalion 101 in Poland, with one exception: there were no deportations to death camps, only shooting actions. The first series of reports came from Lieutenant Deuerlein, gendarmerie commander in the countryside surrounding Brest-Litovsk. In October 1942 Deuerlein reported:

> On the nineteenth and twentieth of September a Jewish action was carried out in Domatshevo and Tomatshovka through a *Sonderkommando* of the SD, in conjunction with a mounted squadron of gendarmes stationed in Domatshevo and the *Schutz-mannschaft*. A total of 2,900 Jews were shot. . . . After the Jewish action in Domatshevo and Tomatshovka the Jews living in the region are now almost totally destroyed.[55]

The next month he reported "participation in the action against the Jews in the city and region of Brest-Litovsk since October 15. So far some 20,000 Jews have been shot." For his anticipated activities in the near future, he added: "Search for bunkers to be found in the area around Brest-Litovsk. . . . Taking care of [*Erledigung*] the flee-ing Jews still found in the region."[56] One month later the "Jew hunt" was still in progress, as Deuerlein once again reported on his planned activities: "Search for the Jews even now hiding in bunkers in the forests."[57]

The gendarmerie outpost in Mir, also in Belorussia, likewise re-ported the results of its killing activities to headquarters in Baranovi-che. Its commander noted that "560 Jews were shot in the Jewish action carried out in Mir" on August 13, 1942.[58] The gendarmerie commander in Baranoviche thereafter reported to Minsk:

> I have been given general instructions by the *Gebietskommissar* in Baranoviche to clear the area, especially the lowlands, of Jews, so far as the forces at my disposal permit. As a result of the major actions that were carried out in the past months, large numbers of Jews fled and joined groups of bandits. To prevent further escapes, I have eliminated Jews who were still living in the towns of Po-lonka and Mir. Altogether, 719 Jews were shot. In the meantime, 320 Jews who had escaped from the major actions could be recap-tured by the gendarmerie posts and executed after court-martial.[59]

Around Mir the Jew hunt continued. On September 29, 1942, a "patrol of the Mir *Schutzmannschaft*" found in the forest six Jews who "had fled the previous Jew action." They were shot "on the spot."[60] Six weeks later a forester discovered a Jewish bunker. He led a patrol of three German gendarmes and sixty *Schutzmänner* to the site. Five Jews, including the former head of the *Judenrat* of Mir, were hauled from the bunker and shot. "The food"—including 100 kilograms of potatoes—"as well as the tattered clothing were given to the Mir *Schutzmannschaft*."[61]

In short, the role of the precinct-level police recruited on Soviet territory in the Final Solution seems scarcely distinguishable from that of German reserve police in Poland. The precinct-level *Schutz-männer* were not the eager pogromists and collaborators of midsum-mer 1941, just as the German reserve police were not career SS and policemen but post-1939 conscripts. The role and behavior of the Ukrainian and Belorussian auxiliary police in carrying out the Final Solution do not, I think, lend support to the notion of "specifically German behavioral modes."

I would like to make one other cross-cultural comparison, as yet insufficiently documented, that is even more suggestive. Reserve Police Battalion 101 was composed almost entirely of Germans from the Hamburg region, including some men from Bremen, Bremerhaven, and Wilhelmshaven, as well as a few Holsteiners from Rendsburg who felt like relative outsiders. In addition, however, the battalion included a contingent of policemen from Luxemburg, which had been annexed to the Third Reich in 1940. The presence of the Luxemburgers in Reserve Police Battalion 101 offers the historian the unusual opportunity for a "controlled experiment" to measure the impact of the same situational factors on men of differing cultural and ethnic background.

The problem is a scarcity of testimony. Unfortunately, the Luxemburgers of Reserve Police Battalion 101 were not among those interrogated in the 1960s, and only one witness described their participation in the battalion's activities in any detail. According to this witness, the Luxemburgers belonged to Lieutenant Buchmann's platoon in first company and were particularly active in the roundups before the first massacre at Jozefow. This was a period in late June and early July of 1942, when the trains were not running to Belzec, and Jews in the southern Lublin district were being concentrated in transit ghettos such as Piaski and Izbica. On the night before the initial massacre at Jozefow, Lieutenant Buchmann was the sole officer who said he could not order his men to shoot unarmed women and children and asked for a different assignment. He was put in charge of taking the work Jews to Lublin, and, according to the witness, the Luxemburgers under his command provided the guard. Hence they did not participate in the massacre.[62]

Thereafter Lieutenant Buchmann continued to refuse participation in any Jewish action. However, those in his platoon were not exempted. Under the command of the first sergeant, who was a "110 percent Nazi" and a real "go-getter,"[63] the Luxemburgers in particular became quite involved. According to the witness, the company captain took considerable care in selecting personnel for assignments. "In general the elderly remained behind," he noted. In contrast, "*the Luxemburgers were in fact present at every action.* With these people it was a matter of career police officials from the state of Luxemburg, who were all young men in their twenties" (emphasis mine). Despite their absence at Jozefow, it would appear that the Luxemburgers became the shock troops of first company simply because of their younger age and greater police experience and training—the absence of "specifically German behavioral modes" and singular German antisemitism notwithstanding.

This evidence requires qualification, however. The company captain in question was with the battalion in Poland for less than four months, and thus testimony about the captain and the Luxemburgers does not apply to the later period and may not hold true for the more voluntaristic Jew hunts. There is at least a highly suggestive argument from silence, however. While many witnesses could still remember the nonshooters in the battalion twenty years later (though it was not always in their interest to do so), the Luxemburgers attracted no comment whatsoever. One must ask: did the Luxemburgers stir no memories and cause no comment in the 1960s precisely because in 1942 they had behaved like most of their German comrades?

Let me conclude briefly. If the studies of Kershaw, Kulka, and Bankier are valid and most Germans did not share the fanatical antisemitism of Adolf Hitler and the hard-core Nazis, then an argument taking a singular German antisemitism to explain the murderous actions of low-level perpetrators does not hold up. If the Nazi regime could find executioners for millions of non-Jewish victims, the centrality of antisemitism as the crucial motive for the German perpetrators is also called into question. If tens of thousands of local policemen in Belorussia and the Ukraine—taken as needed by the Germans, who were desperate for help and offered a variety of inducements—basically performed the same duties and behaved in the same way as their German counterparts in Poland, then the argument of "specifically German behavioral modes" likewise fails. And finally, if Luxemburgers in Reserve Police Battalion 101 did not behave differently from their German comrades, then the immediate "situational" factors to which I gave considerable attention in the conclusion of my book—much to the displeasure of my critics—must be given even greater weight. The preponderance of evidence, I would still argue, suggests that in trying to understand the vast majority of the perpetrators, we are dealing not with "ordinary Germans" but with "ordinary men."

Allan Fenigstein

Reconceptualizing the Psychology of the Perpetrators

AT THE CORE OF ANY ATTEMPT TO EXPLAIN THE MASS DESTRUCTION of European Jewry is the question of the behavior of the perpetrators: how to understand those who actively prepared and implemented the Holocaust, the systematic extermination of six million Jews. In examining the perpetrators, I will focus not so much on the Nazi elite who were ultimately responsible for creating the "final solution to the Jewish question" but were far removed from the actual occurrence of torture and death; rather, I look at the rank and file who directly perpetrated the atrocities, and whose scale of involvement was astounding. It has been estimated that, including Nazi organizations such as the Gestapo, the *Schutzstaffel* (SS), the *Sicherheitsdienst* (SD), and the *Sturmabteilung* (SA), over two hundred thousand rank-and-file members of Hitler's regime committed crimes before and during the war.[1]

What psychological mechanisms transformed ordinary, otherwise unremarkable citizens of Germany into people capable of destroying the lives of innocent Jewish civilians? Were these Germans predisposed, as a result of some deep-seated, repressed antipathy, toward fervent prejudice and obedience of a malevolent authority, as suggested by Theodor Adorno and his associates in their work on the "authoritarian personality"?[2] Did the bureaucratic pressures compel atrocities in spite of powerful moral and emotional resistance to those actions, as demonstrated in Stanley Milgram's classic studies on obedience to authority?[3] Both of these perspectives, which have dominated contemporary psychological approaches to the Holocaust, have some glaring conceptual inadequacies. In particular, these paradigms focus almost exclusively on the attitudes and behaviors of *individuals,* whereas the event we are struggling to explain must be understood, fundamentally, as involving two *groups,* Jews and Nazis. Although the intergroup nature may be self-evident, its implications for an understanding of the Holocaust have not been fully developed. After reviewing the problems with the individual-centered approaches, I will offer a different analysis, one interpreting Holocaust as an intergroup phenomenon, in the hope of providing a better understanding of the psychology of the perpetrators.

THE AUTHORITARIAN PERSONALITY

German society has long been characterized by its dominant values of tradition, order, and respect for authority. In the decade after World War II, Adorno's research group at Berkeley, all survivors of the Holocaust, believed they had discovered a particular kind of personality structure—"authoritarianism"—that, consistent with previous characterizations of German culture, predisposed the affected individuals toward totalitarian dogma and unquestioning obedience. More importantly, prejudice and discrimination were the product of authoritarianism, these authors were convinced, and studying it could significantly contribute to an understanding of the Holocaust.

Their work rested on the fundamental assumption that political and social attitudes, and racial prejudices in particular, were largely an expression of deep-lying, disturbed tendencies in personality. As Freudians, Adorno and associates viewed personality development as the result of the repression and redirection of instinctive needs that come into conflict with the constraints of family and society. Parents who are obsessed with rules, duty, convention, and authority, they argued, secure dependence and obedience, in effect, by emotional blackmail that makes their children simultaneously revere and despise them. The parents become idealized, and the children's hatred for them is repressed, eventually finding its expression elsewhere. Idealization of the parents is then generalized to all authority figures, as is the repression of criticism. The grown children instead direct their criticism toward out-groups who are of lower status and lesser power. Other repressed aspects of the personality, such as sexuality and malice, are then projected as out-group characteristics, which in turn serve to rationalize the selection of out-groups as legitimate targets for aggression. Thus, repressed aggression toward authority is displaced onto the out-group.

In essence, the theory argues that when the ordinary balance between parental discipline and individual self-expression is upset by an overly harsh and restrictive disciplinary regime, as presumably was the case for many Germans, the child develops an "authoritarian personality." In this personality syndrome, the individual respects and defers to authority figures, is overly concerned with rank and status, is intolerant of ambiguity and uncertainty, has a need for a clearly defined and rigidly structured world, and expresses hostility toward and discrimination against weaker others. The authoritarian, in other words, is predisposed toward prejudice and a hatred of minority groups. Some early studies of SS members did, in fact, identify the authoritarian quality of the family as a possible predisposing factor in their later Nazi leanings.[4]

AUTHORITARIANISM IN NAZI GERMANY

In the postwar era, this theory stimulated a massive research effort into the nature and origins of racial prejudice, attracting both firm adherents and trenchant critics. While many of the specific methodological details of that controversy are beyond the scope of this paper,[5] some of the conceptual problems involved in attempting to explain the Holocaust in terms of individual, disturbed personalities can be addressed here. In general, the attempt to depict those who obeyed the order to massacre Jews as mentally sick or dysfunctional, completely different from "ordinary" people, has not been very successful.[6] Although some Nazis probably could be described this way, the overall psychiatric evidence suggests that many perpetrators were in fact quite ordinary. Psychological tests, interviews, and case histories have revealed that most rank-and-file Nazis were very average men who, for the most part, had lived quiet and respectable lives. As psychiatrist Robert Jay Lifton has observed, what was horrifying about them was not who they were but rather what they did.[7]

The Holocaust could not have happened without the active participation of massive numbers of Germans—not only those who committed the murders but those who performed the countless other tasks, from manufacturing the gas to assembling the trains, that also constituted the Holocaust[8]—and the acquiescence of countless more ordinary citizens whose passive complicity in the escalating anti-Jewish persecution was a necessary precondition for the implementation of the Final Solution.[9] Yet although antisemitic attitudes and actions prevailed among hundreds of thousands of Germans, research has shown that they differed greatly in most psychological traits, and that the authoritarian personality was not nearly as widespread among the Nazis as researchers had anticipated;[10] thus, this personality explanation fails to account for the extraordinary pervasiveness of both explicit prejudice and implicit assent to the atrocities within Nazi Germany. German antipathy toward Jews simply cannot be explained as a function of specific personality characteristics when those characteristics were represented in at best only a small segment of the population. In addition, a focus on relatively stable personality structures cannot account for sudden leaps in prejudicial attitudes. Despite a long cultural history of prejudice and discrimination toward Jews, the steep growth of antisemitism took place in Nazi Germany over the course of only a decade or so[11]— much too quickly for a whole generation of German families to have adopted new forms of child-rearing practices giving rise to authoritarian personalities.

Consistent with a voluminous psychological literature, these arguments suggest that we are much more likely to find sources of prejudice by looking at powerful sociocultural factors,[12] such as the prevailing ideology and societal norms in Nazi Germany, than in individual personality factors.

SITUATIONAL INFLUENCES ON THE INDIVIDUAL

A second psychological approach has been to explain the behavior of the perpetrators as resulting from powerful situational or external forces operating on the individual. The best-known and most controversial experiment associated with this perspective is that of Milgram on the power of obedience. Milgram asked ordinary, mentally healthy, primarily male subjects, drawn from a broad spectrum of socioeconomic and educational backgrounds, to participate in a study on "learning" in which they, as the "teacher," were to administer punishment—in the form of increasingly severe electrical shocks—to another participant, the "learner," out of sight, whenever the learner failed to answer a question correctly. Although each teacher submitted to a low-level, but quite unpleasant, sample shock (to heighten the realism of the situation), no other shocks were actually delivered during the experiment. But the teacher did not know that; for that person, the situation was extremely realistic and tense. As the supposed shocks grew more intense, the learner/victim's prerecorded reactions became more excruciating. Early in the procedure, the victim shouted that the shocks were becoming too painful. That was soon followed by a demand to be let out of the experiment. Next the victim cried out that he could no longer stand the pain. Eventually, he began yelling that he would not provide any more answers and insisted that he be freed. Over the course of the next set of shocks, there were agonized screams, and finally silence. In trying to decide what to do during the research, many subjects turned to the experimenter for instructions. The response was that the experiment must continue and that the experimenter would take "full responsibility."

How far did subjects go in obeying the experimenter? The now well-known and still startling finding was that 65 percent of the subjects were willing to punish another person with an almost lethal dose of electricity at the bidding of the experimenter, despite the facts that the victim had done nothing to merit such severe punishment and the experimenter had no special powers to enforce his orders. The fascination that attends Milgram's studies derives from what it implies about the nature of evil: that is, about how easily normal individuals possessing no malevolence can carry out inhumane commands. The implication is that *anyone*—not just Nazis and their sympathizers or collaborators—would have willingly participated in the attempted annihilation of the Jewish people. Another lesson of this research is that ordinary people simply doing their jobs, without any particular malice or hostility, can become agents in a terribly destructive process.

As Milgram recognized, there were enormous disparities in circumstances and consequences between the artificial laboratory situation and the all-too-real horrors of Nazi Germany. For example, whereas Milgram's subjects were assured that no permanent physical damage would be done to their victims, and the victims were not systematically devalued prior to their victimization, in contrast, Nazi killers knew they were destroying human life (although an intense propaganda program had at least partially succeeded in portraying those lives as unworthy of life). Still, Milgram believed that similar psychological processes were centrally involved:

> A commonly offered explanation [of these research findings] is that those who shocked the victim at the most severe level were monsters, the sadistic fringe of society. But if one considers that almost two-thirds of the participants fall into the category of "obedient" subjects, and that they represented ordinary people, . . . the argument becomes very shaky. This issue is highly reminiscent of Hannah Arendt's contention, offered in *Eichmann in Jerusalem,* that the prosecution's effort to depict Eichmann as a sadistic monster was fundamentally wrong, that he came closer to being an uninspired bureaucrat who simply sat at his desk and did his job. . . . After witnessing hundreds of ordinary persons submit to the authority in our own experiments, I must conclude that Arendt's conception of the "banality of evil" comes closer to the truth than one might dare imagine.[13]

A crucial factor in Milgram's analysis of obedience is a socialization theory that makes obedience a basic element in the structure of social life. In this view, ordinary persons become well practiced in adopting the mentality of an agent who, in an essentially mindless fashion, performs an action authorized by someone else. The most far-reaching consequence of this submission to authority is the disappearance of a sense of responsibility for one's actions. The subjects in the experiment attribute all initiative to the experimenter, and the obedient subjects see themselves simply as instruments of the experimenter, and in no way morally accountable for their actions. This "agentic" state, as Milgram described it, is not merely a thin alibi; it represents a fundamental change in an individual's mode of thinking and self-understanding.

Milgram's perspective certainly has some appeal. His argument is frighteningly evocative of the "I was just following orders" heard repeatedly at the Nuremberg trials. Also consistent with Milgram's position is the generally high value placed on obedience to authority in Nazi ideology and German culture,[14] as is Arendt's analysis of Eichmann as a career-oriented bureaucrat.[15] Raul Hilberg's argument—that what made the Nazis' success in carrying out genocide on such a scale possible was countless bureaucrats and agencies applying their practiced skills and standard procedures to the task at hand—may also be offered in support of Milgram's thesis.[16] Finally,

Christopher Browning, in his study of Reserve Police Battalion 101, suggests that although none of Milgram's studies exactly paralleled the historical situation of Nazi Germany, "nonetheless many of Milgram's insights find graphic confirmation in the behavior and [subsequent] testimony of the men" who carried out shootings and deportations of thousands of Jews.[17]

OBEDIENCE PRESSURES IN NAZI GERMANY

A number of factors, however, caution us against unquestioningly accepting Milgram's analysis by analogy. For one, on the basis of their behavioral reactions, we might question whether the destructive obedience observed in laboratory subjects involved the same psychological processes guiding the Nazi killers. Milgram's subjects were not like Eichmann; they did not act like mechanistic bureaucrats. Almost everyone participating in the experiments experienced great tension, distress, and conflict while shocking the victim. Eichmann showed no corresponding difficulty in carrying out his orders.[18]

These varying reactions may have been due, however, not to differences in the underlying obedience process but to differences in the situations. Eichmann only had to sit at his desk to participate in mass murder. He rarely experienced, in any direct, personal way, the consequences of his action. (When he did, touring the concentration camps, even he was sickened.) In contrast, the subjects in Milgram's experiment received graphic and immediate aural evidence of the effect of the shocks they dutifully administered. Perhaps a more appropriate comparison of psychological mechanisms would be between Milgram's findings and the responses of the Reserve Police, men who confronted the effects of their actions directly and extremely explicitly—they literally became, in Browning's words, "saturated in the blood of their victims."[19]

Browning argues that pressures to obey authority, "even to the point of performing repugnant actions in violation of 'universally accepted' moral norms," were crucial in turning the "ordinary men" of Reserve Police Battalion 101 into participants in mass murder. He even suggests that the massacre they carried out in one day at Jozefow, where fifteen hundred men, women, and children were systematically slaughtered by gunfire, might have been "a kind of radical Milgram experiment that took place in a Polish forest with real killers and victims." [20] How is this proposal to be evaluated? There is no question that, faced with orders to commit atrocities, the policemen carried them out. But to what extent did their compliance reflect deference to authority?

As Browning acknowledges, arriving at a definitive answer is extremely difficult: several levels of authority were operating, as were myriad other factors, including careerism and pressures to conform. Despite these complexities and the variations from Milgram's experimental conditions, however, many findings from the laboratory are indeed consistent with the behavior of the Reserve Police. For example, direct proximity to the killing reduced compliance; and when the policemen's work only involved rounding up the victims on "Jew-hunts" and forcing them onto the trains that would take them to the death camps, this division of labor removed any feeling of responsibility for the victims' ultimate fate. That comparable findings emerged from Milgram's laboratory perhaps render his insights even more impressive.

Where Was Conscience?

However, before concluding that similar psychological processes were at work, we must scrutinize some significant points of departure between Milgram's research and the events at Jozefow. A critical assumption of the Milgram experiment was that obedience pressures are necessary to compel destructive actions *in the face of powerful moral resistance to those actions.* As Milgram argued, the power of obedience can be effectively demonstrated only when it is opposed by another powerful force (such as the moral imperative against harming an innocent other) that works in the direction of disobedience; in the absence of moral opposition to an action, obedience is unnecessary as an explanation for that action. [21]

In Milgram's studies, the extreme tension and distress exhibited by virtually all his subjects testifies to the moral conflict they experienced, between the demands of a legitimate authority to harm an innocent other and the demands of conscience not to do so. (These reactions, however, should not obscure the basic lesson of the research: despite their moral qualms, subjects continued to obey the order to harm an innocent victim.) Although no quantitative analysis is provided, Milgram reports that "many" subjects also felt they had acted against their own moral values, voiced disapproval and denounced their actions as wrong, and drew attention to the victim's suffering.[22]

The operation of any similar psychological processes among the men of Reserve Police Battalion 101, then, would be evidenced by an expression of similar moral concerns. In their actions and testimonies, however, such evidence is demonstrably lacking. There were a few men in the battalion—twelve out of a total of almost five hundred—who, from the beginning, extricated themselves from the impending mass murder; a few more removed themselves from the killing squads only after they had already committed several murders; and some managed on occasion to avoid killing when an opportunity arose, for example, when there was no direct surveillance. In all, perhaps 10 to 20 percent sought to evade the killings, once the shootings began.[23] This means, of course, that at least 80 percent of those called upon to shoot continued to do so until the last Jew had been killed—and often with a sense of relish and bravado that clearly belied the presence of moral restraints.[24]

Was the reluctance of the few evaders motivated by moral concerns or by empathy with their victims' plight? Browning admits that in their testimonies, given twenty to twenty-five years after the fact (and after considerable opportunity for reflection), "those who quit shooting . . . overwhelmingly cited sheer physical revulsion as the prime motive, but did not express any ethical principle behind this revulsion."[25] A particularly telling and egregious, but not uncommon, illustration of where the killers' concerns were comes from the testimony of one of the evaders, who described the horrifying results of the killing action as follows: " *The shooters* were gruesomely besmirched with blood, brains, and bone splinters; it hung on *their* clothing" (my emphasis).[26]

Although Browning points to other indications that perpetrators had a sense of moral wrongdoing, I find few of those arguments compelling. For example, the men of Reserve Police Battalion 101 are often described as bearing an enormous psychological burden, but the precise nature of that burden remains to be explained: their own testimony suggests that it resulted not from principled moral opposition to the destruction of innocent lives but rather from the sheer horror and grisliness of the mass slaughter. (Browning himself acknowledges this, and there is far more evidence than can be presented here.) Browning describes a feeling of "shame" that pervaded the room when the men returned to their barracks, presumably related to a sense of moral transgression, but he also finds that "by silent consensus . . . the massacre was simply not discussed" by the men, preventing overt indications of such shame.[27]

Despite the fact that the policemen's own testimonies rarely indicated any ethically motivated opposition to the murders, Browning argued that the "absence of such does not mean that their revulsion did not have its origins in . . . humane instincts."[28] However, any evidence of these "humane instincts" is lacking. That these former Nazis failed to express any ethical qualms about their participation in the brutal murders of unarmed, unresisting civilians is especially striking given the circumstances under which their testimonies were made. Speaking to representatives of the criminal justice system in a democratic Germany, these men had powerful motives to express remorse, whether genuine or fabricated, in the hope of mitigating their guilt and minimizing their punishment. It is difficult to escape the conclusion that their not expressing remorse must be taken at face value: these men simply did not feel that they had performed "repugnant actions in violation of 'universally accepted' moral norms."

The failure of the Reserve Police to voice any moral opposition to the killing of Jews is critical to the present analysis in two ways. First, it represents a crucial difference between Milgram's subjects, many of whom were reluctant to participate and who experienced moral distress over their destructive actions, and these Nazi perpetrators, whose reluctance to kill, if it existed at all, was a matter not of principled conscience but of physical disgust. And second, it undermines the need to cite obedience as an explanation. That is, when people perform actions they do not consider wrong, there need not be external causes, such as situational pressures, for their behavior.

Thus, it is highly doubtful that the Nazi executioners were subject to the same psychological processes observed in laboratory studies of obedience. In the laboratory, obedience pressures were necessary in order to overcome subjects' moral resistance; moral resistance was largely nonexistent in the men of Reserve Police Battalion 101. Given their backgrounds as ordinary Germans who had not been specifically selected for the task of mass murder by reason of personality or allegiance to the Nazi regime, we might reasonably assume that the Reserve Police were not especially eager to kill (or thought likely to kill). But their actions at Jozefow, and their subsequent testimony, suggest that, nevertheless, the overwhelming majority of them were also not inwardly opposed to the mass murder of Jews.

Was the Killing Mechanistic?

The concept of obedience, as formulated by Milgram and used by Arendt and Browning, suggests an image of the Nazi executioners as dutiful agents mechanically carrying out the murderous commands of the leader, without malevolence toward their victims. Was Nazi behavior in fact detached and emotionless? Arendt's characterization of Eichmann has been seriously questioned by a number of critics, who point out that Eichmann pursued his goal of shipping to the camps as many Jews as possible with a zealousness and perseverance that clearly went beyond the call of duty.[29] For example, he timed many large-scale actions against the Jews to coincide with their religious holidays, presumably to intensify their suffering. Arendt herself, in apparent contradiction of her Eichmann thesis, elsewhere offers some horrifying descriptions of Nazi torture and murder, clearly acknowledging that there was another face to the Holocaust than that of the dispassionate bureaucrat.[30]

Browning, as well, in describing the behavior of Reserve Police Battalion 101, repeatedly illustrates their penchant for cruelty, barbarism, and sadism toward Jews. In one case, for example, totally naked Jews, preferably old and bearded men, were forced to crawl in front of their intended graves and sustain beatings with clubs, before being shot. Again, it should be noted that these perpetrators were not generally SS men or ardent supporters of Hitler's regime. They were, for the most part, ordinary Germans (25 percent of whom were Nazi party members) who presumably had no unusually virulent antisemitism or obvious inclination to murder. Yet when the time came, they proved themselves capable of killing Jews with dedication and zeal. In general, the historical evidence on the inventiveness and enthusiasm with which the Nazis degraded, tortured, and killed their victims suggests that while Milgram's findings about obedience may account for a few rare instances of duty in the face of inner resistance, his research misses the mark entirely when it comes to explaining the more zealous cruelties that so defined the Holocaust.

Was Authority Absolute?

A simplistic authoritarian explanation, suggesting absolute obedience to absolute authority, has been challenged by Raul Hilberg. While emphasizing the bureaucratic nature of the Nazi regime, he notes that Milgram's conception of a bureaucracy involved a strictly totalitarian system, with a clearly defined hierarchy. The bureaucratic structure that destroyed European Jewry, on the other hand, was remarkably decentralized, with many of the far-reaching decisions and innovations originating among officials serving in middle or even lower positions of responsibility.[31]

The polycratic nature of the Nazi system is further exposed by an examination of the nature and consequences of disobedience in the Reserve Police and the *Einsatzgruppen*.[32] The men drafted into the mobile killing squads of the *Einsatzgruppen*, when ordered to kill defenseless Jews en masse, dispatching them by machine-gun fire into mass graves, for the most part complied. What impelled these men to slaughter? Were they simply following orders? Were they acting under coercion? We can gain some insight by looking at an attendant but largely neglected question: what happened to those SS men who were unwilling to continue killing Jews and decided not to participate? Examining the circumstances in which SS men and ordinary Nazis could avoid killing, and the men who did so, might elucidate the extent to which obedience pressures were necessary to make such slaughter possible.

It has been widely assumed that if an SS man refused to carry out a killing order, he himself would be killed. This assumption is largely based on the repeated and emphatic assertion of this contention by defendants in postwar trials. In addition, given the brutality and fanaticism of the SS, it might seem reasonable to assume that this externally directed terror could easily be turned inward, to punish those who refused to comply. But these assumptions are mistaken. There is not a single instance on record of harsh punishment ever being used, or even being possible, against one not obeying a killing order.[33] Thus, the likelihood of anyone in the SS or the Reserve Police suffering punishment for refusing to kill Jews was small or nonexistent; and if it did occur on rare occasions, it was not widely known. In fact, if anything, the killers knew that they were permitted to transfer from their killing units. Himmler himself had issued a written order to that effect, with the understanding that only those dedicated to the task should be killing Jews. At some level, Himmler believed that only the most fervent Nazis, deeply committed to the cause, could carry out the essential but difficult (in the sense of physical revulsion) task of extermination. Failure did not make the person a criminal; it was merely a matter of shame and disgrace for his not measuring up to the Nazi ideal.

An important emphasis of Browning's study is on the opportunities the men of this police battalion had to avoid their task of mass murder. That the perpetrators knew they had a choice of participating or not participating is made explicit by the testimony of one of the Reserve Police: "It was in no way the case that those who did not want to or could not carry out the shooting of human beings with their own hands could not keep themselves out of this task. No strict control was being carried out here."[34] The same point is made by Commander Ohlendorf of *Einsatzgruppe* D, who testified at Nuremberg that he "had sufficient occasion to see how many men of my *Gruppe* did not agree to this [killing] order in their inner opinion. Thus I forbade the participation in these executions on the part of some of these men and sent them back to Germany."[35] Again, it should be understood that "inner opinion" was not necessarily a matter of conscience. In one case, the SS officer requesting a transfer made it clear that his incapacity to continue killing resulted not from any principled disapproval but rather from physical revulsion. He was deeply ashamed of his inability to "sacrifice himself to the very last for the cause of Germany," but did not want to "disgrace Germany's image" by "presenting the spectacle of one . . . who has succumbed to cowardice."[36] This Nazi did not oppose the extermination of the Jews out of moral considerations. In fact, every indication was that he believed in the justice of the *Einsatzgruppe's* task; he simply could not endure the goriness of the killing.

These observations seriously weaken any argument that the executioners were effectively coerced into killing or were at the mercy of unyielding obedience pressures. The murderers were able to influence their own fate. The order to kill was not absolutely compelling. Those who were unwilling could stop; those who did not extricate themselves, therefore, were choosing to participate in the killings.

To return briefly to the comparison with Milgram: the nature of authority in the laboratory situation was also not absolute; subjects could have quit at any time. That many did not is testimony to the power of authority, even when it is not absolute, and perhaps a rejoinder to the problem raised concerning the less-than-absolute authority at Jozefow. But to reiterate: what is most important about the behavior of Milgram's subjects, and most impressive about the power of obedience, is not simply that subjects obeyed (even a weak) authority but that obedience occurred *despite significant moral opposition*. Milgram's subjects may have obeyed a malevolent authority, but unlike the Nazi perpetrators they were not willing participants; they were not responding to malevolent drives within themselves. Can the willing participation of so many men in the Nazi genocidal program also be explained as merely a matter of duty and discipline, devoid of any hatred or hostility toward their victims?

THE QUESTION OF RESPONSIBILITY

Beyond the problems already discussed, the concepts of the authoritarian personality and of obedience raise difficult questions about assigning blame to the perpetrators. In essence, both research traditions explain human inhumanity by identifying psychological factors, traceable either to familial history or to specific situational constraints, that effectively predispose an individual toward destructive obedience. In the presence of a malevolent authority, this disposition presumably becomes a corrosive poison that destroys the individual's sense of self and humanity. Thus, these theories emphasize powerful forces, either unconscious or external in origin, that in some way diminish personal responsibility for one's own immoral actions. Unconscious forces are beyond one's conscious control and represent, in effect, a separate and uncontrollable part of the individual. The obedient killer is also responding to forces outside his control. His murderous actions cannot be explained in terms of conscience, because he has presumably undergone some extraordinary psychological transformation in which a "new (agentic) creature replaces autonomous man, unhindered by the limitations of individual morality."[37]

When I discuss Milgram's experiments with students, I ask them, "Were the subjects responsible for their actions?" Initially, the students answer no, incredulous that I would even ask this question. But this soon gives way to an absolute certainty in the perception of, and indeed the need to perceive, Milgram's subjects as indeed morally responsible for their actions. The students implicitly recognize that moral responsibility is not a property that can be abdicated, but is an inescapable element of participation in an immoral enterprise.

Beyond these anecdotal observations, research findings, too, have challenged the explanatory viability of an "agentic" state that removes or denies a sense of conscience and responsibility for one's actions. During postexperimental interviews, the obedient subjects in Milgram's research were just as likely as the defiant ones to accept personal responsibility for their actions. Several other studies have similarly found reason to question whether the shedding of responsibility is a concomitant of obedience.[38] In summary, both phenomenological considerations and empirical evidence suggest that, if we are to develop a psychology that recognizes the inescapability of moral responsibility, we must rule out any theory that routinely exempts normal individuals from responsibility for their own heinous acts.

SOCIAL IDENTITY THEORY

For an alternative approach to a psychological understanding of the behavior of the Nazi murderers, we must fundamentally shift the focus of our analysis. Both Adorno's person-centered approach and Milgram's situation-centered approach are primarily concerned with the actions of individuals as *individuals,* while the main issue here, the annihilation of Jews by Nazis, involves the actions of individuals as *group members.* The Holocaust not only has been historically defined in terms of Nazis and Jews; it was experienced in those same terms by the victims and perpetrators.

Any interpersonal event will be influenced by the characteristics of the individuals involved, but if the encounter is perceived in terms of group membership, the interpersonal effects will be overwhelmed by the paramount categorization of "us versus them." To illustrate the point, Henri Tajfel, a major theorist in the field of intergroup relations, writes: "The selections for the gas ovens in the concentration camps were undoubtedly affected, to some extent, by the personal characteristics of those selected, by the individual whims or personalities of the selectors, or by the personal relationships which may have developed here or there. But all this hardly amounts to more than a wrinkle if our aim is to describe and understand the most significant, general aspects of what happened." [39] That is, the individual thoughts, feelings, and actions of the perpetrators on the whole were far more a matter of their shared group identity as Nazis (or Nazi sympathizers) than of their personal characteristics.

Tajfel's choice of example was not random. He was one of the few who survived the Nazi terror—who, as he described it, "came in from very cold and very far"—and he never forgot the extremities that must ultimately be explained. After the war, his interests turned to social psychology, and eventually and not surprisingly came to focus squarely on the issue of prejudice. The theory he originated and developed with his colleagues, which has come to be known as "social identity theory," is largely a European product, and this, together with his own personal history, adds a great deal of credibility to the theory because of the European history of group conflict. It is perhaps telling that this work has not yet achieved a comparable status in American psychology.

Tajfel and his colleagues developed a theory of group antagonism based on psychological processes that may well be universal and ineradicable. In essence, the theory identifies two fundamental tendencies: first, to categorize the world into in-groups and out-groups, and second, to nourish that differentiation through in-group favoritism and out-group derogation. The source of these tendencies is then traced to the individual's effort to achieve and maintain positive self-esteem, a drive so deep-seated and so basic that it is difficult to imagine its absence. [40]

Although the ultimate goal of Tajfel's work was to explain enormously catastrophic events, his starting point was a rather modest, somewhat artificial, but thought-provoking laboratory demonstration. Social psychology had long studied group conflict as an outcome of realistic competition for limited resources, but Tajfel suspected that, even in the absence of competition, conflict was likely to emerge, so long as the groups saw themselves, even in some small, insignificant way, as different. The basic experimental procedure devised by Tajfel to test that idea has come to be known as the "minimal group paradigm," and in numerous replications the same essential finding has emerged: regardless of how "minimal" or meaningless the difference between groups, the mere process of categorization into groups is sufficient to create a marked preference for members of one's own group. When social categories are imposed on individuals—even when those categorizations are done on a random, trivial, or ad hoc basis, such as the flip of a coin; even when there is no prior social contact or conflict between the groups or individuals involved; even when there is no discernible relation to self-interest; even when the participants remain anonymous to each other—the minimal categorization process creates the perception of in-groups and out-groups, and results in discriminatory intergroup behavior, as well as biases in the way group members perceive and evaluate themselves and others.

Tajfel and his coworkers did not expect to find this minimal group effect. The minimal situation had initially been created as a kind of baseline condition in which no group effects would occur—after all, there was no meaning to these minimal groups. The experimenters' intention had been to systematically introduce additional group-forming properties until discrimination did occur. What they had not anticipated was that, even in this baseline condition, bias and discrimination would emerge from meanings that the participants *themselves* imposed on the groups. In different studies, this in-group favoritism has been manifested as unequal allocations of resources, more favorable ratings of in-group characteristics, selective memory, biased evaluations of group performances, and biased attributions, such that the in-group is associated with good things and the out-group with bad ones.[41] All these findings have shown that neither attraction nor interdependence are necessary conditions for group formation; simply imposing a shared membership category can be sufficient to generate a group mentality. The effect is also rather mysterious in that very few participants were aware of their biased tendencies.

Subjects in this paradigm were given an opportunity to distribute monetary rewards. They were not permitted to determine their own rewards, but their predominant strategy was still a selfish one: they tried to maximize rewards for other members of the in-group, despite the lack of any obvious connection to those people, and despite the recognition that this strategy was essentially unfair. One of

Tajfel's most consistent and psychologically telling findings was the preference for a maximal in-group advantage over the out-group, even at the sacrifice of a larger total of in-group rewards; that is, more important than the absolute size of the group's resources was the need to establish the greatest *relative* advantage over the other. (In this context, it is interesting to think about the Nazis' willingness to divert valuable resources to the extermination process at great cost to the larger war effort.)[42]

Why should group formation result in this spontaneous, virtually automatic in-group bias? What is the basis of the apparently gratuitous discrimination in these most gratuitous of groups? Tajfel initially suggested norms as an explanation, since group categorizations in most cultures might evoke associations with competitive norms. But normative explanations are too general, and they fail to account for the existence of alternative "fairness" or "equity" norms, or for variations in behavior due to situational factors.

Fundamental cognitive processes involving categorical differentiation have also been offered as an explanation. If different classifications are imposed on two sets of stimuli, any stimuli, they exaggerate people's judgments of the differences between those stimuli. For categories to be cognitively useful (in ordering and simplifying information), they need to discriminate clearly between classes. Judgmental biases facilitate that process by sharpening the distinction (while at the same time blurring the differences within classes). In the minimal group situation, the arbitrary categories, although real, are ill defined; categorical differentiation—in the form of in-group bias—may then facilitate the distinction between categories.

The problem with the categorization approach, however, is that although it can explain why groups become more distinctive from each other, it does not explain why that distinctiveness is so often valued positively for the in-group and negatively for the out-group. A new concept was needed to explain that positive distinctiveness. So Tajfel and a colleague developed the notion of *social identity*.[43]

Categorization does not just order and simplify the world: it also serves to define who people are. Tajfel and Turner's fundamental insight was that when people become members of a group, any group, their sense of identity immediately and almost reflexively becomes closely bound up with their in-group membership. Any aspect of an individual's self-concept that is based on social group or category

memberships, together with the emotional and evaluative consequences of those memberships, will define that person's social
identity.

Although the concept of social identity has a long history, Tajfel
and his colleagues were the first to recognize that social identity processes have significant implications for an understanding of intergroup hostility and conflict. Their basic argument was as follows:
to the extent that people are motivated to evaluate themselves positively, and insofar as they define themselves in terms of their group,
they will be motivated to view their group positively; that is, to seek
a positive social identity. Since a group's worth is evaluated primarily
through comparison with other groups, a positive social identity requires that one's own group be favorably different, or positively distinct, from relevant comparison groups. Because intergroup comparisons indirectly contribute to individual self-esteem, groups attempt
to differentiate themselves in a positive direction from the others
through in-group biases that ultimately increase individual members' self-esteem.

In effect, therefore, in-group favoritism and out-group derogation enhance the status of the in-group while diminishing that of
the out-group, thus fostering positive social identity. Even in the absence of realistic conflicts of interest, hostility can develop between
groups as a result of the competition for mutual distinctiveness and
enhanced self-esteem. To take an example far removed from our current concerns, yet illuminating in its irony: two groups that are both
engaged, let's say, in a common humanitarian effort (that would be
greatly aided by cooperation between the groups) may find themselves at odds or even in conflict in a way that, ultimately, can be
understood as a rivalry in their drives for positive distinctiveness.

THE JEW IN NAZI IDEOLOGY AND NAZI IDENTITY

Social identity theory suggests a fundamental reanalysis of the nature
and consequences of identity among the perpetrators of the Holocaust. When group membership is salient, there is a transition from
personal to social identity; that is, a shift in self-definition, away
from personal and idiosyncratic characteristics, and toward category
memberships and adoption of the category's common or critical attributes.[44] From this perspective, it may be insufficient and perhaps

inappropriate to examine the Nazi perpetrators as products of their individual histories. In the context of the Holocaust, it might be more appropriate to consider them as having undergone a genuine process of identification with Nazism, to the point where Nazism became their central, social identity. The essential element in that process would then be a shared social categorization of themselves as Nazis in contrast to Jews. Did such an identity exist?

The basic elements of Nazi ideology and policy do seem to offer strong evidence of a Nazi identity defined, in large part, through differentiation from the "other," that is, the Jew. Hatred of the Jews was a central, compelling element of Hitler's mind, and of Nazi ideology.[45] The propaganda for that ideology was an explicit, multifaceted attempt to depict the Jewish people as "other." Essential to Nazi ideology was the claim that Aryans were racially superior to the racially inferior Jewish *Untermenschen*. As Claudia Koonz has argued, the language and respectability of eugenics succeeded in getting the masses to accept a radically new identity expressed in terms of binary racial concepts, and to dissociate themselves from the targeted Jewish subgroup.[46] Depictions of Jews as diseased, as vermin and lice, as the embodiment of vileness and filth, were widely disseminated through antisemitic newspapers, such as Julius Streicher's notorious *Der Stürmer* (with a circulation of nearly half a million), and displays on special notice boards in towns and villages. Cartoons and editorials held Jews responsible for every kind of social and economic ill and suggested that only through their elimination could health be restored to the German body politic.[47] That this incessant propaganda affected all levels of German society is documented by Jürgen Hagemann.[48] It is also suggested by Thomas Keneally's anecdote about some old drinking friends of Oskar Schindler who, in trying to make sense of the exceptional behavior the industrialist showed in risking his life to protect Jews, "thought of him as the victim of a Jewish virus. It was no metaphor; they believed it in literal terms. . . . Some area of the brain had fallen under a thrall that was half bacterium, half magic."[49]

Although many historians believe that antisemitic indoctrination, depicting the Jews as racially inferior and as the incarnation of evil bent on destroying the German people, was a necessary precondition for their mass murder,[50] Browning, in his analysis of how the "ordinary men" of Reserve Police Battalion 101 became murderers, raises serious challenges to that argument. More specifically, Browning questions the extent to which the conscious inculcation of Nazi doctrines shaped the behavior of Reserve Police Battalion 101, expressing significant "doubts about the adequacy of the . . . indoctrination [process] as an explanation for [their] becoming killers."[51] In effect, by questioning the role of ideological indoctrination, Browning is attempting to argue that the murderous actions of the Reserve Police were motivated not by murderous intent directed at an ideological enemy, but rather by immediate situational factors, such as obedience pressures. The deficiencies of the obedience argument have already been addressed; now we turn to an examination of the deficiencies in Browning's argument alleging the inadequacy of the indoctrination process. The major problem in his analysis is that much of the evidence he cites is either inconsistent or open to alternative interpretations that, in effect, undermine his position. Thus, while expressing skepticism about the extent to which the Reserve Police were subject to indoctrination, Browning, in apparent contradiction of his own thesis, also acknowledges that (1) this group was, ultimately, under the command of Himmler, who set a premium on ideological indoctrination against the political and racial enemies of the Third Reich; and (2) racial ideology was a pervasive part of the training of the Reserve Police. In similar fashion, other contradictions may be identified in Browning's presentation of the evidence bearing on the issue of indoctrination.

Specific Indoctrination Materials

Despite his admission that the racist perspective was evident in some of the indoctrination materials directed at the Reserve Police, including serials and pamphlets addressing topics such as the "end of the Jews," "the removal of this parasitical race," and "a Europe free of Jews," Browning, nevertheless, was able to reach the conclusion that there was relatively little (preserved) material that was "devoted explicitly to antisemitism."[52] In addition, he argued that racial propaganda discussing the "end" or "removal" of the Jews, which to some might appear to be blatantly and malevolently exhorting their destruction, was, in Browning's view, simply (and innocently?) intended to encourage Nazis to have more children (this despite his recognition that such encouragement was certainly irrelevant to many of the middle-aged reservists who were unlikely to have more children, and probably of limited relevance to anyone actively engaged in combat).[53]

Were There Explicit Orders to Kill?

Another source of Browning's skepticism regarding the role of Nazi indoctrination in the police killings was the apparent absence of explicit orders directing the Reserve Police to ruthlessly slaughter the unarmed, unresisting, innocent Jewish civilians of Jozefow. Again, this conclusion is somewhat perplexing in view of the evidence he cites. Browning acknowledges that explicit instructions to ruthlessly and mercilessly kill women and children were part of the guidelines for the Order Police, but then he suggests that these guidelines were limited only to targets who could be construed as "suspects" engaged in active "partisan warfare" against the Nazis, and that the Jews of Jozefow could not possibly have been construed in that way.[54] This interpretation seems highly suspect; in view of the unrelenting propaganda depicting Jews in general as the enemy, it would seem reasonable to at least consider the possibility that these victims could be regarded as partisans, in which case the killing instructions would, indeed, have been applicable. That is, a slightly different reading of the documents suggests that indoctrination materials supporting the slaughter at Jozefow may very well have existed, although not at the level of specificity sought by Browning.

Cultural Indoctrination

Even in the absence of specific materials, it is difficult to ignore other forms of indoctrination. Browning himself repeatedly acknowledges that the men of the Reserve Police were immersed in a ubiquitous cultural value system that was infused with vehement and unrelenting anti-Jewish propaganda, vilifying and demonizing the hated Jews and preparing the Germans for their destruction.[55] It is especially difficult, then, to understand how the role of ideology among these men can be questioned, when Browning identifies the political culture in which they lived for almost a decade as one in which "the denigration of Jews and the proclamation of Germanic racial superiority was so constant, so pervasive, so relentless, that it *must have shaped the general attitudes of masses of people in Germany, including the average reserve policeman"* (emphasis mine).[56]

In summary, Browning's argument that the murderous actions of the Reserve Police were unrelated to Nazi ideology was based, in large part, on his particular reading of the evidence, which suggested that (1) indoctrination materials directed toward the police were relatively rare; or (2) these materials were innocent in their intent; or (3) they were not specifically directed toward the actual victims of the Reserve Police. In response, it must be said that these interpretations are, at the very least, suspect: it is certainly possible, if not eminently reasonable, to regard the materials that Browning uncovered as specifically promulgating the murder of innocent Jews; to do otherwise is to offer an extraordinarily controversial reading of Nazi documents that, on final analysis, questions their murderous intent. In addition, Browning's denial of ideological indoctrination of the Reserve Police can only be made by ignoring the virulently antisemitic cultural milieu in which the police were raised. Given these considerations, it would not be difficult to argue, on the basis of Browning's own research but contrary to his thesis, that sufficiently compelling evidence exists for the idea that the Reserve Police were indoctrinated, by Nazi culture, Nazi ideology, and Nazi documents, with murderous intent toward the Jewish enemy.

SOCIAL IDENTITY AND THE BEHAVIOR OF THE PERPETRATORS

Even when Browning conceded the possibility that antisemitic attitudes or understandings may have existed among the police, he persists in his claim that they "could not help explain the actions of Reserve Police Battalion 101," who "were singularly unprepared for and surprised by the murderous task that awaited them." Browning clearly recognized that the men of the Reserve Police were "immersed in a deluge of racist and antisemitic propaganda" and "imbued in particular with a sense of their own superiority and racial kinship as well as Jewish inferiority and otherness";[57] he also suggested "it is doubtful that [the men] were immune to . . . the incessant proclamation of German superiority and incitement of contempt and hatred for the Jewish enemy."[58] Despite these assertions, and largely because of the presumed absence of specific documentation exhorting the police to brutally kill Jews (a presumption which is now suspect), Browning argued that Nazi ideology and indoctrination could not have "explicitly prepared [the Reserve Police] for the task of killing Jews."[59]

From the perspective of social identity theory, it is precisely such insidious propaganda and indoctrination that made it possible for the Nazis to exclude the Jews from their circle of human obligation and responsibility. According to the theory, the ideologically fundamental racial dichotomy of "us" as opposed to "them," and notions of superiority to the inferior "other," are crucial to the emergence of fierce enmity between groups. These ideas, together with an image of Jews as the enemy, the diabolical adversary that was bombing German women and children (as the commander of Reserve Police Battalion 101 told his men), could unquestionably have paved the way for the killing of Jews.

That the Jews, an utterly defenseless people, could be portrayed as a dangerous enemy when in fact, in the words of one Nazi commander, "the shooting of the Jews was not a matter of destroying a threat . . . it was simply a matter of destroying Jews for the sake of destroying Jews,"[60] suggests a great deal about the ease with which profoundly antisemitic beliefs were inculcated into Nazi minds. Tajfel's theory has identified a deeply rooted, destructive tendency to divide the world into "us" versus "them, " even on the basis of totally arbitrary and trivial differentiations. Imagine, then, given the penetration of antisemitic ideas into the national consciousness, how prepared the Nazis were to perceive and act on enemy images.

Several other factors heightened their need to differentiate. The traditional German sense of cultural superiority had been severely shaken. Not only had the loss of World War I destroyed Germany's power and prestige, but the severity of the Versailles Treaty had caused great humiliation. Severe economic hardships, as well as a great deal of political and social instability, created uncertainty, self-doubt, vulnerability, and a weakening of the sense of national identity. These difficult interwar conditions posed enormous threats to both personal and societal self-concepts.[61]

Social identity theory suggests a powerful, almost "natural" means of dealing with such collective self-doubt: the devaluation of others. Not only does derogation enhance the in-group's tenuous self-concept through comparisons with the devalued out-group; it also provides a scapegoat for all of the ills that threaten the group's social identity, implicitly promising that problems can be overcome through action against those who caused them. In Germany, Jews were blamed for whatever had gone wrong: war, moral corruption, economic distress, defeat, and postwar humiliation; Jews were the disease, the enemy, the "other" that had to be expurgated or "cleansed" to make the culture healthy again.[62]

There were other important consequences of this social identity strategy. In the face of economic, political, and social chaos, Germans sought order and meaning in their lives. Hitler—like other paranoid demagogues—offered an appealing, attractively simple view of the world as irreconcilably split between "us" and "them," between absolute good and evil, with Jews as the absolute enemy. Identifying an enemy "other" is also a powerful force in solidifying a previously fractured group, connecting them through a common enemy that must be destroyed for a better world to emerge.[63] Nazi ideology gave Germans a sense of significance, restored their belief in cultural superiority, and provided hope for the future. At a time of severe national identity crisis, Germans did not have to be rabidly ideological antisemites to be drawn to Nazism.[64] The masses were identifying with a leadership whose primary appeal was the promise of a strong and proud Germany; but because antisemitism was at the core of that desperately sought social identity, it, too, became a central part of that identification.

Any relevant out-group may be selected to buttress a weakened societal self-concept, according to social identity theory, but certain groups are more likely to be scapegoats or ideological enemies in times of difficulty. Germany had a long history of devaluation, discrimination, and mistreatment of Jews. The deep structure of the culture—the stereotypes and images ingrained in its literature, art, and historical consciousness—provided a ready and powerful antisemitic milieu that well prepared Hitler's followers to use the Jews to serve their psychological needs.

SOCIAL IDENTITY AND SOCIAL PROCESSES

When social identity predominates, individuals come to see themselves as relatively interchangeable with other in-group members.

That is, despite great variations in the personal characteristics of the participants, they exhibit marked uniformity of attitudes and behaviors both within the in-group and toward the out-group. This has important implications for understanding both the nature of identity and the processes of social influence operating within groups. Although personal identity may be less salient in group circumstances, the emergence of a social identity should not be construed as any loss of self, but rather as a developmental change in which the individual internalizes and takes on the identity of the group.[65] This conceptualization of group or social identity contrasts markedly with Gustav LeBon's previous analysis of group behavior, which essentially argued that individual identity is somehow destroyed in a group or crowd situation.[66] That turn-of-the century analysis began with the assumption that the self is a unique property of the individual; thus, when attention is removed from self (as in a crowd), the only alternative is a state of deindividuation, that is, no self and therefore no basis for behavioral standards. Social identity theory, in contrast, introduces the possibility that social conditions that remove attention from personal aspects of the self refocus it onto social aspects of identity or common category memberships, which then become the essence of the individual's personal identity and the basis of behavioral control. If anything, the individual's sense of self, now redefined in group terms, rather than being diminished in a group actually becomes clearer and stronger, as a result of both in-group biases and the group's social support. Conjure up an image of a thousand *Hitlerjugend,* absolutely interchangeable externally yet each experiencing fierce pride in his own identity as a member of this privileged group.[67]

LeBon further argued that the anonymity, contagion, and suggestibility endemic to crowds caused people to lose not only their identity but their rationality as well, and to operate instead on the basis of a "group mind." Under the influence of this collective mentality, and freed from normal social constraints, people's base destructive instincts can be released, resulting in a decline into barbarity. Although the concept of "group mind" has largely been discredited, LeBon's ideas about anonymity and deindividuation still enjoy considerable currency in contemporary explanations of collective behavior, which continue to emphasize the loss of identity, reduced individual responsibility, and the absence of "normal" personal and social controls causing irrational and destructive behavior.[68] In particular, Milgram's analysis of destructive obedience, suggesting that individuals are led into violence by forces outside their control and for which they are no longer responsible, is very reminiscent of these concepts.

There are, however, several problems in this model of the group as a dehumanizing force, with its emphasis on the negative consequences of group membership. Groups can sometimes *enhance* the productive or prosocial actions of its members. That is, whether people's actions in a group become antisocial seems to depend not so much on the anonymity of the group as on the norms prevailing within the situation, and the norms in turn are largely determined by the identity of a particular group and by the actions that enhance that identity.[69] Group behavior may, in fact, not be as irrational and uncontrolled as LeBon suggested: some mobs and rioters are clearly selective in their violence, singling out appropriate or preferred targets in a manner inconsistent with the notion of deep-rooted and uncontrollable antisocial instincts.[70] In addition, such behavior, rather than reflecting a loss of identity, often seems to involve a new found sense of pride.

Social identity theory offers a radically different analysis of behavior in a group context from LeBon's. Immersion in a group, instead of deregulating the individual's behavior, brings into play strong social and identity considerations. Under conditions where distinct social categories are salient, and people perceive themselves in terms of those categories, individuals' behavior becomes significant primarily as part of a collective response. Appropriate conduct, then, is conduct that adheres to the norms and attributes of the relevant social identity.

What does this analysis imply about the Nazi perpetrators? The other theories—which emphasize uncontrollable and unconscious personality dysfunctions, or a bureaucratically induced degeneration into a mindless "agentic" state—reflect their originators' difficulty accepting the idea that so many *ordinary* men could have participated in mass murder. According to those approaches, there must be some fundamentally irrational, *extraordinary* process to explain this perverse behavior. In contrast, social identity theory recognizes that (in the words of George Kren and Leon Rappoport) "far from being irrational, the Holocaust can only be epitomized in terms of excessive rationality."[71] Not only were the perpetrators fully cognizant of their actions, it suggests, but these actions satisfied an inner logic that was consistent with the murderers' psychological self-interest.

Nazi ideology created a social identity that conceived of Jews as a lower form of life, the embodiment of an absolute, immutable evil. This form of Jew-hatred had direct implications for the Nazis' sense of their own superiority: it was antisemitism in the service of selfishness. In time, of course, this ideology provided individuals with all the justification they needed to participate in mass murder. But in an important sense, the critical moment of moral choice came not with the act of brutality but with the acceptance of the original lie, the claim of superiority. In effect, the psychological burden of killing was lightened by one's knowledge that it served not only Nazi ideology but one's own self-esteem.

This argument highlights a crucial distinction between obedience and social identity as the psychological mechanism that transformed ordinary Germans into brutal murderers. If the mechanism had been obedience, then the critical moment of moral choice should have occurred just before the act of murder. But that would have been evidenced by a moral reluctance to kill. The absence of any such reluctance undermines the role of obedience. It also suggests that the killings were not perceived in moral terms, that is, as immoral acts. By the time the murders were committed, the victims had already lost their humanity in the eyes of the killers, as a result of Nazi propaganda and the dictates of social identity; thus, the killings had no moral force, but were instead serving other purposes. The killing did not simply destroy the enemy: in the process, it asserted the perpetrators' own superiority, which may explain their willing and dedicated participation.

The collective atrocities of the Nazis, according to social identity theory, can be directly related to the ideological content of their individual social identities. Nazi leaders may well have understood this relationship: the SS employed group identification rituals, with special nicknames and a special language, not only to heighten the men's in-group bond, but also to prepare them for their official roles as murderers.[72] For Nazis, performing atrocities consistent with their social identity as Nazis was not simply a matter of obediently carrying out the orders of authority; fundamentally, it must be understood as behavior that reinforced the status of their group, their internalized ideology, and their own identities. Only thus could Himmler perceive a thousand Jewish corpses as "a page of glory in our [Nazi] history."

ON THE BANALITY OF EVIL

According to theorists of obedience and banality, the Nazi perpetrators were somehow indifferent to the meaning and consequences of their actions, and without hatred or ideological malice toward their victims. The evidence, however, suggests otherwise. Personalized cruelty toward Jews was the rule, not the exception, and cannot be described as dispassionate. Nor can indifference be claimed when those actions obviously benefited the perpetrators—psychologically, economically, or otherwise.

If we construe human behavior in terms of irrational processes or a deindividuated loss of self, we are left with questions of ambiguous motive and moral culpability. But we can remove any ambiguity about selfhood and conscious control by reconceptualizing the perpetrators in terms of social identity theory, by pointing to motives that are conscious, controllable, and self-serving. This reconception makes it clear that the behavior of the perpetrators was ultimately self-interested. Immoral actions in the service of self-interest cannot be described as banal: they are unambiguously evil and entail unequivocal moral responsibility.

Social identity theory accepts that ordinary people can commit extraordinary atrocities. As with other attempts to explain perpetrator behavior, it emphasizes ordinary psychological processes, normal human tendencies, as a basic source of the human capacity for mass destruction. As Ervin Staub suggests, evil that arises out of ordinary thinking and is committed by ordinary people is the norm, not the anomaly.[73]

Here, rather than depicting the Nazis as extraordinary (although the magnitude of their crime certainly was), I have attempted to bring some balance to our understanding of the ordinariness of genocide. The concept of "ordinary" is complex and problematic. To some extent, it is defined by the cultural and social context. The behavior of the Nazi perpetrators was "ordinary" only within the confines of the extraordinary political culture they inhabited. Nazi Germany's lethal view of the Jews, together with the personal and social benefits this view provided, were the mainsprings of Nazi barbarism among "ordinary" Germans.

Dina Porat

Jewish Decision-Making during the Holocaust

HISTORICAL RESEARCH ABOUT DECISION-MAKING DURING WORLD WAR II and the Holocaust has primarily dealt with decisions of the German leadership and the high echelons of the Nazi party. Even before the famous *Historikerstreit* and the debate between the "intentionalists" and the "functionalists," a vast body of literature had addressed the question of when and how it was decided to murder the Jews of Europe.[1] At the same time, although researchers have referred to decisions by Jews, they have not examined the processes of individual or group decision-making among Jews. The reasons are perhaps twofold. First, for many years the Jewish communities and their leaders were seen, in the prevailing interpretations—as developed in the early sixties by Raul Hilberg, Hannah Arendt, and Bruno Bettelheim—as passive actors for whom the crucial decisions were made by an external force, the Germans.[2] Undoubtedly, such interpretations did encourage other historians, especially Israelis in the late sixties and seventies, to detail the inner organization and functioning of Jewish communities, thus presenting them as the active and attentive publics that they indeed were.[3] But no studies on decision-making ensued. And there is a second, enduring obstacle to research on Jewish decision-making: the lack of original material and documentation. Today's historians may know, more or less, *what* decisions Jewish communities reached but cannot locate adequate material on *how*. In part this is because most records kept by Jews during the Holocaust were lost, but primarily it is because most of the deliberations and discussions that preceded the decisions were not recorded, and were necessarily kept secret, known to only a few people. The problem, therefore, is both historiographical and methodological.

In this essay I examine a number of decisions taken by Jews in order to see whether the extraordinary events of the Holocaust inspired unique ways of reaching decisions. Did the unprecedented situation shatter old, familiar methods and give rise to new ones? Four such cases—two in Nazi-occupied Europe and two others in the outside world—will serve as examples. In the first sample case, the Jewish Council in the Kovno ghetto decided to make public the German order to gather the entire ghetto population in one place, despite the fears that such a gathering would be a prelude to a fateful *Aktion*. Second, a youth-movement leader in the ghetto of Vilna decided to call for self-defense, having reached the then-unsubstantiated conclusion that there existed a German plan for the systematic killing of European Jewry. Third, the leadership of the *Yishuv* (the Zionist community in Palestine during the British Mandate) decided not to establish a new large and independent rescue committee, instead making do with enlarging an existing, problematic one. And fourth, a Jewish-American leader decided to wait for confirmation of the systematic killing of the Jews of Europe before announcing it, letting the information stay unpublished in the meantime. These four cases were chosen because relevant material is available, and because they illustrate a systematic decision-making process, based, at a minimum, on, first, the gathering of data and information; second, assessing previous experience; and, third, consultations with others who had faced similar situations.

THE JEWISH COUNCIL IN KOVNO

On October 24, 1941, a car entered the ghetto of Kovno, Lithuania, carrying two Gestapo officials in charge of the ghetto. Their appearance caused unusual concern, because they did not head for the *Ältestenrat* (Jewish Council) offices, nor to the Jewish police or the German ghetto guard, their usual destinations. Instead, in one survivor's words, they "toured various places . . . tarried a while in Demokratu Square," the largest of the local squares, and vanished. The next day, on the Jews' Sabbath, they returned, accompanied by higher officials, and commanded the Jewish Council to announce that all ghetto inhabitants, then numbering about 27,000, were to assemble before these officials for a muster in Demokratu Square three days later, in the early morning. The rationale offered was that the workers and their families would get better food rations, while the others would be separated and removed into the "small ghetto" to "avoid jealousy."[4]

Fortunately, the detailed diary of the Jewish Council's secretary (Avraham Tory, then Golub) survived the war. This is one of the few surviving Holocaust diaries in which the writer as an individual is secondary: his role as the council's secretary is the main theme. (It should be added that the memoirs of the vice-chairman of the council, lawyer Leib Garfinkel, written in Israel in the late fifties, corroborate the secretary's diary in the main points.)[5] The diary records how a Jewish community and its leaders tried to analyze their situation and reach a correct, albeit tragic, decision about how to respond to the terrifying order of October 1941. What was the real aim of that summons to assemble all the Jews? Was the Jewish Council ordered to publish the announcement because the Nazis felt that ghetto Jews trusted their leaders? If so, Tory writes, "had the council the right to comply with [the] order and publish it, thereby becoming an accomplice in an act which might spell disaster?"[6]

Almost immediately, the Kovno council rejected the idea of not publishing the announcement the Germans demanded, fearing that a refusal might risk the lives of thousands, bring about other unknown but certainly disastrous consequences, and have long-term moral, if not also historical, implications. Moreover, the council members remembered very well how, about five weeks before, they had been ordered to distribute 5,000 work certificates among the ghetto craftsmen when the ghetto population numbered 30,000 people. The Jewish population had immediately nicknamed these "life certificates," feeling rather than knowing the intention behind such a distribution. The first reaction among the council members had been to return the certificates to the Germans. Yet under pressure from the craftsmen, who claimed that no one had the right to deny them this chance to live, the members had decided to start distributing the certificates—but only to the actual craftsmen in person. After distribution had started amid tumult and panic, the Germans had suddenly canceled their instructions.[7] With this recent incident in mind, the council now rejected the idea that it withhold the announcement.

The second step was to request to meet again with the German official in charge of the ghetto, to get more detailed information.

The request was granted, and the German officer met with the council's chairman, who asked if a muster was needed just to change the distribution of food rations: the council was ready to vouch for an exact fulfillment of the German orders without one. As Tory records, the chairman pleaded with the German official to tell him "the whole truth behind the roll call." The official answered that solidarity among Jews would preclude the distribution of additional food to workers' families only, leaving the Gestapo with just one choice: to enforce this "purely administrative measure."[8] The chairman countered by hinting that Germany might lose the war, in which case the Jewish people would express its gratitude provided that the German official now answered honestly. Since the official stuck to his original version, and none of the council members believed this was a "purely administrative measure," the problem remained unsolved. Moreover, rumors reached the ghetto from various Lithuanian sources that Soviet prisoners of war, excavating pits in a nearby fortress used as a prison and place of execution, had found that 3,000 children, women, elderly, and sick had already been killed.[9]

At this stage, it seems, the Jewish Council already knew or at least guessed the German intentions. The Lithuanian Jewish community had been the first in Europe to be hit by the "Final Solution," immediately following the German invasion of Soviet Russia in June 1941. By the end of October more than 10,000 Jews had already been killed by the Lithuanians and Germans in Kovno alone. Coupled with the information about the pit graves, what, other than wholesale murder of the ghetto's nonworking population, could the summons foretell?

Given the intensifying atmosphere of impending disaster, the council now also had to worry that once the ghetto inhabitants became aware of its deliberations, many would resort to acts of despair, including not showing up for the muster, which might bring down more punishment on others. Still unable to decide whether to make the announcement public, the council took a third step and urgently asked the chief rabbi's advice. The old rabbi, after spending nearly twelve hours reading relevant halachic (Judaic legal) sources on similar situations in Jewish history, reached a conclusion. In such cases, he said, when the existence of the entire community is jeopardized and only part can be rescued, it is the obligation of the communal leaders to shoulder responsibility and rescue that part.[10]

Following the rabbi's ruling, the council members gathered and decided to publish the German command. On October 28 the Jews gathered as ordered, the Germans then selected 9,000 of them in Demokratu Square, removed them to the "small ghetto," and, on the following day in the Ninth Fort, murdered them all. One-third of the ghetto population was killed.[11]

Later, other rabbis and a number of public figures in the ghetto criticized the chief rabbi's decision. In their opinion, the council should not have published the decree, because that act turned its members into collaborators who helped, even if unwillingly, to carry out a plot against the ghetto. Some added that as the ghetto was doomed in any case, the council should have preferred the old Jewish rule of "dying rather than crossing," and forfeited their lives rather than hand Jews over to the authorities to be killed. Maimonides and the Mishnah had ruled that no Jew ever hand over another Jew only because that person is a Jew.[12]

Was the decision of the Kovno *Ältestenrat* the result of a systematic process of decision-making? Here gathering data was difficult: the opponent's intentions were kept secret or masked, and information on the killings in other Lithuanian Jewish communities had not yet reached the Kovno ghetto. Still, the council members could have guessed the meaning of the 10,000 previous murders, the distribution of "life certificates," and the digging of pits. As for previous experience, the rabbi found similarities with former situations that could have served as precedents, but could he and his listeners have known that this similarity was only very general, and that they were faced with a unique historical event. Consultation with Jews in the same situation in other ghettos was, of course, out of the question.

It seems, however, that the council sought the chief rabbi's opinion not because they were rooted in Jewish traditional concepts and knew no other channels of action.[13] On the contrary, the three principal members were secular and active Zionists, who ideologically rejected the rabbi's overriding authority. Rather, they turned to him in order to share the terrible responsibility with someone to whom other sections of the community deferred, to get his support and blessing at such a time, and to see whether Jewish tradition had a better response to the dilemma than Zionism or secularism. Their course of action had been determined, in fact, five weeks earlier when they had decided, albeit under pressure, to go ahead and distribute the certificates. The old chief rabbi simply helped reaffirm that decision with his tools: historical precedent and Halacha.

THE YOUTH MOVEMENTS IN THE VILNA GHETTO

The second case concerns the earliest known decision by any Jewish group in a ghetto to take up arms against the Germans.[14] This occurred in Vilna on New Year's Eve 1941–42. The decision was based on some Jews' estimation that the Nazi party and its leaders were beginning to carry out a systematic plan to murder (in the contemporary words of Abba Kovner) "all the Jews of Europe."[15] Given this, an uprising would be an alternative, more dignified way of dying. How was it that this particular Jewish group clearly saw, only a few months after the German invasion, that it was doomed? In answering this question, we are fortunate to have a variety of protocols and testimonies minutely describing the process that led to the decision to revolt.

An important background factor was the unique nature and degree of organization of the Jewish community in Vilna. Before the Second World War, the Vilna community numbered about 50,000. The city was nicknamed the "Jerusalem of Lithuania" for the vibrant richness of its Jewish cultural and ideological life. Some 14,000 refugees augmented the community during the first six months of the war, most of them from the elite of Polish Jewry: in addition to leaders, writers, and rabbis, there arrived a few thousand youth movement members. During the year of Soviet rule in Lithuania (from June 1940 to June 1941) Jewish organizations were banned and dissolved, and the few remaining public activities were driven underground. The youth groups—local members and especially the Polish refugees—formed an umbrella organization, which included seven Zionist movements.[16] When the Germans entered Vilna in June, the Jewish population totaled 57,000. This active and organized Jewish community, representing a variety of opinions and beliefs—mostly lower class and tending strongly to the left and to political involvement—had developed a strong political awareness. This awareness was coupled with the youth movement's tradition of shared contemplation and lengthy, systematic discussion of political phenomena, traditions that had intensified during the underground period of Soviet occupation. Together these formed a context for the exchange of ideas and information, and for decision-making.

The actual decision of New Year's Eve resulted not from one sole piece of information but from the accumulation of many small ones. These bits and pieces added up to an inkling of the nature of the Nazi killing program. This happened even though, first, to date Lithuanians, not Germans, had done most of the nearby killing; second, in Vilna, as in Kovno, the killings in the rural towns would become known only months later; third, the Vilna youth movement leaders had news that the large ghetto in Warsaw was carrying on, despite hunger and disease, and that a work ghetto with better conditions existed in Bialystok, so one could dismiss the killings in Vilna as the whim of a lunatic local German commander; fourth, the Germans claimed to be leading an anticommunist onslaught, and communists were admittedly numerous in Jewish Vilna; and fifth, the Germans were doing their best, as always, to delude and deceive. Despite all these factors, the young activists' analysis of available information led them to conclude that the killing was not random or arbitrary. Youth group members hiding both in and outside town, most notably in a monastery outside Vilna, had formed an unofficial network that brought information into the ghetto. They organized sites to meet and discuss news within as well as outside the ghetto. The leaders of this movement gradually reached the conclusion that the Jews of Vilna were being systematically killed.[17]

During July and August of 1941 about 10,000 Jews had been killed. Community leaders pondered whether the Germans aimed at wiping out all the Jews in Lithuania, though information about other communities was not yet available in Vilna. The former secretary of the community, on the basis of the same information, even revealed in private to two youth movement members: "They plan to kill us all, all East European Jews." The possibility that all the millions of East European Jews were targeted was discussed as well among youth leaders hiding in the monastery. Abba Kovner, a prominent leader of the Zionist movement Hashomer Hatsair, was already planning to establish a unit of fighters. Kovner had recognized the necessity of (as he later wrote) telling the Jewish public "the bitter and cruel truth regarding the plan to completely annihilate the Jews of Eastern Europe."[18] During September and early October, 12,000 more Vilna Jews were killed. Some youth leaders assembled to analyze the situation. Hashomer Hatsair gathered twenty members for a meeting in the ghetto; the umbrella organization met in small groups in a public kitchen they had established; and the remaining Communist party leaders did the same. Female members of the youth movements went out into the surrounding area to gather information on developments outside the ghetto.[19] In October and early November, another 11,000 were killed, mostly through a selection based on the prior distribution of another kind of "life certificate." The distribution pattern indicated long-term German planning, and the various ghetto organizations increased their meetings about the possibility of taking action, separately or together. Though the wave of killing subsided, December marked the transition from meetings mainly among members of individual movements to umbrella meetings and even larger ones. There the idea crystallized that not only those Jews taken out of the Vilna ghetto were being killed, not only the Jews of Lithuania, nor even only East European Jews, but that the target was in fact "all the Jews of Europe."

This assessment, proclaimed aloud for the first time by Abba Kovner on the night of December 31, 1941, in a gathering of about 150 members of all youth movements, could not have been based on direct or comprehensive information. The killings were then being carried out only in the former Soviet areas. Deportations had not yet started from the Polish ghettos or from Western and Southern Europe, and most of the death camps had not yet been built. Very little information on the killings in the ex-Soviet areas could have reached Vilna. The assessment formulated by Kovner was more of a hunch, an intuition, an unknowingly realistic glance into the abyss. Throughout the months from July to December, hunches had been a step or two ahead of solid data. When the ghetto leaders found out about the Jews of Vilna, they were already thinking about Lithuania or even Eastern Europe; and when they found out about Lithuania and a bit about Byelorussia, Kovner was writing about all the Jews in Europe. At the turn of the year, his idea was not simply accepted out of the blue by his comrades; it had already filtered down slowly, first to some of them as individuals, then as a remote possibility whispered among close friends, then in small groups of a given youth movement, and only then, when the terrible possibility came closer, in larger forums. In other words, Kovner expressed verbally and publicly a thought that could have already been vaguely considered by others but had been too threatening to express openly, certainly not in the harsh terms he now used: "Hitler plans to murder all the Jews of Europe."

The tools that enabled a youth movement leader of twenty-three to come to this far-reaching conclusion—and enabled the group to decide as a consequence to revolt—were the history and tradition of the Jewish community in Vilna and of the youth movements in particular. These factors included the groups' former organizations and their underground experience; the close ties among members, sometimes closer than family ties, that motivated them to risk their lives; their tradition of discussing and analyzing each detail, trying to foresee political developments; their romantic and uncompromising youth; the loss of their families in most cases, which made them independent personally and at the same time dependent on each other as their last human resort; their deep concern for the image of their movements in the future annals of Jewish history and especially in the collective memory of the Zionist *Yishuv* in Palestine; the charisma of Kovner himself, who was part of the process and yet stood apart by virtue of his leadership and insight. All these factors shaped the decision to revolt. It grew not only out of a sense of doom but also out of the gathering of information (though limited and contradictory) and perspicacious intuition and imagination.

THE JEWISH AGENCY IN PALESTINE

So far we have examined examples of decision-making from Nazi-occupied Europe. Let us now look at two other examples, taken from the experiences of Jews in the free world: in the offices of the *Yishuv* institutions in Palestine, and in the offices of the U.S. State Department.

The third case concerns the decision reached in Palestine, in mid-January 1943, *not* to establish a new, large committee to handle the *Yishuv's* rescue work. Instead it was decided to perpetuate the existing four-member Committee for Polish Jewry, simply adding eight more members to represent three additional bodies in the *Yishuv*. Why and how was this decision reached, and which decision-making tools were employed?

The Committee for Polish Jewry had been established by the Jewish Agency back in 1940, when the *Yishuv* leaders assumed that the appropriate response to the main problem created by the Germans was to render political and economic aid to the Jews of Poland. In 1940, Germany's final anti-Jewish policies were still being elaborated, and the ghettos—characterized by hunger, hard labor, disease, and the deprivation of basic rights, and established to that point only in Poland—represented the worst situation of which outside Jewish observers could conceive. According to their logic, the essential tasks were the dispatch of food parcels and medicines, accompanied by political struggle to ensure postwar Jewish rights. But in November 1942, the Jewish Agency Executive formally announced that a systematic murder of European Jewry was taking place. The announcement shocked the *Yishuv*. One idea for stepping up rescue work, voiced the following day, was to establish a new, larger rescue committee, equipped with sufficient financial resources and headed by prominent enough figures to make its efforts efficient and serious.

After long and tiresome negotiations, a committee of twelve was set up in mid-January 1943, seven weeks after the announcement was published. Included were the four former members of the Committee for Polish Jewry, all of whom were on the Jewish Agency Executive as well; another prominent member of the executive, who had joined the four right after the agency's announcement in November; two representatives of the religious party Agudat Israel, three from the National Council, which served as an umbrella for most of the organizations in the *Yishuv* on domestic affairs; and two from the right-wing Revisionist party.

This new committee, named the United Rescue Committee Affiliated to the Jewish Agency, represented all organs and parties, from the Left to the Right, and its members were well known in the *Yishuv*. The Jewish Agency Executive was satisfied, because five of its members were included, so that the agency could go on closely monitoring the committee's work. Thus the "United" in the committee's name indeed reflected its composition.[20]

Almost immediately, however, the new committee was severely challenged, in two long and stormy meetings: one of the National Council, the other of the Zionist Executive, the supreme organ of the movement between Zionist congresses. The main charge against the twelve-member committee was that its core members had been notably inactive since their initial appointments to the Committee for Polish Jewry and were, like the new members, overburdened with other obligations. Moreover, the critics alleged, a coalition of opposing forces could paralyze the committee's work.

The participants in the two meetings were unanimous in their demands: an entirely new rescue committee was needed, with members who would devote themselves wholly to the needs of besieged European Jewry and, as chair, a public figure who would command the respect of all sections of the *Yishuv.* (This demand thus implied that the present head of the committee, Yitzhak Gruenbaum, was not such a figure.)

Subsequently, an ad hoc committee to "reorganize" the rescue committee was appointed, with David Ben-Gurion, then chairman of the Jewish Agency, playing a prominent role. When this ad hoc "reorganization committee" completed its deliberations, it presented the Zionist Executive with two options: either constitute a new committee or, as favored by the ad hoc committee, augment the twelve-member committee with a few more public figures. The second option was adopted, despite the vehement preference voiced by most members of the National Council and the Zionist Executive (albeit as individuals and activists rather than officially) in favor of the first.[21]

This outcome was more than a political maneuver aimed at keeping the rescue committee under the supervision of the Jewish Agency, although it was that, too. Establishing a totally new committee would have entailed long negotiations with the main bodies in the *Yishuv* (fifty-four parties and associations were listed by the 1944 elections to the National Council, in a population numbering less than half a million!). The structure, financing, and scope of authority of the new body would all have had to be negotiated and arranged, and recall that the negotiations for the establishment of the twelve-member committee had already taken seven weeks. Also, the five members of the Jewish Agency Executive at the center of the twelve-member committee were already involved in rescue work in their respective other capacities: one was head of the *Yishuv*'s Immigration Department, taking care of immigration certificates and contact with delegates abroad, another was secretary of the Political Department, maintaining contact with governments and international bodies, and so on. In other words, starting a new organ from scratch would have necessitated creating all these ties afresh, wasting time and effort and duplicating work already being done. The proposed new committee was an ideal that clashed with reality.[22]

Furthermore, at that stage the *Yishuv* and its leaders did not know whether large-scale rescue work was at all possible; nor, if it were, did they know how and from where to arrange it. They had no idea if rescue work could be done with the Allies, or without them. The scale and horror of the Nazi crimes against the Jews left the *Yishuv* bewildered, so much so that the matter of choosing between the two committees seems to have been rendered academic (to judge by the feelings expressed in the Zionist Executive meetings).

Another consideration was the probable role of unofficial, clandestine work. During the British Mandate the *Yishuv* had managed to carry out operations underground, illegally, whenever necessary. These had generally been executed by clandestine units, or by a small number of trusted activists, with the blessing of the *Yishuv* authorities but without their direct, formal involvement. There was no doubt that rescue operations would also entail clandestine work, perhaps even more important than the formal political work. It was equally clear that a clandestine body could operate equally well either with or without a new committee. Also, the Jewish Agency treasurer pledged, behind the scenes, to *Yishuv* delegates in neutral countries and to other leaders in the *Yishuv,* that should any pending rescue plans prove realistic, the agency would immediately allocate the necessary funds whether or not there were a new committee.[23]

The decision not to establish a new, larger rescue committee has since been criticized as a grave mistake, as proof of the *Yishuv*'s alleged indifference toward the plight of Jews in Europe. But the discussions prior to the decision involved many *Yishuv* leaders, all speaking with great concern for the fate of European Jewry. These very leaders decided against a new committee for pragmatic and realistic reasons, not just as a result of Ben-Gurion's maneuver. His strategy could be interpreted today not as an attempt to avoid rescue work but rather as an effort to keep such operations under the control of the *Yishuv*'s central political body.

Indeed, foremost among the factors influencing the decision was the sociopolitical structure of the Zionist community in Palestine. Initially swayed by news from Europe to consider a new committee, the leaders ultimately rejected that option because of years of experience running *Yishuv* institutions, in which informality, secrecy, and personal ties were essential. Moreover, the Jewish Agency was the political body empowered by the World Zionist Organization to build a "national home" for the Jewish people, and its chairman was unlikely to let a task so important for the future of Zionism as the rescue of European Jewry be handled by others, even if the possibility of rescue was not yet guaranteed.

STEPHEN WISE IN THE UNITED STATES

Our fourth example of wartime decision-making involves Jewish leadership in the United States: "one of the most tragic moments of my life," Rabbi Stephen Wise calls it in his autobiography *Challenging Years*. On August 28, 1942, Wise received the now-famous cable from Gerhart Riegner, director of the World Jewish Congress office. The cable relayed the information he had gotten from a reliable German source that (as Wise later recalled) "a plan had been discussed in Hitler's headquarters for the extermination of all Jews in Nazi-occupied lands. These Jews . . . were to be deported to concentration camps in Eastern Europe and then exterminated through prussic acid and crematoria . . . in one blow." [24]

Having received this news August 1, Riegner had originally cabled the American and British consulates in Geneva on August 8, asking that they immediately inform Wise, as president of the World Jewish Congress, and also Sidney Silverman (chairman of that body's British section), the U.S. administration, and all the Allied governments. The American legation in Berne did in turn cable the U.S. State Department, which replied by telegraph that it was "disinclined to deliver the message in question in view of the apparently unsubstantiated character of the information." [25] Luckily, Silverman got Riegner's cable from the British Foreign Office and transmitted it directly to Wise on August 28. On September 2, Wise, unaware that the State Department had already seen the cable, sent the news on to Sumner Welles, then undersecretary of state, who asked Wise not to release it until an attempt had been made to confirm it. Wise consented.

Three months later, on November 24, data arrived at the State Department fully substantiating Riegner's cable and other reports it had received in the meantime. Wise was summoned and notified that the fresh communiqués "confirm and justify your deepest fears."[26] Welles now encouraged him to release this news to the press, and Wise immediately did.

The question is: why did Wise agree to wait for three long months—from September 2 to November 24—until getting permission to publicize the German plan? During these three months the murder of Jews, especially Polish Jews, continued in full force, most notably in the camps of Belzec, Maidanek, and Treblinka. Every day counted. What made him concur on the spot with Welles's request to wait? What experience and prior information influenced his decision?

To answer this question, we must take into consideration a few details missing from Wise's autobiography. Having agreed to wait, Wise nevertheless took action. He notified a number of clergy functionaries and some secretaries of state.[27] He likewise notified President Roosevelt, through Justice Felix Frankfurter, to whom he wrote on September 4 about the Riegner cable, asking him to "share the knowledge of this horror."[28] Wise disclosed the content of the cable to Jewish leaders, such as Henry Morgenthau, Jr., and formed an emergency committee with Agudat Israel leaders such as Jacob Rosenheim, who had received a parallel cable from Switzerland and had forwarded it right away to President and Eleanor Roosevelt.[29] The emergency committee also asked Welles to have American intelligence check into the latest report from the Warsaw ghetto that about 100,000 Jews had been evacuated from the ghetto. Besides his work with the emergency committee, Wise continued to meet with U.S. officials, asking them to transmit information, approach the pope, ship food to Europe, and so on, although with meager results. He continued meeting Jewish leaders as well, and accumulated news corroborating the reports of Riegner and others.

These were all "desperate . . . behind-the-scenes efforts to develop some sort of action to help the doomed Jews . . . and to ease [Wise's] own psychological burden," as historian David Wyman puts it.[30] Indeed, Wise drew Justice Frankfurter's attention to the heavy burden of silence: "Have you noted that I have kept the thing out of the press up to this time, thus accepting a great responsibility if the threat should be executed . . . ?"[31] Wise did not initiate a strong public campaign and did not try to get American Jewry to unite and focus on the issue with the seriousness that it deserved, although he was under pressure to do so and must have believed wholeheartedly that such steps were advisable.

Wise was too far from the scene of events to be able to obtain news through independent channels. He was wavering, much like the Zionist leaders in Palestine at the same time, between despair and hope—in his case, hope produced by the reassuring words of American officials who explained that the German measures taken against Jews might simply be part of the war effort and that shipping food might be enough to alleviate their plight.[32] But as time went by and reports accumulated, despair gained the upper hand and Wise's "psychological burden" became heavier.

Since he had no precedent to guide him and was dependent on outside information, in making this vital decision of whether to publicize the truth and break his word, he had to rely on his experience and worldview. An essential part of these was his unbridled admiration for the "chief," or the "boss," as he used to refer to President Roosevelt. Since 1936 (Wise writes in his autobiography) he had "felt free to take to the President my knowledge and views on the Nazi situation—and from then on I found the President sympathetic and eager to be of help." Wise felt that Roosevelt "grasped what was occurring with more feeling and understanding" than some Jews manifested, and certainly more than "certain gentlemen in the State Department." "There is no place in the lives or thoughts of true Americans for antisemitism," the president wrote to Wise, who in turn later commented that the "so-called Rooseveltian 'friendliness to Jews' was not a token of pro-Jewishness but of his Americanism," of his being "a friend of men and man. No one was more genuinely free from religious prejudice and racial bigotry."[33] One could go on and on quoting Wise's expressions of admiration for his "boss."

If Roosevelt was such an unwavering pillar of democracy and human rights, then Wise just had to wait for the right moment to reveal to him the news from Europe, because then it would be in the best possible hands, those of the "foremost and finest figure in the political world today."[34] There are no indications in Wise's diary and letters that this certainty—or his firm belief in reform and progress, including the progress in the status of Jews in the non-Jewish world—was eroded by doubts as time passed without a word from

the State Department, even though a supposedly sympathetic, helpful president sat in the White House. Information did come concur-
rently from other sources; and suggestions for aid and rescue that
Wise made while waiting for the cable to be confirmed (such as formal American appeals, exchange programs or the shipping of food)
were in effect, though not formally, turned down both by the president and his "gentlemen in the State Department." In other words,
Wise remained a captive of his old convictions and his belief in values he hoped existed where he sought them. As a result, he was left
with no means with which to make a better decision about when to
publicize the disastrous truth.

CONCLUSION

Perhaps the very phrase "decision-making" imperfectly suits the conditions Jews had to face during the Holocaust. The usual compo-
nents of communal or national decision-making—such as committees, agendas, protocols, systematic thought based on previously
gathered information and consultations, and discussion based on
priorities and the setting of goals—were nonexistent for them. Jews
had to react to plans made against them, and could identify these
measures only gradually, as they were being implemented.

The Jewish people as one entity could not reach conclusive decisions. No leadership at the time was acceptable to all of its factions.
The World Jewish Congress had only started operating on the eve
of the war. The World Zionist Organization represented only 10
percent of Jewry. The Bund and the Communist party were not generally acceptable options. No body or organ or leader existed that
could come forth and decide for all. Even within its separate sectors
(the Jewish communities in occupied Europe, in the free world, and
in the *Yishuv*), not all bodies and parties took part in the decisions,
owing to either the war situation, the limitations imposed by the
Germans, or the lack of internal unity and leadership.

The four cases outlined here, which represent diverse slices of
Jewish life during the Holocaust years, show that the unique events
of the time did *not* equip individuals or communities with new tools
for decision-making. The quick, unpredictable flow of events pre-
cluded the creation of new approaches. Therefore, decisions were

made on the basis of factors that had guided decision-making during former, quieter periods.

It is my conclusion, then, that Jewish decisions were determined mainly by the expectations and practices that were formed before the Holocaust and the war and maintained during these calamitous events. Within Europe, the Kovno community leaders regarded themselves as appointed by the community and therefore responsible for its safety regardless of their previous political and religious convictions. They felt, rather than actually had the means to be, responsible for their community, and the goal informing all their decisions was to rescue as many people as possible. The Vilna youth movement leaders perceived themselves, as a result of their ideological education, as guardians of their movements' image and place in history. Headed by Abba Kovner, they were convinced, once they faced the reality of annihilation, that the attempts to rescue part of the Jewish population would fail. Therefore, saving the people's self-respect, through self-defense, became their top priority. These different perceptions of the rescue possibilities were the root of possible clashes between Jewish councils and youth movements in the ghettos. The question common to both was: what would be left of the Jewish people after the war?

Outside Europe, the *Yishuv* leaders claimed to be the vanguard of the Jewish nation, offering and leading the only possible solution for national liberation. It was their task, they believed, to rescue at least part of the nation—for the sake of those rescued, for the future of the *Yishuv* and Zionism, and for their image as rescuers. Yet they found themselves entangled in a net of debilitating factors: their limited sources of information, the Allies' indifference, the Nazis' determination, a world war. An additional factor linked them and American rabbi Wise: the belief that the democratic and humane values of Western civilization, represented by the Allies during the war, pertained as well to the Jewish people, a long-standing contributor to the achievements of this culture. Zionism believed in a future based on the underlying principle of the equality of all individuals and nations. Wise perceived himself as an open-minded liberal living in a trustworthy society, led by leaders who seriously took his people's fate into consideration. Had both the *Yishuv* leaders and Wise questioned this belief when the Holocaust began, perhaps their decisions would have been different. But established beliefs and images could not be speedily shaken, and so they served as the basis for decisions even in these unprecedented circumstances. Jewish communities and leaders had to reach unprecedented decisions, but could only rely on their former experiences. In such a tumultuous time, they had no chance to develop new, more effective decision-making processes.

II. R · E · S · O · U · R · C · E · S

Judith Tydor Baumel

Gender and Family Studies of the Holocaust: A Historiographical Overview

INTRODUCTION

IN THE BEGINNING THERE WAS ANNE FRANK. SINCE HER DIARY WAS first published, in 1947, millions of readers have been introduced to the inner world of the Holocaust's most famous victim.[1] Initially, some did not connect her with that cataclysm, never before having heard the term; others intentionally universalized her story, portraying it as a symbol of humanity in a world filled with oppression and terror. However, the *Diary of a Young Girl,* as the 1950 English-language edition was entitled, is first and foremost the story of a Jewish child (and later young woman), living in hiding with her family, during the Holocaust. Many of its better-known entries focus on the dynamics of mothers, children, and family in wartime. It might therefore be natural to guess that the interest surrounding its publication must have quickly inspired a number of gender and family studies examining Jewish life under Nazi domination.[2] What happened in reality? When did historians begin to pursue gender and family studies (or child-oriented studies) of the Holocaust? How has the examination of family and women's culture been integrated into other ongoing Holocaust research? Why have researchers initially concentrated on certain aspects of these topics while completely ignoring others? These questions and their answers are the focus of this essay.

Any serious survey of gender and family Holocaust research necessitates a few basic definitions. The term "Holocaust" entered the English language in the late 1950s to refer to the fate of Jews under Nazism. Thus, by definition, gender and family studies of the Holocaust, as opposed to Second World War, must concentrate primarily upon Jewish women, children, and families in Nazi lands. Following the recent growth of interest in refugees and postwar survivors, the field of "Holocaust studies" has expanded to include these topics as well. Consequently, we will also mention those studies concentrating upon female or young refugees and survivors.[3]

THE FIRST WAVE OF HISTORIOGRAPHY (LATE 1940s)

The first books on women, children, and family life under Nazism began to appear in Germany shortly after the end of the war.[4] However, for the most part, their subjects were Germans living in the Third Reich and not Jews under Nazi domination.[5] Non-Jewish women and children from Nazi-occupied lands (as opposed to Germany proper) were likewise excluded from most historical research until the late 1970s; one exception was Kiryl Sosnowsky's pioneering study in 1962 documenting the fate of Polish children in Nazi-occupied Eastern Europe.[6] There were the numerous volumes written on women and youth in the European resistance movements.[7] But most of this resistance literature cannot be considered family- or gender-oriented, as its primary focus is resistance, not women or family. Furthermore, while these studies deal with Nazi Germany or the war, few of them could truly be labeled "Holocaust research" per se.

When did the study of *Jewish* women and children begin? While the phrase "gender and family studies of the Holocaust" is new, the phenomenon the phrase describes is not. More than half a century ago, using a technique that had become popular in interwar Polish social research, Emmanuel Ringelblum began studying the lives of women and children in the Warsaw ghetto. During 1941 and 1942, the staff of his clandestine "Oneg Shabbat" archives distributed questionnaires to women, inquiring into their lives as women, mothers, and wives under ghetto conditions. The respondents' answers, together with the researcher's own historical observations, were intended to serve as the basis for a comprehensive examination of ghetto family life. However, before Ringelblum could bring this project to fruition the ghetto was liquidated and the subjects of his study sent to Treblinka. Today, only a handful of questionnaires and some preliminary conclusions remain as testimony to this early attempt at a gender and family study of the Holocaust.[8]

The first wave of publications about Jewish women, children, and family during the Holocaust began within a year of the war's end. During the early postwar period (1945–48), little synthetic Holocaust research of any type was pursued. Those historical essays that appeared usually documented life in ghettos and concentration camps. Only a few of these focused on women's experiences—for example, Denise Dufurnier's 1948 study of the women's camp at Ravensbrück.[9] What did characterize the early postwar period was *memoirs:* first-person stories by survivors who had experienced life in hiding, ghettos, camps, and the resistance.

Broadly speaking, it appears that more memoirs were written by women than by men. Was this because women had a heightened historical consciousness, a greater need to record their experiences? Was it just because more of them survived the Holocaust? There is no way to be certain. The disproportion may also stem from the fact that women were often granted a longer recovery period than men before having to rejoin productive society. Thus, after an initial stage of physical rehabilitation, women could devote more time to emotional healing, recording their wartime experiences as part of a postwar catharsis.

Some of the better-known memoirs published during these years are those by Ruzhka Korchak and Zivia Lubetkin, both members of East European Zionist underground movements; Olga Lengyl and Gisella Perl, Jewish doctors who had survived Auschwitz; and Auschwitz survivor Kitty Hart, as well as the diaries of Mary Berg and Justina Davidson—and of course, the posthumously published diary of Anne Frank.[10]

It is interesting that many of the memoirists of this early period—as opposed to the authors of more randomly preserved wartime diaries—had been pivotal figures in the Eastern European Jewish resistance movements or were camp functionaries. Not only did women in these groups have a better chance of survival, their stories were also considered of greater public interest than those of "ordinary" survivors. This was particularly true in the case of memoirs written in Palestine (and later Israel) by former activists in the underground Zionist movements. For more than two decades after the Second World War, the Israeli public remained "resistance-oriented," not approving of what it considered the passive, "Diaspora" behavior of most other Holocaust victims. These were the years when the accusation of Jews "going like sheep to the slaughter" was hurled in the face of more than one Holocaust survivor in Israel.[11] This was also the period when the Holocaust memorial day in Israel was still entitled *Yom Hashoah Vehamered,* Holocaust and Resistance Memorial Day (as opposed to the name adopted later, *Yom Hashoah Vehagevurah,* Holocaust and Heroism Memorial Day), thus placing the armed uprisings on a plane equal to that of other Holocaust experiences.[12] These were also the years when Israeli political movements encouraged members who had belonged to the Zionist resistance in Europe to record their memoirs for posterity.[13] Again, it appears that initially more women than men took up this challenge.

What characterizes the early memoirs by women who had survived the Holocaust? First, their authenticity. Memoirs written right after the war often more accurately describe authors' experiences than later recollections, as memory had not yet been blurred by the passage of time. Second, they contain little moralizing. Although often referring to the author's ideological background and the impact of ideology on experience, early memoirs were usually a factual, if emotional, reconstruction of an individual's wartime experiences, devoid of the moral preaching or sweeping conclusions that characterize many later Holocaust memoirs. Third, many concentrate on experiences that belonged solely to women's culture, such as rape and childbirth, this at a time when it was uncommon to conceptualize gender. Fourth, a majority take September 1939 as a starting point, with only a short description of the authors' prewar life. In this they differ from early men's memoirs, which usually devote at least a few paragraphs to the interwar period. Finally, virtually all of the women's memoirs from this period emphasize the role of female self-help and mutual assistance in their authors' survival. This solidarity would later help scholars in analyzing women in wartime— for example, in the recent studies on women's mutual assistance during the war, particularly in women's camps[14]—as an explanation of their ability to survive under conditions often worse than the ones men were forced to endure.

The first wave of publications focusing upon Jewish *youth* during the Holocaust followed a different pattern from those on women, with their strength in autobiographical writings. Only a handful of children's diaries survived the war, and most were not published until the 1960s or even later.[15] The same holds true for young peoples' memoirs. During the early postwar years most child survivors had not yet reached the stage of writing memoirs (although at least one appeared in Poland as early as 1946).[16] But whereas in the late 1940s no Holocaust-related gender studies were being conducted, two research projects involving children were already under way.

The first was headed by Ernst Papanek, a German-Jewish educator who had found refuge in France and later in the United States. In 1945 Papanek was commissioned by Columbia University's School of Social Work to examine the history and acclimatization of child Holocaust refugees in America. Columbia University made his preliminary findings available in 1946. Papanek then appropriated the source material for his personal collection. Eventually, the collection was donated to the New York Public Library, where it became a gold mine for scholars seeking documentary sources on the history of refugee children in the United States.[17]

The second research project on children was conducted by Mark Dworzecky, a Lithuanian physician who abandoned medicine after the war to devote the rest of his life to Holocaust research. Dworzecky's work, unlike Papanek's, focused on children in ghettos. In early 1942, Dworzecky had begun documenting the health and welfare of Jewish children in the Vilna ghetto, where he was incarcerated. In 1946 he published his first articles on the fate of Jewish children and families under Hitler.[18] Although not of standard historiographical quality and often medically oriented, these articles constitute an early academic study about children and families.

Both Papanek's and Dworzecky's studies were based on circumscribed sources: in one case, material provided by the child refugees themselves; in the other, Jewish wartime and postwar observations on life in ghettos. This main source material was supplemented by the readily available German documentation, captured by the Allies, on which most early postwar studies are based. Neither project could use Jewish sources such as children's diaries, registers of welfare organizations, or communal records, as these either had been destroyed or were as yet unavailable.

THE 1950s AND 1960s

The second group of publications about women, children, and family began to appear in the early 1950s and continued for almost two decades. These years are often considered a semidormant period between two waves of "Holocaust consciousness," the first encompassing the immediate postwar period and the second beginning in the mid-1970s. With the exception of Raul Hilberg's monumental work based primarily upon German documentation,[19] little systematic research—and virtually no gender or family studies—was conducted until the late 1960s. There were some sociohistorical studies about refugee children during the Holocaust (many of which were commissioned by child welfare organizations to mark milestones in the institutions' history). Three examples are Kathryn Close's *Transplanted Children,* about refugee children in the United States; Norman Bentwich's *They Found Refuge,* describing the rescue of 10,000 children from Central Europe to England; and Recha Freier's *Let the Children Come,* telling the story of the Youth Aliyah movement.[20] These studies were based largely on non-German documentation, such as those of Jewish child welfare organizations in France, England, Israel, and the United States (unlike the earlier studies on children, which were forced to rely primarily on firsthand Jewish observations, supplemented by Nazi documentation). But on the negative side, that the studies were commissioned by the same organizations whose achievements they were supposed to document often influenced the authors' conclusions. Also, the authors were usually unable to interview more than a few children, so their studies could not provide a balanced analysis.

As for Holocaust memoirs, these appeared sporadically throughout the decades in question, growing in number from the late 1960s.[21] A high proportion of the women's memoirs published were by resistance members or wartime functionaries, as earlier. Several collections of children's testimonies also appeared now: two examples are Karen Gershon's "collective autobiography" of German-Jewish refugees in Britain, published in 1956 under the title *We Came as Children,* and Inge Deutschkron's . . . *denn ihrer war die Hölle,* based primarily on children's testimonies from the Auschwitz trial, held in Frankfurt in 1964.[22] Another volume, encompassing testimonies of both women and children who survived Nazi camps, is Georgina Bellak's *Donne e bambini nei lageri nazisti,* published in Milan in 1960. These first-person accounts provide the very dimension that is missing in the studies of refugee organizations—that which could only be provided by the survivors themselves. Another interesting memoir combining women's and children's Holocaust-related experiences is *My Hundred Children,* Lena Kuchler-Zilberman's account of her postwar attempts to rehabilitate Jewish children in Eastern Europe.[23] Originally published in Hebrew and later translated into English, this book had a great impact on early Holocaust consciousness in Israel in the 1960s.

Why was there such a dearth of Holocaust scholarship and memoirs in the 1950s and 1960s? Several factors worked against the publication of memoirs. First, many survivors had overcome their immediate psychological need to bear witness and were now busy rebuilding their lives.[24] Second, some who had originally intended to record their stories began to realize that their audience was dwindling or almost nonexistent. Then one must bear in mind the sociological and cultural framework in which many of the survivors—particularly the young ones—functioned. Until the growth of American multiculturalism in the early 1970s, a great number of survivors attempted to play down their past in order to assimilate into the culture of their adopted country; thus, while there were probably those who recorded their memoirs for private purposes, few were willing to actually publish the results and emphasize their foreign origins. Finally, there was the economic aspect of publication. Prior to the mid-1970s, when a resurgence of interest put the topic back on the literary map, few publishing houses considered Holocaust books to be a lucrative venture; therefore, they did not actively solicit manuscripts from survivors, as they would a decade or so later. The lack of synthetic Holocaust research during those decades—particularly on topics concerning gender and family—can be connected to the scholarly and cultural climates of the period. The state of source material, dearth of memoirs, lack of historical awareness of the importance of gender and family history, and even political considerations all made unlikely the systematic study of women's and children's Holocaust history.

The absence of such Holocaust studies contrasts sharply with the extensive research then being conducted on *German* women, children, and families under Nazism. One explanation cites the Nazi preoccupation with motherhood and feminism as providing the impetus for the postwar gender and family studies. A second conjecture places these studies within the context of the postwar research on life under fascism. Examinations of women and children under Nazism were, in these two views, just another facet of broader research and not forerunners of gender and family studies as we know them today. A third explanation concentrates on source availability. The profusion of Nazi documentation regarding German women and youth made these topics extremely fruitful areas of research. Finally, one must not overlook the cultural fact that German interest in topics concerning women and family dates back to the early years of the Weimar Republic, and thus it was natural for postwar scholars to continue where their predecessors had left off.

THE 1970s AND AFTER

A third wave of publications began in the mid-1970s. This new group reflected two international phenomena: the growing interest in issues pertaining to the Holocaust, and the academic development of women's and family studies. Three major categories of Holocaust literature dealing with gender and family now appeared: individual memoirs, collected testimonies, and academic studies.

Ever since the end of the war, the overwhelming bulk of Holocaust literature had consisted of survivors' memoirs. With the development of ethnic pride and "Holocaust awareness" in the mid- to late 1970s, dozens more memoirs began to appear. This "Holocaust awareness" featured significant historical, sociological, and psychological study of the Holocaust, which was both influenced by and in turn left its mark on the arts and the media. The success of the NBC miniseries *Holocaust,* and the subsequent debate over its merits, including responses by survivors, contributed to this development. Many survivors who had previously toyed with the idea of recording their experiences now took up the challenge in a world more receptive to their stories. Others, who had never considered such a venture, were encouraged to do so by friends, family, Holocaust centers, and astute literary agents.

Women's memoirs appearing from the mid-1970s onward strongly emphasized gender-related experiences. Like the earlier memoirists, survivors writing in the 1970s and 1980s emphasized the uniqueness of female experience during the Holocaust. Once again, almost all cite women's mutual assistance as a primary factor in their survival. But while earlier women's memoirs usually begin with the outbreak of war, most later memoirs include a certain number of prewar experiences. This expanded chronological framework usually stemmed from the heightened sense of historical awareness that temporal distance can provide. The reader is given necessary background material and also introduced to Jewish women's culture during the interwar period. This group of memoirs is characterized in addition by comparative modesty in sexual matters. Although they tend to be emotionally revealing, many are reticent about female sexuality and physical intimacy among women. This contrasts sharply with literature written in the 1940s and 1950s, which is often surprisingly revealing about such matters. One conjecture as to the cause of this difference notes that "Stalag" literature (sexually explicit, even pornographic stories set in prison camps), at its zenith during the earlier period, had created a tone and cultural framework for all Holocaust literature then appearing; another connects it with the authenticity of early memoirs, whose authors did not attempt to "beautify" their experiences for their potential audience. A final characteristic of memoirs from the 1970s—both men's and women's—is the absence of ideological ballast. While frequently tinged with religious or moralistic overtones, most are devoid of the ideological beliefs that accompanied many of the earlier publications. This is because memoirs were now being written by "ordinary survivors," as opposed to political ideologues or resistance members.

What characterized the women writing Holocaust memoirs after the mid-1970s? They were survivors of concentration camps, ghettos, transit camps, family camps; had lived in hiding, assumed false identities, fought among the partisans; had written before, had never written before, had written for their families only. In short, any and every type of female survivor—and for that matter, male survivor—was writing Holocaust memoirs. The same held true for memoirs by people who had been children in the 1940s. Some who had never considered putting their stories into print were suddenly publishing intimate recollections of their prewar and wartime experiences. Many of these erstwhile children were now entering their sixth decade and finally able to devote time to dealing with their past. Part of their catharsis assumed written form, creating children's Holocaust memoirs written thirty years or more after the fact.[25]

The second type of literature from the 1970s is collected volumes of women's and children's testimonies.[26] Three examples are Lore Shelley's *Secretaries of Death,* the story of the Jews who worked at the political bureau at Auschwitz; my own *Voices from the Canada Commando,* giving the testimony of female Jews who worked in Auschwitz's sorting barracks between 1942 and 1944; and Azriel Eisenberg's *The Lost Generation,* categorizing into eighteen types the children's experiences that appear in testimonies and published literature.[27] Some collected memoirs are annotated, others are solely narrative. All provide valuable source material for gender and family historians examining Holocaust-related experiences.

These collected volumes differ from earlier individual memoirs in several ways. First, almost all were prepared by historians and other scholars, not just by the survivors themselves. Thus they heralded a surge of academic interest in gender and family studies of the Holocaust. Second, most required the cooperation of a group of survivors willing to bare their private experiences for the public. This could occur only during a period of heightened Holocaust awareness, when participants understood the importance of making their stories known. Finally, the collected testimonies are usually thematic, and so pave the way for subsequent academic research.

In addition to the individual and collective memoirs, a third category began to appear from the mid-1970s onward: true analytical research. Four examples of academic studies about children are Joseph Walk's book on the education of German-Jewish children in the Third Reich, Chaim Shatzker's articles about Jewish youth movements during the Holocaust, my studies of the rescue and resettlement of Jewish refugee children in the United States and England, and Deborah Dwork's study on Jewish children under Nazism.[28] All of these attempt to view children as subjects and not solely objects of history, adding a new dimension to child-oriented Holocaust research. All are by scholars familiar with both Jewish and non-Jewish sources; most rely on both written and oral documentation; and, most important, many adopt an interdisciplinary approach.

Among the scholarly historical studies about women to have ap-

peared in the late 1970s and since are Marion Kaplan's social histories of Jewish women and families in prewar Germany, biographies
of German-Jewish women writing in exile by Gabriele Kreis and Andreas Lixi-Purcell, Joan Ringelheim's essays probing the framework
for gender-oriented Holocaust studies, and my articles on mutual
assistance among women during the Holocaust. Another group of
studies examines the changing role of Jewish women in Germany
from *Kristallnacht* until the final deportation of German Jews in
1943.[29] For the first time, a number of such gender-oriented studies
have now been written by historians who are *not* survivors of the
Holocaust. Furthermore, with few exceptions, these studies treat the
Holocaust from a predominantly historical perspective as opposed
to a personal perspective. Most draw on the numerous memoirs and
diaries that have become available over the past two decades. Some
adopt an interdisciplinary approach, integrating the methods of the
social sciences into a humanities framework. Finally, all are typical
of the new wave of historical gender and family studies appearing
since the late 1970s in making women and children into subjects,
not just marginal objects, of history.[30]

CONCLUSIONS

In the preceding discussion we have examined three cycles of publications in family and gender Holocaust studies. We have shown how
the first books dealing with women and children during the Holocaust were usually memoirs by, or studies conducted by, survivors.
Although memoirs and diaries continued to be published and even
grew in number, they were later also augmented by analytical studies, part of the second cycle of publications. Finally, a new group of
historians, most born after the end of the Second World War, are
now involved in synthetic gender and Holocaust family research,
conceptualizing these topics historically.

But our survey leaves several questions yet unanswered. What
generated each of these cycles? Were they connected to world events,
or to new historical interpretations or other academic developments?
What common denominators exist among the topics chosen for research? What limitations hindered their examination and analysis?

In my opinion, the various surges of interest seem to have been
completely unrelated to world events connected to the Holocaust,

the war, Jewish identity, or Jewish survival. Neither the Kasztner (1954) nor Eichmann (1961) trials spurred specific Holocaust research on women, children, and families. The same is true of the ratification of relations between Israel and Germany, the Israeli debate over accepting German restitution, and the Six-Day (1967) and Yom Kippur (1973) Wars. The only factors that appear to have generated new interest in these topics were the broader development of "Holocaust awareness" during the mid-1970s and the simultaneous growth of general academic interest in women's culture and family studies.[31]

As interest in Holocaust family and gender studies grew, it assumed distinctive forms depending upon the availability of sources, researchers' personal inclinations, and the popularity of a particular subject. Many studies began more as appendixes to the general Holocaust research then being conducted than as independent historical examinations. For example, the studies from the late 1970s on refugees in the free world gave birth to research in the 1980s on refugee children and women in exile. Similarly, research of the mid-1980s on religious life during the Holocaust has now yielded studies on Orthodox women's groups in ghettos and camps. Thus it appears that gender and family studies of the Holocaust have been primarily reactive, responding to existing research patterns and academic areas of interest. Nevertheless, it is interesting to note that most gender and family research has remained within the realm of social history, barely touching on areas many historians consider the heart of Holocaust research: the Final Solution, Jewish leadership, and so on. Consequently, the topics of gender and family generally remain marginalized from "mainstream,""hard core" Holocaust scholarship.

Why have synthetic gender and family studies of the Holocaust taken so long to begin to appear? Two factors are topic awareness and source availability, as for all Holocaust studies. But while general Holocaust research began to flourish during the early 1970s after Jewish source material became available, the problem of sources is much more acute for gender and family studies. These rely heavily on oral documentation and memoirs, material that was slow to appear in quantity. Thus, the field has only recently taken its place on the academic map. Owing to the growing awareness of feminist and family history and the abundance of newly available sources, historians are finally just beginning to integrate the examination of family and women's culture into general, mainstream Holocaust research.

Numerous challenges face the historians specializing in gender and family research of the Holocaust. One is to actively seek sources and topics instead of only responding to existing ones. Another is to give their research an interdisciplinary focus, as most of their primary sources, such as memoirs and testimonies, are best studied on the interdisciplinary level. Finally, whereas several of the early gender studies on the Holocaust tended excessively toward speculative tangents (for example, the early claim that women suffered *more* than men and not *differently*), serious historians must avoid such pitfalls, concentrating instead on analytically probing their designated topic.

Research concerning women during the Holocaust is still in its infancy. That pertaining to children and family life is better developed; this is primarily a reflection of the superior source availability. There are many topics that remain to be covered. Little has been written about the rescue of children by resistance organizations.[32] Research has begun on the question of women as leaders during the Holocaust.[33] Other projects in their infancy concern women's religious lives during the Holocaust,[34] motherhood in camps and ghettos,[35] women's and children's culture during the Holocaust, and the Jewish woman in Nazi ideology.[36]

The question of research themes brings our historiographical survey to a close. What direction will the new research on gender and family take? Will it be incorporated into existing fields of research, such as studies of the resistance movement, rescue activities, and the displaced persons problem, or will it become an independent academic discipline? Will the choice of themes depend on the historian's personal inclination, or will there be an attempt to coordinate research and share information in order to avoid duplication and to streamline projects? These are but a few of the issues facing Holocaust women's culture and family history in the years to come.

Dan Laor

The Legacy of the Survivors:
Holocaust Literature in Israel

ISRAELI LITERATURE HAS ALWAYS BEEN OBSESSED WITH THE HOLO-
caust. On November 27, 1942—just a few days after the first official
news about the systematic extermination of European Jewry had
reached Palestine—poet Nathan Alterman published in the daily
Ha'aretz a poem entitled *"Mikol ha-Amim"* ("From All Peoples").
"For Thou didst choose us from all peoples / Thou didst love us and
favor us," protests Alterman against God, following a pattern that
had been established by Hayim Nachman Bialik in his classic poem
written after the Kishinev pogrom of 1903. "For Thou didst choose
us from all peoples, / Norwegians, Czechs and Britons," Alterman
writes, but alas, this was not a choice for life, but for death and annihilation.[1]

Alterman's poetic masterpiece can be seen as the beginning of
Israeli writing about the Holocaust, as writers belonging to the *Yishuv* (the Jewish settlement in Palestine) responded to a national catastrophe that had managed to skip over their own land. From that
point on, the Holocaust became a major issue for Israeli literature.
Year after year, more Israeli writers—including those born after the
war, such as David Grossman, the author of *Ayen Erekh Ahava* (*See
Under Love*, 1986)—join the circle of those responding to the Holocaust. The claim of some social and literary critics as to the relative
"silence" of Israeli literature with regard to the Holocaust is un-
founded.[2]

Among Israeli writers on the Holocaust, there is one group
whose overall contribution to the corpus of Israeli literature is
unique: survivors, those who managed to reach the shores of Israel
in the late 1940s and the 1950s. Some had no formal education and

little or no knowledge of Hebrew. They came from many countries—Poland, Hungary, Lithuania, Russia, Romania—each having been exposed to the Holocaust in some way: in a ghetto, a concentration camp, a forest among the partisans, in refuge in Siberia, or in a hiding place in a Christian monastery. They had experienced the pre-Holocaust years in Europe, the dark years of the war itself, and their individual as well as collective attempts to emerge from the ruins of the Holocaust and integrate into life again—first in Europe, later in the land of Israel. Unlike other Israeli writers (even those who felt tremendous empathy for the victims, a feeling that, to be sure, led to the creation of some important literary works), these individuals were the victims themselves. Having survived the Holocaust, they were committed to the imperative to bear witness. "If someone else could have written my stories," said survivor Elie Wiesel, "I would not have written them. I have written them in order to testify." The writer-survivors can therefore be seen as the most outspoken producers of what Wiesel calls "the literature of testimony," contributing to the constantly growing awareness in Israeli society of the nature of the Holocaust.[3]

Here I will examine writer-survivors in Israeli literature through four of their leading representatives: Abba Kovner, Ka.Tzetnik (Yehiel Dinur), Aharon Appelfeld, and Dan Pagis.[4]

Abba Kovner (1919–87) was long regarded by the Israeli public as the living symbol of the Holocaust. During the war years, he headed the underground organization in the Vilna ghetto. Later he commanded a partisan brigade and was an organizer of the *Beriha* movement to Palestine, where he immigrated in 1945. There Kovner soon became a major public figure: a member of the kibbutz movement, an officer in the new Israeli army, and one of the most articulate public speakers on matters concerning the Holocaust. In his poetry, which is largely devoted to the Holocaust, Kovner acted very much as a "poet-prophet." In critic Stephen Spender's words, Kovner "does not write simply as an individual artist expressing his exceptional sensibility. . . . Instead, he is the voice of the people. . . . His purposes are didactic and mystical, not aesthetic."[5] The major achievements in Kovner's literary treatment of the Holocaust are three long narrative poems. This poetic form enabled him to address the wide scope of Jewish collective experience during that period. (It is worth noting that the genre of the long narrative poem is widely

accepted among Holocaust poets as an appropriate medium for coping with the magnitude of their subject.)[6]

Kovner's first Holocaust-related work was *Ad Lo Or* ("Until
Dawn"), a "partisan poem" he had planned in a prison cell in Cairo
in 1946, where the British had incarcerated him for illegal attempts
to organize reprisals against the Germans, and written down and
published soon after his release.[7] The action takes place in the forests
in the course of one long night, dramatizing the Jewish partisans'
war of revenge against the Nazis as well as their struggle against the
elements—the forest, the wind, the night, and the swamp. A few
years later, Kovner apparently felt ready to face the theme of the
ghetto and its destruction. *Ha mafteah Zalal* ("The Key Sank," a title
alluding to a legend about the destruction of the Second Temple)
was first published in 1950, the revised version in 1965.[8] This work
was the first attempt in Hebrew poetry to present an epic of a ghetto
in the Nazi period. It depicts the idyllic and illusory prewar years,
war and occupation, the construction of the ghetto, daily life in the
ghetto, the gradual murder of its inhabitants, the resistance, and,
finally, the days of liberation—symbolized by the return of the survivor from the forests to face the ashes of the annihilated ghetto. Kovner's third work of this sort was *Ahoti Ketana* (*My Little Sister*), published in 1967, with its English version introducing Kovner's poetry
for the first time outside the Hebrew-speaking world.[9] This moving
text describes the lot of a Jewish girl who flees the Nazis and finds
refuge in a Dominican monastery, where she is saved physically but
lost to the Jewish people. The figure of the little sister—who in one
critic's words stands for "all little sisters, born and unborn, who were
swallowed by the Holocaust"[10]—is borrowed by Kovner from the
Song of Songs (4:9, 5:1), traditionally interpreted as an allegory
about the love between God and the people Israel.[11] The poem can
therefore be regarded as an anatomy of Jewish victimization, in
which the poet protests (through the ironic use of a biblical allusion)
God's breaking the covenant, which exposed God's own people to
the brutality—as well as mercy—of Christendom.

Though Kovner obviously well understands the complexity of
the Holocaust, he emerges in his writings and in his public appearances as heavily indebted to the heroic code of that period. This is,
indeed, the moral heritage he took from the Jewish resistance movement, in which he played a historic role. His partisan poem is a trib-

ute to Jewish heroism in World War II. "The Key Sank" reveals a particular interest in the conflict between the warriors and the masses, presented as a major characteristic of life in the ghetto. This heroic code was soon to be carried by him—and by other members of the underground movement—onto the Israeli scene. As a former leader of the Hashomer Hatsair youth movement in Vilna and a renowned fighter of Nazis, Kovner easily found his way into the top echelon of Israeli society, and then his literary work became more and more engaged with the rebirth of modern Israel. For example, he created a multivolume novel on Israel's War of Independence, the first part published as early as 1953.[12] His Holocaust poems should be read as part of a larger body of literature that includes fiction, poetry, and many essays related to Jewish national revival. In this respect, Kovner, the survivor of the Vilna ghetto, perhaps more than anyone else is associated with the common Zionist notion of the linkage between Holocaust and "redemption" in modern Jewish history.[13] This concept materializes in some of his other works, particularly in his post-1967 war poem *Hupa Bamidbar* ("A Canopy in the Desert"), which can be interpreted as a sequel to *My Little Sister*. The poem focuses on the voyage of the narrator-survivor, who is also the would-be bridegroom, into the Sinai Desert, the cradle of the Israeli nation, where the canopy missing from the wedding in his previous poem is set up—a symbol for the recovery of the covenant that had been violated during the Holocaust.[14]

While Kovner was producing his first major Holocaust poem in his prison cell in Cairo, another survivor was writing his own first book of testimony in a small hospital room in Italy, to which he had been taken sometime after his liberation from Auschwitz. This was Yehiel Dinur (b. 1917), better known by his pseudonym Ka.Tzetnik, and the book was his first novel, *Salamandra*, originally written in Yiddish and published in Hebrew translation in Israel in 1947 (it is known in English as *Sunrise over Hell*).[15]

"Why do you use this pseudonym?" the author was asked by Israeli attorney general Gideon Hausner, who put him on the stand in the Eichmann trial. And he replied:

> It is no pen name, I do not regard myself as a writer of literature. My writings are the chronicles of the planet Auschwitz. I was there

for about two years. Time does not run there as it does here on earth. Every fraction of a second there passes on a different scale of time. The inhabitants of this planet had no names; they had no parents; they were not born there and they did not beget children. They breathed according to different laws of nature. They did not live nor did they die according to the laws of this world. Their name was "Number . . . Katzetnik." . . . And I believe with all my heart that I should continue to bear this name Ka.Tzetnik, so long as the world has not been roused, after the crucifixion of a nation, to wipe out this evil, as it was once roused after the crucifixion of one person.

This testimony did not last long. When the prosecutor presented Dinur in his Auschwitz prisoner garb, he managed to utter only: "They always went away from me, they left me, and in the look of their eyes was this injunction. . . . For almost two years they went from me, always leaving me behind. I can see them, they are gazing at me, I see them . . ." Describes the attorney general: "That was as far as he got. He rose, wavered back and forth on the witness stand, and collapsed on the floor. He was carried to hospital, where it took him several days to recover from the shock. I did not dare to put him on the stand again." [16]

Nothing better illustrates Dinur's personality than this dramatic episode, undoubtedly one of the highlights of the Eichmann trial. Ever since his liberation from Auschwitz, Dinur has completely dedicated his life to the writing and rewriting of his Holocaust experience. Managing for many years to live in anonymity (until the Eichmann trial almost nobody knew who "Ka.Tzetnik" really was), Dinur cultivated a solitary lifestyle in order to keep the memories of Auschwitz fresh in his mind, so he would be able to live up to his commitment to give a complete testimony about what he had seen and gone through. "I have to disconnect myself from the rest of the world," he once said in a rare published interview, "in order to go back and live once again something of the horrors of Auschwitz. I made a circle around myself. I don't want to cross it. I don't want others to cross it. . . . Otherwise I will not be able to write." [17]

Dinur's most recent book, published in 1987, is a detailed report about psychiatric treatment he underwent in Holland. He was given LSD in order to cure him of the nightmares that had haunted him since his liberation from Auschwitz.

Though Dinur has declared time and again that he does not write "literature," it is literature that he writes, and that literature has a well-defined direction. One can call it "naturalism," because Dinur's claim for authenticity in the treatment of the Holocaust, and particularly Auschwitz, is realized by an "objective" and detailed description of the physical and human environment; a constant appeal to the ugly, abominable, and somber aspects of life; an obsessive exposure of sexual desire; and compassion toward the poor and the miserable. Critic Hana Yaoz has defined Dinur's métier as "the art of nausea." She adds that few Holocaust writers have considered naturalism to be the appropriate medium for rendering their experience.[18]

Dinur's stance is manifest in three major books, which form the core of his novelistic cycle *A Chronicle of a Jewish Family in the Twentieth Century*.[19] In *Sunrise over Hell*, for example, set partly in the ghetto and partly in Auschwitz, Dinur presents in great detail scenes of brutality and physical torture (including beating to death); a mother cutting the throat of her child and then committing suicide to avoid further persecution; heaps of corpses piled in the crematorium; the ugly, diseased and deformed look of the camp prisoners, particularly the *Mussulmänner*, those who have lost hope and are near death, presented in this novel as the epitome of human degradation. Two of Dinur's later novels—*Beit ha-Bubot* (*House of Dolls*, 1953) and *Karu Lo Piepel* (*Piepel*, 1961)—focus on the concentration camp guards' common practice of using inmate women and children for their own sexual pleasure.[20] Violence and brutality are represented together with sexual exploitation and sexual perversion, a mode of presentation that exposes both the misery and dehumanization of the victims and the vulgarity, indeed bestiality, of the victimizers. These novels, too, are filled with nauseating scenes, reaching their climax in an episode where starving prisoners, gathering in the camp latrine, are eating human flesh, the corpse of a fellow prisoner. Dinur strove to find a poetics that would adequately represent what he defined as "the other planet"—referring directly to Auschwitz but also to the Holocaust world at large—whose mode of existence, according to his claims, has very little to do with the world in which we normally live.

It is therefore not surprising that the appearance of Ka.Tzetnik's writings on the Israeli scene had a strong impact. Readers' encounter with these texts served as a shock treatment and helped them grasp something of the horrors of the Nazi period. When the new edition of *Salamandra* appeared in 1971, reviewer Gideon Talpaz vividly recalled how the first edition of 1946 had practically "shattered" its readers.[21] And when Ka.Tzetnik published his second novel, the poet K. A. Bertini, himself a survivor, credited the writer for his ability to stage the horrors of the Holocaust far beyond *The House of Dolls*.[22] Journalist Raphael Bashan calls Ka.Tzetnik's books "shocking, exciting, shuddering, opening a window onto hell itself, daringly tearing the conspiracy of silence" around the Holocaust.[23]

For many years Ka.Tzetnik's books were an important part of Holocaust education in Israel. They were recommended reading for high school students, and widely circulated by the Israeli Defense Force's chief education officer to be read by the military. Nevertheless, Ka.Tzetnik has never been accepted by the Israeli literary establishment as a writer of stature whose art transcends its subject matter: most of his works were published by marginal publishing houses; he has never won any literary prize; and he has not been treated in depth by Israel's major critics. And though nobody would put it in writing, it seems that his crude naturalism, his "art of nausea," his melodramatic tendency, and an overall lack of craftsmanship alienated readers from his writing—in spite of its effectiveness—and prevented its inclusion in the literary canon on the Holocaust.

A totally different position is that of Aharon Appelfeld, who has gained an outstanding reputation since the 1970s both in Israel and abroad. One can even say that with the diminishing popularity of Ka.Tzetnik and the passing away of Abba Kovner in 1987, Appelfeld has emerged as the most vital presence in Holocaust literature in Israel today.

Born in Bukovina (then Romania) in 1932, Appelfeld was only eight years old when the war started and fourteen when it ended. At the beginning of the war, he was deported to a work camp in Transnistria (a region in southwest Ukraine), where he was separated from his parents. Later he fled the camp, hid in the forests of the Ukraine for three years, and finally served in a series of Red Army units. After the war, he made his way to a displaced persons camp in Italy and in 1946 to Palestine. Thus, Appelfeld, although a child survivor, had neither lived in a ghetto nor experienced the reality of a death camp. These biographical facts must be taken into consideration in comparing his oeuvre to that of other Holocaust writers.

Yet Appelfeld's uniqueness is due mainly to his poetics, which is diametrically opposed to that of Ka.Tzetnik.[24] Appelfeld purposely avoids treating the horrors of the Holocaust; indeed, he almost avoids the Holocaust itself. Despite the horrors of the camps in Transnistria—tens of thousands of displaced persons brought there by force; camp prisoners exploited in forced labor; thousands suffering and often dying from diseases, hunger, and cold; mass murder of Jews in some of the camps carried out by the German *Einsatzgruppe D* with the help of local Ukrainians[25]—at least some of which he must have witnessed, nothing of this infiltrates Appelfeld's prose. In his stories, novellas, and short novels one finds hardly any mention of Nazis, concentration camps, torture, forced labor, ghettos, revolt, partisans, mass murder, crematoria. Strangely enough, Appelfeld's writings, considered by many as the epitome of Holocaust literature today, are notable for the very absence of anything usually associated with what we refer to as the "Holocaust." Appelfeld's novel *Mesilat ha-Barzel* ("The Railway," 1991) may serve as an example.[26] It is a story about a man in his late fifties who has spent the four decades since the end of the war traveling on trains, coming again and again to the same recurring destinations. This absurd situation—which reminds one of Kafka's novels as well as Camus's *L'Étranger*—reflects the existential restlessness of the survivor, who has never really found the way back to normal life. Even the man's successful attempt to kill a former Nazi officer, to avenge the death of his parents, does not change this pattern, for nothing can really emancipate him from the bondage to his past. This innovative treatment of the social and mental state of the survivor also occurs in other stories, such as "1946," which represents the collective physical and moral disintegration of a group of Jewish refugees on the shores of Italy soon after their emergence from the camps and forests;[27] and, for example, his famous short novel *Bartfus Ben Almavet* (*The Immortal Bartfus*), a portrayal of a survivor who refuses to conform to the norms of bourgeois society—wife, kids, social responsibility—and even looks back with a certain nostalgia to his war years in the forests, where he had gained his "immortality" through his day-to-day struggle and his triumph over the Angel of Death.[28]

The other major theme of Appelfeld's fiction is Jewish life in Eastern Central Europe in the 1930s. In *Baddenheim, Ir Nofesh* (*Baddenheim, 1939*), the novella with which Appelfeld made his debut in the English-speaking world in 1978, a group of Jews vacations at an Austrian summer resort. Their indulgence in daily pleasures makes them unable to respond seriously to the signs of doom all around them. Yet this collective *dolce vita* suddenly comes to an end in the final episode, when all the vacationers are taken into a train, leading them to an unknown (to them) destination.[29] Appelfeld takes a similar perspective in his novel *Tor ha-Pela'ot* (*The Age of Wonders*), whose first and major section describes the lot of an upper-middle-class Jewish family from the vantage point of a child. The father—a famous German-language writer—remains committed to the values of German culture despite the growing antisemitism to which he is exposed time and again. The ironic denouement of the story comes in the second section, when the child, now an adult, makes a postwar visit to his native town and realizes that even though the town is by now completely *Judenrein,* it is still a stronghold of antisemitism.[30] And finally, from 1985, there is *Be'et uve-Ona Ahat* (*The Healer*), another novel about an assimilated Jewish family, in which the question of identity is a source of constant tension among its members. Rejecting his wife and daughter's growing attachment to a Hasidic healer somewhere in the Carpathian Mountains, the highly assimilated father, Mr. Katz, finally makes his way back to Vienna, only to realize that the *Anschluss* has successfully taken place and the Jewish population, including himself, is no longer tolerated in the Austrian capital.[31]

In his own way, Appelfeld avoids entering into the depths of horror. Philip Roth has even gone so far as to say that "his literary subject is not the Holocaust." But Roth's statement can be accepted only in the strictest sense of the word.[32] For the Holocaust is the *terminus ad quo* of at least half of Appelfeld's fiction, as well as the *terminus ad quem* of the other half. Appelfeld is always treating either the world of the survivors, who miraculously emerged from the inferno though they never freed themselves of that trauma, or the world of prewar Jews who were blindly led into that inferno, exposing the futility of their ideal of becoming part of European civilization. In both cases, the Holocaust is the filter through which Appelfeld faces the issue of Jewish destiny in the twentieth century, a kind of Rorschach test through which contemporary Jewish life and recent history are screened. "There is a very great literary difficulty," Appelfeld once said: "how to deal with horror itself . . . whether horror in its pure form and artistic expression can somehow go together." He then said what sounds very much like a poetic credo: "What I have tried to do all these years was to encircle the horror, to mark its boundaries. I have tried to show how much it nourished the past and how relevant it has been as far as our future is concerned."[33]

The imperative to tell, so crucial among writer-survivors, brings us to the late poet Dan Pagis (1930–86), whose biography is similar to that of Appelfeld. Born in Radautz, Bukovina, a city mentioned only once in his writing, Pagis spent four years of his childhood totally alone in a German concentration camp. By that time his mother was already dead and his father had been living in Palestine for many years. After the liberation he migrated to Palestine, where he managed to achieve a magnificent scholarly and literary career.

For many years Pagis avoided any reference to the Holocaust in his public life or his writing. A drastic and perhaps unavoidable change in his attitude occurred in mid-career. In a 1986 interview, the poet described an experience he had had during a visit to New York in 1967. He had happened to meet distant relatives who in their home had preserved some objects from his own family home in Bukovina: "The room looked exactly like the house of my grandfather in which I had grown up. For years I had tried to ignore the subject of the Holocaust, but the sight of the room, which appalled me, enabled and even forced me to write poems on this subject."[34] Immediately afterward, beginning with his 1970 book of poems *Gilgul* (*Metamorphosis*), the Holocaust, thus far excluded from his writing, became a major factor in shaping the poet's worldview and his poetic discourse.[35]

One poem in particular, "Written in Pencil in the Sealed Railway-Car," stands as the hallmark of this book, indeed of Pagis's Holocaust poetry. It has been circulated in the English-speaking

world through a translation by Stephen Mitchell, and reads as
follows:

> here in this carload
> i am eve
> with abel my son
> if you see my other son
> cain son of man
> tell him that i[36]

Both "the sealed railway-car" and the "carload" are immediately associated with the Nazi war against the Jews, particularly with the
mass transports to the death camps. The title gives the poem a sense
of authenticity; the text is a record or document, a few lines inscribed by someone on the walls of the railway car as it made its way
to death. The Hebrew original for the word "written" in the title is
katuv vehatum, "signed and sealed," an allusion to the famous liturgy
recited on the Day of Atonement, suggesting the verdict for life or
death issued by God on that day. Yet soon the speaker is identified
as Eve, seen here in the company of her son Abel, sending a message
to her other son Cain; Cain and Abel are frequent figures in Pagis's
Holocaust poetry. By making this reference to the Book of Genesis,
the poet charges the concrete situation so well dramatized in the
poem with a general overview of the catastrophe that came upon the
"family of man": the victimization of human life (Eve, let us remember, is "the mother of all living" [Gen. 3:20]) by a murderous force
that is, paradoxically, a human being himself (the Hebrew for "son
of man" is *ben adam,* carrying a triple meaning: son of Adam, son
of man, human being). The climax of the poem, its interrupted
ending—"tell him that i"—brilliantly illuminates the horror of the
situation. The railway car, we may assume, has reached its final
destination, and the speaker, facing death, is unable even to complete her cry of anguish. The poem ends in a terrifying moment of
silence.

Seven short but well-wrought lines, fewer than twenty carefully
chosen words in the original, strict omission of punctuation, an art-
ful command of poetic devices, and above all a great poet's touch are
the ingredients from which Dan Pagis produces this classic work.
Translated into many European languages, anthologized, interpreted

by numerous critics, this poem is taught in Israeli schools and, even more significantly, often cited in public Holocaust commemorations. "Written in Pencil in the Sealed Railway-Car" is by now a widely accepted text in Israeli ritualization of the Holocaust. Yet it should be remembered that this work is just one small part of Pagis's impressive body of Holocaust poems from *Metamorphosis* and later books. These are mostly short lyrical poems, in which the simplicity, skill, and inventive treatment of the subject manage, on the one hand, to create horror with an astonishingly "human" effect and, on the other hand, to transcend the text, making a moral or philosophical statement about either victim or victimizer and offering new perspectives on the meaning of the Holocaust. Indeed, "Written in a Pencil in a Sealed Railway-Car," as well as some other poems by Pagis, implicitly challenge Theodor Adorno's declaration that writing poetry after Auschwitz is "barbaric" (" *Nach Auschwitz ein gedicht zu Schreiben ist barbarish*").[37]

As we can see, Pagis's poetics is the opposite of that of Abba Kovner, who adopted the persona of the poet-prophet of both the Holocaust (emphasizing its heroism) and Jewish national revival. And presumably Pagis would not have felt comfortable with the so-called literature of atrocity cultivated by a writer such as Ka.Tzetnik. There is, however, some similarity between the sensibilities of Pagis and Appelfeld—both of them natives of Bukovina, child survivors, and late disciples of the Central European literary tradition—though Pagis seems not to share Appelfeld's taboo against working with materials associated with the Holocaust per se.

In spite of this impressive variety, all these writers have one thing in common—they are survivors of the Holocaust who, through imaginative literature, constantly try to speak about their experience, each in his own literary code: Kovner is the poet-prophet; Ka.Tzetnik produces novels of atrocity; Appelfeld writes a continuous narrative on the Jewish condition in an era that has known the Holocaust; and Pagis leads us to the heart of darkness through the sophisticated medium of the short lyrical poem. As a group these writers, together with others not mentioned here, function as emissaries from what Ka.Tzetnik has defined as "the other planet," each trying to tell us what it was all about. Their presence is of great importance not only to Israeli literature but to Israeli life and culture as well; they provide precious testimony crucial for the remembrance of an era that we Israelis ought to remember and come to grips with. By shaping and reshaping our national consciousness, they make us more capable of handling the past, of facing the future.

Lawrence Baron

Teaching about the New Psychosocial Research on Rescuers in Holocaust Courses

PSYCHOSOCIAL INTERPRETATIONS OF THE BEHAVIOR OF THE PERPETRA-
tors and victims of the Holocaust have long been central to its study
and teaching. On SS conduct, Holocaust courses usually cite Stanley
Milgram's or similar clinical experiments on obedience as one possible explanation of why seemingly normal Germans obeyed murderous orders; on survival in the concentration camps, Bruno Bettelheim's and Viktor Frankl's analyses of inmates' coping mechanisms
have been contrasted to the theories advanced by Terrence Des Pres
or Lawrence Langer.[1] But until recently, there was no body of psychosocial literature on the motivations of gentiles who saved Jews.
Thus, the rescue of Jews was taught from a comparative national
perspective that usually focused on Denmark as the atypical case of
collective solidarity with the persecuted Jews.[2] Coverage of "righteous gentiles" in class lectures and readings tended to be limited to
narratives about their good deeds, and failed to probe further into
their backgrounds, beliefs, and personalities.[3] Students learned
something about rescue activities but almost nothing about the traits
and values of the rescuers themselves.[4] Philip Hallie's *Lest Innocent
Blood Be Shed* stands out as an notable exception precisely because it
delves deeply into the prior lives and moral convictions of its protag-
onists.[5]

Perry London's 1970 pilot study of "Christians who saved Jews"
heralded the beginning of serious systematic inquiry into the psychological and sociological origins of ethical courage under life-
threatening conditions.[6] The 1980s witnessed the beginning of a
spate of significant articles and books that examined which qualities
and experiences distinguished the rescuers from the vast majority of

their neighbors who abandoned Jews to their genocidal fate in Nazi-occupied Europe. The best-known scholars involved in this research have been Eva Fleischner, Eva Fogelman, Douglas Huneke, Mordecai Paldiel, Pearl and Sam Oliner, Andre Stein, and Nechama Tec.[7]

Most of this steadily growing body of research relies primarily on intensive interviews, qualitative or quantitative, with rescuers. The transcripts of their responses have been subjected to content or statistical analysis to determine if there were recurring combinations of factors that contributed to their decisions to help Jews. In some of the studies, these data have been compared with information from interviews of control groups—contemporaries who either ignored the plight of the Jews or exploited it for personal gain. These studies have contrasted the differences discerned between the two groups to highlight the qualities that may have prompted rescuers to risk their own lives on behalf of Jews.[8]

Despite their disagreements over the causal importance of particular variables, a consensus has emerged that the extraordinary altruism displayed by most rescuers was anchored in *ordinary* attitudes and patterns of conduct that had been developed throughout their lives. Thus, Nechama Tec maintains, "Helping behavior was an integral part of their lifestyle, which explains why they engaged in this behavior without premeditation."[9] Pearl and Sam Oliner likewise conclude: "Helping Jews was less a decision made at a critical juncture than a choice prefigured by an established character and way of life."[10] Echoing the same theme, Eva Fogelman writes: "This humanitarian response sprang from a core of firmly held inner values."[11] And while Mordecai Paldiel argues that the remarkable goodness manifested by the "righteous gentiles" was elicited by the extreme situation in which they found themselves, he, too, admits that it was "nourished by other factors at the root" of their personalities.[12]

In my opinion, this is the most important lesson that teaching about the rescuers conveys: namely, that the attributes that compelled them to save Jews are common virtues that can be cultivated in our daily lives. We often romanticize the rescuers, unproductively, as adventurous and valorous heroes confronting the Nazi behemoth. The attention paid to Raoul Wallenberg's daring exploits illustrates this point. Regardless of his personal courage, cunning, and motives, his success in shielding tens of thousands of Hungarian Jews stemmed largely from his diplomatic status and the external support he received. To students, he sounds like a mythical figure with little relevance to their own lives.[13] The other way we minimize the lessons to be learned from the rescuers is by viewing their actions as an impromptu response to an emergency situation. This is the implicit message conveyed by the movie *Schindler's List:* if an amoral profiteer such as Oskar Schindler could be converted into an altruist, then there must be little continuity between one's normal ethics and one's reaction to crises such as Jewish suffering in the Holocaust.[14] Integrating the new psychosocial theories about rescuers into the teaching of the Holocaust can provide students with credible role models, whose deeds arose out of their key personality traits and values. Their decisions to rescue Jews demonstrate that there were viable moral alternatives to complicity in, or passivity toward, the slaughter of European Jewry.

Although students should be exposed to the new interpretations of why rescuers saved Jews, teachers need to heed researchers' warnings that (as Fogelman writes) "any attempt to isolate a single all-encompassing motivational factor to explain rescuers' decisions or conduct in extreme, high-risk situations is doomed to oversimplify a complex, multifaceted behavior."[15] None of the psychosocial scholarship has claimed that there exists a simple formula for creating people who will jeopardize their lives and those of their families to protect an innocent minority. Researchers in this field recognize that there were many bystanders with backgrounds and traits identical to those of the rescuers, and caution that it is merely statistically more likely that someone with these qualities would intervene on behalf of a Jew than someone lacking them.[16]

With that caveat in mind, let us now turn to a brief overview of the major theories that have been advanced to explain why rescuers aided Jews. Perry London postulates that some rescuers saw themselves as social outsiders and therefore tended to be more sympathetic to the suffering of the Jews.[17] Nechama Tec similarly reports that most of the Polish rescuers in her sample were socially marginal; but rather than considering this a source of their empathy for other outcasts, she maintains that social separateness heightened their sense of autonomy and individuality, enabling them to follow the dictates of their conscience regardless of the prevailing hostility or indifference toward the Jews in Poland.[18] My own research on Dutch

rescuers suggests that the marginality theory is more applicable to
countries such as Poland, where native antisemitism was strong and
most Jews unassimilated, than to Denmark, France, Holland, and
Italy, where antisemitism was considerably weaker and Jews more
acculturated.[19] But in France, historical memories of discrimination
and ostracism clearly provided one reason for the collective support
extended to the Jews by a persecuted minority such as the Huguenot
community of Le Chambon.[20]

Though most rescuers felt a sense of belonging to their communities, individuality and independence were common traits among
rescuers, Fogelman and the Oliners have found.[21] Fogelman argues
that parents of rescuers had engendered a sense of competence, independence, and self-confidence in their children.[22] Similarly, the
Oliners subsume independence under the category of "personal po-
tency," in which they also include adventurousness, decisiveness,
self-confidence, and a willingness to take chances and assume responsibility for affecting the situations faced in life. They trace these
qualities back to strong, cohesive family bonds and to parenting that
stressed both caring for others and self-reliance. They attribute such
successful child-rearing to consistent and rational disciplinary methods that enabled the child to learn inductively and avoided physical
or verbal abuse.[23] Yet the centrality of independence to rescue should
not be misconstrued as a blanket endorsement of rugged individual-
ism or nonconformity. Only 11 percent of the rescuers in the Oliners' sample acted primarily on the basis of their own autonomously
derived principles.[24]

Instead, rescues were more likely among people who belonged
to groups that perceived the rescue of Jews or resistance to Nazism
as natural outgrowths of core values to which they were already dedicated. Over half of the Oliners' sample falls into this category, which
they term "normative altruism." For this kind of rescuer, the moral
tenets advocated by their family and other primary groups shaped
their conscience and sense of duty. Children and adults in these set-
tings constantly witnessed people who played a significant role in
their lives translating espoused principles into practice. In some instances, such rescuers had internalized the ethical principles of their
reference group to such an extent that they independently took the
initiative to save Jews. In most cases, they helped Jews because their
reference group solicited their participation.[25] In Douglas Huneke's

typology of rescuers, both "ideological" and "communal" rescuers possessed similar "normative" motivational dynamics.[26] So did many of the rescuers Eva Fogelman classifies as "ideological or religious moral rescuers," "network rescuers," children who helped their parents save Jews, and "concerned professionals" who lent their expertise to various rescue operations.[27] David Gushee's research focuses on the kinds of "normative" Christian beliefs and congregational priorities that mobilized religious rescuers.[28] The critical lesson learned from such rescuers is that political and religious activism was not something that emerged from previously apathetic and isolated individuals reacting to a crisis; rather it developed among people who *already* were members of churches and parties committed to ideals that Germany and its allies had violated.

The third distinctive class of rescuers consists of those who acted upon emotional attachments to, and sympathy for, Jews. Responding to feelings of personal affection or obligation, a minority of rescuers (16 percent and 28 percent in the Oliners' and Fogelman's studies, respectively) helped Jews they already knew as colleagues, employers, employees, friends, neighbors, or relatives through intermarriage. Their prior ties with specific Jews made it easier for them to empathize with Jewry in general and eventually led some of them to harbor Jews in dire need who were strangers.[29]

A heightened sensitivity to human suffering and an almost instinctive compulsion to alleviate it were what prompted other rescuers to defend Jews. The new scholarship has identified several developmental sources for this acute empathetic and nurturing sensibility, in addition to marginality. Huneke and Fogelman have maintained that this sense of compassion could result from childhood traumas such as serious illness, a physical handicap, or the death of or separation from parents, siblings, or close friends.[30] Francis Grossman and the Oliners have traced concern for others to the receptivity, responsiveness, and caring that rescuers received as children, from their parents or other significant adults in their lives.[31] But, the Oliners also stress, empathy alone was insufficient to move someone to save Jews: rescuers motivated by empathy also exhibited an above-average level of social responsibility and tolerance toward people from different ethnic and religious groups. They usually had learned these qualities from the attitudes expressed by their parents or through previous interactions with individuals from diverse backgrounds.[32]

Whether the ethic of empathy and caring was more prevalent among women than men has been contested. Originally Fogelman claimed that more women than men helped Jews for emotional reasons, citing Carol Gilligan's theory that emotional sensitivity to others is typical of the moral "voice" that develops from traditional female socialization.[33] However, Fogelman has more recently rejected such "stereotypical gender-based assumptions with men as risk takers and women as nurturing and caring helpers."[34] Analyzing their data by gender, the Oliners report that whereas male rescuers approximated the empathy levels of female rescuers, male bystanders scored significantly lower than either female rescuers or bystanders whose empathy scores were similar. Most women, while already very empathic, were more likely to become rescuers if they had prior positive exposure to people outside of their own families and communities. Conversely, male rescuers who had strong moral convictions often needed the extra emotional spur of compassion and pity in order to act upon their beliefs.[35] Whatever the resolution of this debate, it does underscore that morality emanates from both affective and cognitive sources.

Another body of recent research has challenged the psychosocial theories discussed above. This school of thought contends that the rareness of rescue, the uniqueness of the conditions during the Holocaust, and the multiplicity of motivations and traits detected among rescuers place in doubt the validity of any such studies' general behavioral conclusions. Eva Fleischner, for example, finds "no single common motive" among the French Catholic rescuers in her interview pool and observes that there frequently was a discrepancy between their professed ideals and their actions.[36] After interviewing many Dutch rescuers, Andre Stein similarly laments that "a blueprint for goodness" still eludes his grasp.[37] Eric Silver has reached a similar conclusion: "For every case that confirms a particular hypothesis, another can be found that challenges it."[38] According to interviews conducted by Kristen Monroe, most rescuers viewed "themselves as part of a shared humanity" for whom they felt inherently responsible, but her evidence does not validate any of the proposed psychosocial explanations for the formation of a kind of personal identity that compelled rescuers to save Jews.[39]

The most sustained criticism of the new psychosocial research comes from Mordecai Paldiel, the director of Yad Vashem's Department for the Righteous. In his opinion, rescuers' actions were usually the product not of their own initiative but rather of circumstances beyond their control. Many rescuers possessed backgrounds, motivations, personalities, and values contrary to those the new research has claimed to be typical of rescuers, he observes, and he wonders why there were so few rescuers if relatively common factors produced altruistic traits. In Paldiel's view, the high probability of risk and retribution for helping Jews has not been sufficiently taken into account in the new research. Conceding that the psychosocial theories advanced can explain everyday prosocial behavior, he nevertheless deems them inadequate to account for the extraordinary altruism required to defend Jews during the Holocaust. Finally, for Paldiel, the psychosocial approach implies that rescuers made a rational decision to protect Jews. To him, such a deliberate decision-making process would have been a deterrent, given the dangers associated with rescuing Jews. As an alternative theory, Paldiel has posited that the radical altruism exhibited by the rescuers is a latent psychological archetype animated in times of crisis and therefore beyond rational explanation.[40]

Nevertheless, common types of motivations have been identified. Paldiel and Eric Silver both present material that classifies motivations. Paldiel's appendix groups together rescuers who helped Jews for particular reasons. The motivations include religious beliefs, a commitment to the sanctity of life, a sense of moral duty, a "natural" inclination to aid people in need, shame over what others were doing to the Jews, and a conscientious imperative to take sides against the barbarism of Nazi Germany and its allies.[41] Silver devotes each chapter of his book to a situational or motivational factor shared by certain rescuers. The chapters deal with rescue efforts by entire communities, by diplomats, Christian clerics, Moslems, and isolated individuals, and by Germans whose acts of compassion for Jews constituted treason in the eyes of their compatriots.[42]

The approach teachers use to introduce these theories about rescuers to their students will naturally vary depending on the academic level of the class, the time allotted to rescue within the course, and the availability of resource materials. There are now a variety of inexpensive and readily accessible secondary sources that can be assigned.

The paperback editions of Tec's *When Light Pierced the Darkness,* the Oliners' *Altruistic Personality,* and Fogelman's *Conscience and Courage* make good texts for college courses.[43] For those teaching at Christian colleges and universities, David Gushee's *The Righteous Gentiles of the Holocaust* and Hallie's *Lest Innocent Blood Be Shed* raise issues about Christian ethics, institutions, and theology that are bound to stimulate meaningful discussions about the role of faith and organized religion in contemporary society.[44] High school teachers might consider using such readable narratives about rescuers as Milton Meltzer's *Rescue* or Philip Friedman's *Their Brothers' Keepers.*[45] For briefer introductions to the topic, instructors could assign the American Jewish Committee's booklet summarizing the Oliners' conclusions, or selected articles from the special rescuer issues of the magazine *Dimensions,* the volume of *The Humboldt Journal of Social Relations* devoted to altruism and prosocial behavior, the edition of *The World and I* featuring a number of articles about rescuers, or *Remembering for the Future,* an anthology of papers from the 1988 Oxford Conference on the Holocaust.[46] Any of the above articles, photocopied and distributed, will give students a good idea of the various ways scholars have explained why rescuers acted as they did.

Rather than simply accept these theories as true, students should be encouraged to test their validity by applying them to specific rescuers' lives. Selected members of the class might read books that provide some insight into the personalities of the rescuers. Miep Gies's *Anne Frank Remembered,* Hallie's *Lest Innocent Blood Be Shed,* and Douglas Huneke's *The Moses of Rovno* are a few accounts that go beyond just telling the story of what rescuers did, thus enabling students to identify the ideological and psychosocial factors motivating their actions.[47] The Martyr's Memorial and Museum of the Holocaust in Los Angeles has produced an excellent secondary school curriculum for studying Anne Frank that contains a perceptive analysis of two of Anne's helpers.[48] Collections of the testimonies by (or narrative accounts about) various rescuers also allow students to identify the motivations, personality traits, and values that prompted these rescuers. Block and Drucker's *Rescuers: Portraits of Moral Courage in the Holocaust,* Paldiel's *Path of the Righteous,* and Rittner and Myers's *Courage to Care* contain rich source material for such a project.[49] The students doing this assignment should conclude it with a panel discussion about which theories seem valid or invalid in light of their readings.

Documentaries and feature films can serve as another vehicle for getting students to analyze the psychosocial roots of moral action. Eva Fogelman conveniently lists movies concerning the rescue of Jews at the back of her book.[50] After watching *The Courage to Care, The Weapons of Spirit, The Hiding Place,* or any other films dealing with rescuers, students should read whatever has been published by or about the people depicted so as to develop theories about what might have motivated them.[51] Even in the case of Oskar Schindler, whose motivations are difficult to discern in Spielberg's popular movie, there are several published explorations of his transformation into a rescuer that advance plausible explanations.[52]

The unit on the rescuers should come only after much of the history of the Holocaust has been covered. By placing the rescue of Jews in this broader context, students can better appreciate how atypical it was, and can understand how different countries' cultural and political traditions and wartime conditions facilitated or inhibited the extent of rescue there.[53] Yet realizing how limited the rescue of the Jews was can easily foster cynicism and fatalism about the potential for human goodness. To counteract this sense of despair, students need to understand that the willingness of most rescuers to save Jews originated in common traits and values that had been honed on the whetstone of everyday life. As David Gushee reminds us: "What we are learning about how the rescuers came to perform such deeds illustrates the many paths to righteousness, challenging each of us to consider whether we are journeying along even one of them."[54]

Judith E. Doneson

Why Film?

THE MIND CAN SUMMON ASSOCIATIONS THAT SEEM PERPLEXING BUT are in fact logical. So it's not surprising that my musings turned to the "small people" of Germany, the inhabitants of the fictional *Heimat,* early one oppressively hot June morning. With our belongings thrown indiscriminately into the back seat of the car—one of the luxuries of traveling by automobile—we set out from St. Louis, Missouri on Highway 44. I needed to be in Los Angeles, but I did not want to face the mobbed airports and the crammed airplanes only to fly above the stunning landscape of the southwestern United States. As we drove through the myriad of small cities—Big Cabin, Oklahoma; Groom, Texas; Clines Corner, New Mexico; Seligman, Arizona; Barstow, California—stopping now and then for gas or a bite to eat, I thought about the citizens who reside in these towns, removed from the distractions and destructions of the modern city. It brought to mind the fictional inhabitants of Shabbach, located in the Hunsruck region of Germany—the good citizens of Karl Reitz's sixteen-hour film journey *Heimat,* the "small people" for whom the fate of European Jewry meant little as they lived their lives during the Nazi period, though there was a concentration camp on the outskirts of the village.

An article in the British film journal *Sight and Sound* describes the catalyst for Karl Reitz's film: "Over Christmas [1978], German television began to broadcast the American series *Holocaust.* [Reitz] watched it with mounting horror. Here was the history Germany should be remembering—but not like this. This was sentimental, melodramatic; all the real living details had been smoothed out. Reitz set himself to remember more."[1] More for Reitz meant less for European Jewry: the Holocaust was eliminated from *Heimat.* And I thought, praise be the American network that brought us *Holocaust.* It would be nice to presume that because of this miniseries, the occupants of the towns I was now driving through were informed, albeit in a diluted fashion, about what happened to the Jews under the Nazis. Lest one suspect confusion here between real people and fictitious characters, be reminded that in *Heimat* the individuals represent reality, one that allows an excuse for as well as an evasion of the German past, whereas *Holocaust,* in its clumsy, Hollywood style, helps to retell history to those who would forget.

In any discussion on film and the Holocaust, the inevitable difficulty surfaces over the merits (or in many scholarly views, the lack of merits) of Hollywood simulations. Books are written opposing this Hollywood culture, conferences are organized to probe the "limitations of representation" of the Holocaust, and new films are made to fight the trivialized versions of the catastrophe.[2] So in posing the question "why film?" the first issue I address here is the controversy over the perceived exploitive nature of Hollywood interpretations of the Final Solution. This is followed by an analysis of Agnieska Holland's film *Europa, Europa* (1990), which enjoyed an overwhelming reception in the United States, indicating our need to comprehend what lurks beneath the surface of a film, beyond its ability to entertain. And I conclude by addressing various uses of film in the context of the first two concerns.

As early as 1946, the authors of *The Black Book,* a report of Nazi crimes against the Jewish people, predicted: "As the war recedes into the past, the facts of the Nazi inhumanities against the Jews will fade from our memory like the details of a bad dream."[3] This prognostication has not come true, in large part thanks to the efforts of the mass media. Nonetheless, as Anton Kaes continues to wonder: "How can this historical occurrence [the Holocaust], which is less understood the more we know about it, be represented in the mass media of today's entertainment industry?"[4] Kaes would not argue the watershed impact of NBC's *Holocaust,* which was broadcast for the first time in the United States in the spring of 1978 and telecast throughout Western Europe in 1979. This American melodrama, seen by hundreds of millions of viewers, precipitated debates and discussions that forever changed the landscape of memory of the Holocaust in the popular mind. Indeed, in large part due to this docudrama, the Holocaust became the established framework to which most modern catastrophes are compared.[5]

Kaes does not hesitate to condemn, however, the "unabashed commercial exploitation and trivialization of human suffering as exemplified in such television specials as *Playing for Time* and *War and Remembrance,* or in such films as *Sophie's Choice* and *Enemies—A Love Story*—films in which the Holocaust serves more often than not as a backdrop to melodramatic private affairs."[6] *Holocaust* heads his list of dramas capitalizing on the Jewish destruction.

Most of us are aware of the limitations of interpretation in Hollywood productions. We are more challenged and provoked by interpretations such as Hans-Jürgen Syberberg's *Hitler—A Film from Germany* (1978) or Claude Lanzmann's *Shoah* (1985). These films beg to be considered on the philosophical, theoretical, and even aesthetic planes. They are part of a distinctly dissimilar discourse from that of popular culture, one that dictates a separate mode of thinking. Why, then, must they be viewed in direct opposition to conventional Hollywood films?

"I believe that Hans-Jürgen Syberberg's controversial seven-hour film of 1978, self-consciously entitled *Hitler—A Film from Germany,*" writes Anton Kaes, "represents one of the few attempts to come to terms with the Nazi phenomenon in a way that challenges Hollywood story-telling."[7] Yet in his book *On the Misfortune and Fortune of Art in Germany since the Last War* (1991), Syberberg writes that contemporary Western culture is an "unholy alliance of a Jewish leftist esthetic" and that "whoever goes along with the Jews or leftists can make a career." The German magazine *Der Spiegel* was not delicate in its response to Syberberg: "People know today that blood clings to sentences like that. . . . They aren't abstract nonsense, they're criminal."[8] And so, in light of this spurious quarrel—Hollywood popular culture versus a more complex philosophical discourse on film—we must ask ourselves: should there be no moral considerations involved in praising artistic interpretations of the Holocaust and the Nazi period?

The tenacity and fortitude it took for a U.S. television network to produce a nine-and-a-half-hour miniseries on the destruction of European Jewry defies the capitalist imagination.[9] The unanticipated reward was the astonishing success of *Holocaust.* Yes, it is a product of movie conventions and storytelling. Yet many of those who applauded *Holocaust* were themselves survivors. A letter written to Herbert Brodkin, the producer of *Holocaust,* by members of the 1939 Club, Inc., Jewish survivors of the Nazi destruction, stated: "We think you will agree with us that survivors of the Holocaust are entitled to be the film's toughest critics, and their favorable response to the film is a compliment of the highest regard." [10]

It indeed seems nonsensical to defend the notion of "allowing" the Holocaust to enter into the world of popular culture. Many of us have grappled with the uniqueness of this event, and will continue to do so. But reality informs us that a majority of the population does not wish to engage in this philosophical struggle. So in our quest for understanding, we must distinguish between those for whom the Holocaust is an enduring obsession to come to terms with our own humanity and those who are satisfied with a basic comprehension of evil.

Even survivors are caught in this dichotomy. There are survivors who are more articulate, such as Elie Wiesel and Primo Levi. And then there are those who are not part of this elite. If a common survivor wishes to tell his or her story on a tabloid television program, as was done on *A Current Affair,* [11] should someone tell that person not to do it, that this trivializes a person's own history? Another survivor appeared on the NBC show *Unsolved Mysteries* and told of his liberation from the concentration camp. [12] Was this trivialization, or a mini history lesson for the mass audience? At the 1990 UCLA conference "Probing the Limits of Representation," a participant said that "the Final Solution cannot *historically* be written as romance or as comedy." [13] Yet one survivor is hoping to publish his compilation of love letters written to his wife from the Dutch concentration camp of Westerbork. [14]

Celebrating fictional representations of the Holocaust suggests a tale told about Levi Yitzhak, the rebbe of Berdichev. One of Levi Yitzhak's congregants complained to the rebbe that several Jews were praying in an incoherent babble—not pure Hebrew. Levi Yitzhak responded that God understands a baby and God will understand these pious Jews; it is the passion of the prayer that matters. Most popular recreations of the Holocaust are realized with maximum earnestness, even if their vision lacks the sophistication, innovation, and depth of Lanzmann's *Shoah.*

I respect the authority of those engaged in the debate over the limits of representation of the Holocaust. There is, nonetheless, a need for the art of popular culture: it helps to shape memory, to provide a framework of knowledge, and to assist as a catalyst in the search for a more profound awareness, especially for those youths who will eventually study the Holocaust more intensely in a classroom environment. As historian Christopher Browning has observed, one senses when a representation is right or wrong.[15] It is essential, however, to be flexible with one's vision, to be capable of separating the function of more complex films from those built on conventional narratives, rather than comparing them within the same category. In effect, it is paramount to understand the standards of the nonintellectual, or in the view of historian Carl L. Becker, the needs of Mr. Everyman: "Mr. Everyman is stronger than we are, and . . . we must adapt our knowledge to his necessities. . . . [Our research] will be of little import except insofar as it is transmuted into common knowledge."[16]

Clearly, visual media have supplanted the written word as a means of educating the public. Gore Vidal is right to proclaim film the *lingua franca* of the twentieth century.[17] It is therefore crucial, especially among educators, to understand the language of film—to interpret its signs and symbols—in order to explain, beyond mere intuition, wherein might lie the danger or advantages of a particular cinematic approach to the Holocaust. The film *Europa, Europa* offers an excellent cautionary example. It is a film hailed by the American public and critics alike that, when read beyond the level of pleasure, exposes the subtle, perhaps unconscious, but nonetheless extant continuity of negative Jewish imagery.

Polish director Agnieska Holland's *Europa, Europa,* produced in Germany in 1990, is a dramatic film that begins in a small German town with the circumcision of Solomon Perel. The major moments of the tale are punctuated by episodes tied to political events. For instance, following the circumcision scene we see Solly, as he is called by his family, bathing in preparation for his bar mitzvah, when suddenly stones crash through the bathroom window, signaling the onset of *Kristallnacht.* Solly's sister Berthe is murdered in the ensuing pogrom. Solly's father, the proprietor of a shoe store, determines that his family must return to the safety of his birthplace—Lodz, Poland. They live quietly in Lodz until the Nazis invade Poland, at which time the father instructs Solly and his brother Isaak to escape to the Soviet Union.

The two brothers set out for the East, only to be separated early on. Solly finds himself at a Soviet-run orphanage in Grodno. He adapts swiftly to his new environment, learning to speak Russian while becoming a model Communist. But when the German–Soviet pact is shattered in 1941 and the Germans invade Russian territory, Solly is on the run again. He is arrested by a band of German soldiers, who are charmed by Solly and adopt him as a mascot. Solly becomes their translator and comrade-in-arms. He grows particularly close to one soldier—a homosexual. When the friend discovers Solly bathing—and therefore learns his Jewishness—the gay man swears to guard Solly's secret. But then, Solly's protector, along with the entire German unit, is wiped out. Only Solly survives. Using the phone in the trench, he calls the Russians across the battlefield, telling them that he is a Komsomol youth from Grodno, a Jew, and will be killed if the Germans find out. The Russians guide Solly to their position. As he moves to join them, German soldiers appear from nowhere, and joyously hail Solly for capturing the Russians. To repay his "heroics," the German in command not only wants to send Solly to a special school in Germany for Nazi youth but also wants to adopt him.

So Solly, now called Josef Peters by the Germans—or fondly Jupp—is off to school in the Reich. He excels in sports and soldiering exercises, and he falls in love with Leni, a model of young German womanhood. During his school vacation, when he is supposed to visit his adoptive German family, Solly tells his friends that he must see his *Volksdeutsch* family in Lodz. While there, Solly rides the trolley through the Lodz ghetto, the only instance when we see suffering Jews. From Lodz, Solly returns to school, to his life as a young, elite Hitler youth. Shortly after, the Allies begin their bombing, and the war ends. Once more, Solly is a refugee. Despite pleading that he is a Jew, Solly is taken prisoner by Russian soldiers. He is about to be shot when a distant voice calls out his name. It is his brother, Isaak, from whom he had been separated in 1939. And so the two brothers are united.

On the surface, *Europa, Europa* is a frothy film about the escapades of a young Jewish boy and his attempts to disguise his identity in order to ensure his survival. The narrative deals with the vagaries of life as they affect one's fate. Holland views Solly, that is, the real Solomon Perel (more on this below), as quite courageous in terms of his examining his own motives during this period. In her words: "The experience of that generation was so terrible that even the victims have one moment in their biography when they must have done something terrible. It was impossible to survive being completely innocent."[18] Here, perhaps unwittingly, Holland reveals the camouflaged significance of her portrayal of Solly: no one can judge another, for who among us is innocent? And, I claim, this perspective is immoral.

With regard to videotaped testimonies of real survivors, Geoffrey Hartman has suggested: "If we learn anything here it is about life when the search for meaning has to be suspended: we are made to focus on what it was like to exist under conditions in which heroism or moral choice were nearly impossible."[19] Perhaps, therefore, we should not judge Solly. Holland, however, with her assumption that all survivors must have committed at least one horrible action that allowed them to live, clearly delineates her interpretation of victim behavior. Moreover, the film's insistence on its own veracity, when indeed specific signs tell us something is askew, forces us to question not only the truth of the film but also, within the context of the film, the accuracy of Solomon Perel.

We are clearly meant to view *Europa, Europa* as an authentic tale. In the earliest moments, we see on-screen: "What follows is a true story." And the film closes with the real Solomon Perel, the basis of the film's central figure, speaking to us from Israel, where he currently resides.[20] Throughout the saga, there are voice-over inserts, to remind us that "Perel" is reading from his actual account. The film, unquestionably, is structured on the concept of legitimacy: this is Solomon Perel chronicling his story for us.

Certainly Solly, with his sense of self-enjoyment and his strategies for survival at any cost, seems a flimsy character. His comedic adventures during so tragic an era contrast sharply with those of, for instance, the pained younger character in Jerzy Kosinski's novel *The Painted Bird*. The point of Kosinski's novel is that, in those fatal times, be it in fiction or actuality, the young grew old swiftly, obliged to forfeit play and youthful freedom as their lives and those of their families were being swallowed by the Nazi machine. Solly, however, retains a naïveté that allows him to evade history. In fact, his inno-

cence is really that "something terrible" Holland mentions above—
the tool he uses in order to survive. Simultaneously, the crimes of
the perpetrator are alleviated, for, according to Holland, all who endure are in some manner guilty in the face of history—the times
themselves are the enemy.

At this juncture, we might remind ourselves of the insight of
historian Pierre Sorlin about films that deal with history: "Historical
films are concerned with the problems of the present, even if that
concern is expressed only indirectly." [21] It is with Sorlin's dictum in
mind that we turn to several streams in *Europa, Europa* that beg to
be explored. In particular, we must examine the role of circumcision
and images and stereotypes of Jews, both of which reflect a continuity of the negative imagery that helped to initiate the Holocaust; the
portrayal of "good Germans"; and the film's contemporary context.
As we pursue these issues, it will become increasingly evident why
this film is "wrong."

One of the first scenes, we recall, is the celebration of Solly's circumcision. In voice-over, Solly reveals: "You won't believe it, but I
remember my circumcision." Already, one's credulity is taxed. In
fact, John Kotre has indicated, "Most adults . . . can retrieve no
memories from before the age of three or four." [22] Still, the film com-
mences by inviting us to this "memorable" event, and circumcision
becomes the leitmotif of the film.

In *The Jew's Body,* Sander Gilman informs us of scientific discussions in nineteenth-century Europe in which "circumcision became
the key to marking the Jewish body as different within the perime-
ters of 'healthy' or 'diseased.'" [23] We need not expand on the obvious
presence of such beliefs in Nazi Germany in the 1930s and 1940s.
Solly, then, in a German framework, the one that determines his
fate, begins life "diseased," an element that will haunt him in his
struggle for survival.

In several sequences Solly appears bare, forcing us to be conscious of his "otherness." In the *Kristallnacht* scene, for example, he
jumps naked from the bathtub and hides in a barrel until he can
convince a young female neighbor to bring him his clothes. She gives
him a jacket with the Nazi insignia. This launches the gradual blend-
ing of his personality into the enemy's to the point where circumcision is no longer a Jewish rite but the nemesis of his being. It is in
the outfit of a Nazi that Solly confront his dead sister's body. And

his chronicle is foretold: nothing will stop Solly in his quest for survival—not even having to become a Nazi.

Concealing his "disease" consumes Solly. Circumcision evolves
for him from a condition that must be hidden to one he hates. He
must never be discovered with his pants down. While Solly is with
the German soldiers, he is continually forced to suppress desires to
relieve himself or bathe. When at last he finds a moment of privacy
in a barn and prepares himself a hot bath, the gay soldier enters.
Seeing Solly's naked body, the friend is actually relieved to have uncovered another "diseased" soul. (We know, of course, that homosex-
uals were marked for persecution under the Nazi regime.) Later, at
the Nazi youth school, Solly is terrified to bathe until he sees an
Aryan young man exit the shower in underwear. And Solly maneuvers to avoid a physical examination by feigning a toothache. (About
the scenes at the school, however, historian István Deák does not
believe "that a circumcised Jewish boy could have avoided, year after
year, the rigorous medical inspections and the male-bonding nudity
that were regular features of the Hitler Jugend training camps.")[24]

But it is in the context of his relationship with the lovely Leni
that the frustration of hiding his nakedness finally exhausts Solly.
One afternoon Leni asks Solly to make love to her. Wanting desperately to submit, but frightened of being discovered, Solly tells Leni
he has too much respect for her—they must wait. Exasperated, Leni
taunts Solly, declaring him a sissy because he cannot perform. Dev-
astated that he cannot please Leni—and himself—Solly attempts to
reverse his circumcision—to mend it, with a needle and thread—
but in vain. Solly has an irreversible disorder, not only in Nazi eyes
but also now in his view. Instead of hating the Nazis, he hates his
mark of Jewishness that separates him from what he desires. And in
the inverted logic of the film, Leni will not be "spoiled" by a Jew.

At the war's finale, when Solly is miraculously reunited with his
brother, one of the first things they do is urinate together outdoors
for all the world to see. They are free—but nonetheless still "diseased." Otherwise, why his voice-over pronouncement? "From that
moment on, I decided to be only a Jew. Leaving Europe, I emigrated
to Palestine. And when I had sons, I barely hesitated to circumcise
them." The insinuation behind his emigration and his slight hesita-
tion is that despite the war's end, one never knows when circumcision might be considered a negative sign of difference. Solly need

not hide his circumcision in Israel, where the "disease" that had plagued him is epidemic among the entire male population.

Coexisting with the marked motif of circumcision in *Europa, Europa* is the central idea of the supremacy of idealized *beauty.* By the mid-nineteenth century in Europe, Sander Gilman has shown, "all races, according to the ethnology of the day, were described in terms of aesthetics, as either 'ugly' or 'beautiful.'"[25] Gilman goes on: "It is in being visible in 'the body that betrays' that the Jew is most uncomfortable. For visibility means being seen not as an individual but as an Other, one of the 'ugly' race."[26] At the same time, he points out, "Western Jews had been completely acculturated by the end of the nineteenth century and thus bore no easily identifiable external signs of difference."[27] In fact, one of the primary motives in the Nazi antisemitic film *The Eternal Jew* (1940) was to alert the public to the Jew's ability to infiltrate Aryan society. Therefore, the notion of beauty as seen in *Europa, Europa* is not grounded in a typical stereotype like that of the bearded, caftaned Jew, but rather in the dichotomy between beautiful and ugly. Visually, Solomon Perel is never identified as a Jew because he is beautiful in contrast to those unacculturated Jews who were caught because they bore the mark of the "other," that of ugliness. Solly is only revealed if his pants are down.

The fortune that pursues a clothed Solly is his pretty face. We see this in his appeal to women. On the eve of *Kristallnacht,* Solly is assisted by a young girl who defies her father's demands to have nothing to do with Jews. In Lodz, a disfigured Pole (perhaps another stereotype), Basia, is crazy about Solly. At the Communist orphanage in Grodno, the female superior is captivated by Solly. The gay German soldier is beguiled by Solly even before discovering the Jewishness that unites them as outcasts. On the train, the female attendant assigned to escort Solly to his Nazi youth school ecstatically stimulates Solly manually with his pants on, to Solly's delight, as she calls out "Mein Führer!" And Leni, the blonde, blue-eyed thoroughbred, is charmed by Solly, though she never can be his lover. Beyond the level of erotic allure, Solly's appearance affords him the chance to simply exist. When he and other refugees are first accosted by German soldiers, the sergeant in charge retorts: "Amazing to find such a diamond among such filth." And we recall the German officer who sends Solly to school in the Reich and hopes to adopt him after the war.

In spite of Solly's being shielded by his "beauty," paradoxically, the stereotypical ambiguity of the Jew is subtly revealed by the film. Leni, for example, comments to Solly that he has no imagination, a frequent charge against European Jews. One particular scene, which I suspect was meant to ridicule notions of race, actually contains elements of truth within the film's conditions and so leads us to a different conclusion. The instructor of racial anthropology at the Nazi youth school employs Solly as a specimen for illustrating racial purity. "Although his ancestor's blood, over many generations, mingled with that of other races," the teacher exhorts, "one still recognizes his distinct Aryan traits." He knows; but he does not know. This serves to emphasize the danger, in Nazi rhetoric, posed by the Jew: his ability to penetrate the Aryan world. When Leni's mother finds out that Solly is a Jew, she exclaims that she had always thought so. In other words, Solly can "pass," but the eternal nature of the Jew, that *je ne sais quoi* perceived by the school instructor, is detectable, even when the detector is unaware that he or she has penetrated the Aryan "disguise."

The notion of beauty that informs *Europa, Europa,* that is, the non-Jewish visage that grants Solly his life, persists through the last moments of the film. The war has ended and Solly is a prisoner of the Russians. Despite his protestations that he is a Jew, a soldier turns Solly over to a concentration camp survivor—a political prisoner. The prisoner points a gun to Solly's head. Solly squints his eyes, awaiting the blast. Suddenly a voice cries out: "Solek, Solek!" Solly turns to see his bedraggled brother. Solly, because he is "beautiful," has survived the war in an elite Hitler Youth school. Isaak, not so lovely, wears the uniform of a concentration camp inmate. The insinuation is striking. (Still, one factor confounds us: since concealing his circumcised penis preoccupies Solly throughout his journey for survival, when the political prisoner is about to shoot him and his life is threatened, why doesn't Solly simply pull down his pants?)

The idea of beauty as the key to Solly's survival is unmistakable. Whether a Jew can be truly beautiful, however, is unclear. This is evident in that during the film Solly displays no normal signs of aging, even though the action begins when he is thirteen and ends when he is twenty. We ought to see some manifestations of maturing, especially in light of the internal trauma Solly braves every minute of every day in his quest to live. Instead, he sustains his ingenuous mien from the *Kristallnacht* episode until the culmination of the war, as if his authentic face were concealed by a mask, perhaps a symbol of the real disguise—the absence of truth in the tale. For when we see the genuine Solomon Perel in the film's finale, there is no hint of the beautiful boy that was. Given the six million Jews who were slaughtered, the film's portrayal of beauty as an agent of survival is intolerable; it upholds a stereotype that views "normative" beauty as incompatible with the Jew.

Excluding his attractiveness, Solly does manifest characteristics associated with Jews in European circles in the nineteenth and early twentieth centuries. Chief among these is the image of the uprooted Jew who is at home nowhere and "adapts" everywhere—the perennial foreigner. This is illustrated on several occasions in the film when Solly is willing to conform to his "hosts" of the moment, while other potential victims of the Nazis will not forgo their beliefs.

In one scene at the Soviet orphanage, for example, Solly, born into an observant Jewish family, delivers an oration on religion as "the opium of the masses," thereby adapting himself to the behavior of his captors. Zenek, devoutly Catholic, cries out that God does exist; Solly is a dirty Jew, a Christ killer. Zenek also expresses the wish to return to Poland to battle the Germans who killed his brother.

Later, when Solly and Zenek are captured by the Germans, who are charmed by Solly, Zenek yells in Polish that Solly is a Jew. The Germans ask Solly what Zenek said. Solly shrewdly tells the truth, that the Pole called him a Jew. Who would believe, after all, that such a pretty boy is a Jew? Asked if he knows the Pole, Solly responds in the negative. He knows when to lie and when not to. The German directs Solly to ask Zenek what he wants. Solly approaches him saying, "Why, Zenek? Why?"

"Aren't you a Jew? And I'm a Polish fascist? Correct?" counters Zenek. Solly slaps him. A fight ensues. It ends with the Germans crushing Zenek under the wheels of a truck.

Zenek is a loyal Pole. He speaks Polish. He is a member of the Polish family of citizens. Had he been able to speak German, he might have saved his life. Solly speaks Polish. Solly speaks German. He is a citizen of whichever world he inhabits at the moment. Consequently, in this film the loyal citizen is the victim; the one who adapts—the rootless Jew—survives.

In this same sequence of events, the Germans arrest Stalin's son. Solly, employed by the Germans as a translator, interprets the conversation. Stalin's son asks him how he knows Russian. Solly proudly tells him it is from the orphanage at Grodno where he was a Komsomol youth. Stalin's son spits at him and snarls that now he's obeying the Fascist pigs. The main idea: a faithful citizen does not comply with the enemy. Solly, the translator, however, alters his stand when necessary, and even in extreme situations, when he battles for survival, he still signifies the rootless Jew—a negative image.

It might be suggested that because the Jew had no homeland and was consistently viewed as an outsider in Europe, and because the Jew was most threatened by the Nazis, he had to invent any subterfuge in order to survive. Though Zenek and Stalin's son are clearly at extreme risk, the stakes for the Jew are higher. Since Solly never quite understands the danger, however, as he remains blissfully ignorant of the Final Solution, his behavior reflects the negative and commonly accepted view of the rootless, disloyal Jew.

Indeed, it is Solly's gift of "going with the flow" that allows him to remain unconscious of the critical circumstances threatening the Jews of Europe. The German captain who engages Solly as an interpreter asks if he knows against whom they are fighting. Solly guesses: Russia, France, England? No, the captain informs him. The war is being fought against the Jews. Europe must be freed of its Jews. Solly asks the captain if the Jews will be killed. The captain replies that the Jews will be moved to Madagascar, or Siberia—the Führer will find a solution. (Bear in mind that the 1940 Madagascar plan had collapsed; that Solly was first a victim and then a member of the June 1941 German invasion of the Soviet Union; and that the *Einsatzgruppen,* the German mobile killing units that massacred Jewish civilians en masse, accompanied the German soldiers on their move eastward.) Throughout all of his perils, including a "vacation" trip to the Lodz ghetto (where we are presented with a Holocaust stereotype—that of Jews, old and young, staring passively into nothingness), the film persists in sustaining Solly's ignorance of the Final Solution. It clings to his innocence. When toward the end of *Europa, Europa* Solly is captured by the Russians and insists he is a Jew, a soldier holds up a stack of gruesome photos and says to Solly that if he were a Jew, he would look like this. Not shocked, but rather puzzled and defensive, Solly says he thought the Jews were sent to Madagascar. The inference is that if Solly did not know the fate of the Jews, then the "regular Germans" with whom he spent the war were not likely to know either.

Within the film's set of conditions, we should not neglect the "good Germans." Both times Solly's Jewishness surfaces, he is protected: by the homosexual soldier and by Leni's mother. Besides, the film informs us, not only Jews were victims. Leni's father was a war casualty. German cities are bombed. And for the duration of the war, Solly enjoys a camaraderie and friendship with the German soldiers, with the students at the school, and at home with Leni and her mother. In other words, those that are perceived as different from oneself—in this case, distinct from Solly—are really just like him and his family.

In one sequence, Solly and the German soldiers approach a village where they see the bodies of a dead boy and girl swinging from nooses. Some tell Solly to avert his eyes. Others tell him he must see the enemies who killed his German parents (a deception Solly created to explain his wandering status). In voice-over, Solly relates the confusion he harbors: Who is his friend? Who is his enemy? (The Pole knows; Stalin's son knows.) How could they be so kind to him and at the same time kill others so horribly? What set him and them apart? A simple foreskin? In other words, Solly, the Jew, alludes to Hannah Arendt's frequently cited concept of the "banality of evil."

What is the significance of *Europa, Europa* in the 1990s? In *The Jew's Body*, Gilman raises the question whether the Jews, so long the marker of what the Germans were not, play a central role in contemporary Germany; or have they been replaced by other categories, for instance, the Turks? There are similarities between today's image of the "foreigner" and the image of the Jew. The graffiti in Turkish neighborhoods in Berlin—"Zyklon B" or "Off to Auschwitz"—directly evoke the Holocaust.[28] Is *Europa, Europa,* which seems to view Israel as a haven for the Jews, simply inverting its true intent? In intimating that the Jews can only live authentically in Israel, where all the males are circumcised, the film might also insinuate, in a contemporary context, that "foreigners" can live a legitimate existence only in their own lands—that the Turks ought to return to Turkey, likewise the Gypsies to Romania. They are not and cannot be a part of the *Volk*. Germany is not their motherland, not their *Heimat*.

Europa, Europa achieved uncommon success for a film treating the Holocaust. One might hypothesize that this is due to its "cleanliness"—none of the horrors associated with the Holocaust exist in the film's environment. Solly is engaging and lovable, a young, Jewish Indiana Jones. I recognize that the film does not intend to glorify the ideologies that held sway in Nazi Germany; nonetheless, it is a victim, maybe intentionally, of popular negative images that made it easier to destroy European Jewry, and that, evidently, refuse to die.

The warning to educators implied by our analysis of *Europa, Europa* is that they must be informed not only about the history of the Holocaust, about stereotypes and images, but also about the language of film. The question "why film?" consequently is merely rhetorical. More relevant is to consider the vast array of available visual material with an eye toward its potential use.[29]

To some degree, any film can serve a function. My interest, I might add, is not aesthetics but history. The question is not so much what we use as how we use it. For example, with few exceptions, essentially the only original films we have from the Holocaust are Nazi footage intended for antisemitic purposes, or that shot by the liberating armies as they entered the concentration camps. Much debate has ensued on the use of this material and the possible negative impact on the viewers as well as disrespect to the victims. Claude Lanzmann was praised for the absence of such footage in *Shoah*. Yet Lanzmann could enjoy the luxury of not utilizing these images only because they have been recycled in so many films, in one form or another, that they are now icons of World War II. I would contend, however, that these once ubiquitous images are as significant for future generations as they were for mine, which came of age in the 1960s, in facilitating a visual recognition of the inhumanity of the Holocaust. One must simply be familiar with their derivation and history when using them in the classroom.

Would I show NBC's *Holocaust* to a class today? Probably. This miniseries defines a watershed in the study of the Holocaust on a mass scale. It elicited a debate over representations of the destruction of European Jewry that continues into the present. Would I use *Holocaust* in a classroom to teach the history of the Final Solution? No, though at the time of its appearance, at a diluted level, it did just that.

Obviously, one should screen Lanzmann's *Shoah* as a means of educating students about the Holocaust. But there are many other neglected films—conventional compilations of footage that are vitally informative and beneficial for a visual education on the Final Solution. These include Erwin Leiser's *Mein Kampf* (1960), Paul Rotha's *Life of Adolf Hitler* (1961), and Marcel Ophuls's *The Sorrow and the Pity* (1970). In the realm of the fiction film, early works emanating from Eastern Europe in the late 1940s—such as the Polish *Border Street* (1948) and *The Last Stop* (1948) and the Czech film *The Distant Journey* (1949)—offer the first renditions of the Holocaust and in some ways help to establish models, not always positive, for its future representations. In particular we find the paradigm of the weak, passive, feminized Jewish male being protected by a strong Christian/gentile, the "real" male, signifying a male–female relationship. It is portrayed as generally a benevolent, symbiotic coupling, defined by the stereotype of the weak female in need of protection by the strong male. The Jew cannot act on his own behalf. *Schindler's List* (1993), a powerful but sometimes problematic film in which a non-Jew aids defenseless Jews, continues this trend. One should not neglect Charlie Chaplin's *The Great Dictator* (1940)—on its own an important humanitarian document—for an understanding of the role of film in Hollywood during the war. Leni Riefenstahl's documentary *Triumph of the Will* (1935) and the fictional, antisemitic *Jud Süss* (1940) invite an examination of the role of film in Nazi Germany.

The titles are endless. The emphasis must be on knowledge: use a film not because you like it but rather because you understand it. To screen *The Garden of the Finzi-Continis* (1970) requires at least basic awareness of the Italian-Jewish community and Italian Fascism. When one watches *Lacombe, Lucien* (1974) one ought to be familiar with the French collaboration and French Fascism. Knowledge of recurring images and stereotypes of Jews in Western society is essential to being able to present coherently almost any fiction film. Otherwise, why use film indeed.

In this discussion, I have focused on three issues: the limits of representation versus the demands of popular culture, stereotypes and images of Jews as reflected in *Europa, Europa* (which must be considered in all fiction films of the Holocaust), and the use of film by educators. All of these matter when we ask ourselves what we want from film. The following, from the introduction to *From a Ru-*

ined Garden: The Memorial Books of Polish Jewry, is appropriate here as well: "The dead have a power over the living . . . and it is through the living that they find a measure of eternal life."[30] Let us hope that film can fulfill its potential as an agent of memory to remind future generations of those who perished.

III.   A · P · P · L · I · C · A · T · I · O · N · S

Marshall Lee and Michael Steele

The Affective Approach in the Interdisciplinary Holocaust Classroom

A COURSE IN THE HOLOCAUST IS A PROFOUNDLY PERSONAL JOURNEY. Each time either student or professor encounters the material, it is as if anew, with the full burden of re-entering the "Holocaust kingdom." Our own journey as an instructional team happens in a special environment, for at Pacific University we have chosen to teach the Holocaust during our three-week winter term.[1] During these weeks in January students take only one course, so we have the students to ourselves, their attention focused entirely on our course. Over the years we have come to know our students well; many come from rural Western towns, have never had Jewish classmates or friends, and have never confronted the Holocaust, save perhaps in a gilded encounter with *The Diary of Anne Frank*.[2]

Presenting an interdisciplinary Holocaust course within the framework of a three-week term offers certain advantages. We meet all morning, five days a week. With no other academic responsibilities, students concentrate solely on the Holocaust, thus containing the psychic numbing that often negatively affects students' other courses when the Holocaust is taught during ten-week or fifteen-week terms. We divide the morning roughly in half: seventy-five minutes of lecture and seventy-five minutes of discussion of reading assignments. The lectures cover the historical background and supplement the texts; the discussions allow students to respond to their reading of the literary sources. Even with one hundred students, very stimulating discussions take place, given the nature of the literary material.

The paths to becoming scholars involved in Holocaust studies are seldom direct. We both approached the Holocaust from the relative familiarity of our own disciplines: Marshall Lee from modern German history, Michael Steele from minority literature. Colleagues at Pacific University since 1975, we gradually shared information and visited one another's classrooms. As Professor Lee soon found an interest in enriching the historical record with such literary sources as Elie Wiesel's *Night,* so Professor Steele found that Holocaust literature is vastly augmented when supported by historical facts. In 1982 we therefore embarked on an interdisciplinary course: Holocaust History and Literature.[3]

The result of what we do together is far larger than the sum of the parts; it is compounded many times over. The historical material, even when it is as skillfully and movingly presented as by Martin Gilbert in his magisterial book *The Holocaust,* can leave students relatively unmoved. For young people today, such subjects as Hitler, World War II, and the Holocaust are as deeply embedded in the past as the Middle Ages. To bring students face to face with the Holocaust, to make the events of 1933 to 1945 personal and immediate, literature is an indispensable partner to history. Current postmodern literary theories, in particular the "reader-response" approach, according to which the reader need bring no more than an immediate feeling about what he or she has just read to a discussion of the work, fail when faced with Holocaust literature. The historical background—an understanding of the SS, *Einsatzgruppen,* transports, and even the technical details of death camps—must underlie the reading of the literature. Without the vital historical context, the literature of the Holocaust can aspire to little beyond an emotional response.

By itself, the literature of the Holocaust has unquestioned power. *The Diary of Anne Frank* has evoked in generations of youthful readers empathy and sorrow for the young woman whose attic-bound world and adolescent feelings resonate so powerfully on a purely personal human level. The stories of the heroic Oskar Schindler on the one hand, and the equally heroic Janusz Korczak on the other, have universal appeal, for they exemplify the human capacity for good in the midst of evil.[4] Readers are drawn to Jerzy Kosinski's *The Painted Bird* by its very horrors, not in spite of them.[5] The enduring popularity of Bruno Bettelheim's analysis of concentration camp inmates' behavior, however, illustrates what happens when Holocaust literature operates outside of historical context.[6] Bettelheim's conclusions, accusations virtually, about the behavior of Jewish prisoners in the Holocaust stem from his own experiences in Buchenwald and Dachau in 1938–39: i.e., *before* the Holocaust proper. They are irrelevant to experiences of Jews caught in the maelstrom of the Shoah.

Context is vital. Context illumines and explains. Context opens the entire work to the listener, the viewer, the reader. How much deeper is our appreciation of Beethoven's Ninth Symphony in our awareness of his deafness. Georges Seurat's brilliantly stylized *A Sunday Afternoon on the Grand Jatte* marks him as an impressionist of rare ability, but only as we approach the painting do we see Seurat's pointillist technique, involving literally tens of thousands of dots, and only then do we appreciate the true genius of his work. Similarly, readers are moved by Emmanuel Ringelblum's *Notes from the Warsaw Ghetto,*[7] but to appreciate the full weight of Germany's effort to isolate and kill Poland's Jews, to understand the odds arrayed against Ringelblum and those in the ghetto who resisted, this is to be awed by the strength and the power not only of Ringelblum but of every one of his fellow Jews within the ghetto.

Text and context. Over the years, as our students encounter Holocaust literature in historical context, the literature gains a third dimension: the feelings summoned up in the individual reader have somewhere meaningful to fit; they fit into a real world and into actual events larger than the individual reader. Students describe their emotional response in words similar to these: "Ordinarily I would be frightened and angered by what I am reading. This really happened, though, and that makes me more angry and more afraid, since the victims and the perpetrators were people pretty much like us." Here we see one of the two powerful effects of text and context: there is nowhere to hide—these things actually happened. Unlike a reading experience with a Stephen King suspense novel, the students cannot put the text down, take a relieved sigh, and say, "Okay, I'm glad that was made up."

The second powerful effect of combining the literature and history of the Holocaust is the enrichment that literature brings to the historical account. The works of Raul Hilberg or Leni Yahil, for example, are brilliant in their organization and their mastery of detail,[8] but nevertheless the student is removed, the reader somehow remote. Even Gilbert's *The Holocaust,*[9] which we use in our course for reasons enumerated below, slowly numbs students who are over-

whelmed by the book's enormous detail. So we have defined literature in the broadest sense, to include not merely fiction but eyewitness accounts, autobiographical and reportorial statements, and
often documents themselves. It is in their encounter with these materials that students begin to enter into the Holocaust on a more
immediate and personal level.

How does the student's experience become more immediate and
personal? In many ways, the literature breaks through the distance
between the remote historical account and the reader, between past
events and present-day students. For instance, the Holocaust is at
base about families, both perpetrators' and victims' families. Early
on in Nazi Germany, Nazi racial policies affected all German families, Jew and non-Jew. Non-Jewish families participated in scape-
goating Jews, and Jewish families felt the effects. Few students fail to
see the resemblance between their own families' existence and those
about whom they read. When seen through its literature as well as
its history, the Holocaust has an intimacy that pulls students into
the event on a personal level. And this gravitational attraction does
not stop with the family, for the Holocaust was not, in the traditional sense, a war by men against men; as has become abundantly
clear through recent scholarship, it was a war against women and
children as well.[10]

The unique nature of Germany's war against families, against
women and children, challenges and captures students like no other
historical event. The examples of war against women, and indeed
also the roles of women as bystanders and perpetrators, are such an
affront to civilized norms that students face a special challenge: how
do women's roles as life-givers and nurturers square with genocidal
murder, in particular the murder of mothers and children? Only recently have scholars begun to tackle such questions, questions com-
pellingly raised by Gitta Sereny in her chilling work on the Sobibor
and Treblinka commandant Franz Stangl, in which Mrs. Stangl figures prominently in a role supporting her bestial husband.[11] The
more recent works of Vera Laska and Claudia Koonz paint equally
troubling pictures of women victims and women perpetrators.[12] The
power of women's testimony about the Holocaust—victim, bystander, or perpetrator—and the choices they confronted in their
roles, bring students face to face with questions about themselves:
"How would I act in that situation?" "Would I have had the strength

to resist?" "What would I have done with my baby? My children?" It is the duty of the Holocaust educator to confront students with these questions and compassionately to push for answers.[13]

How easy is this for the average student? Not easy. Students quickly encounter the difficulties of the "interpretation" of a text, be it literary or historical. They are not free to interpret it any way they see (or, more likely, feel) it. Context and historical reality take care of that. The typical adolescent American response to Nazis' round-up of Jewish families—"I'd get my gun and shoot them as they came through the door!"—soon gives way in face of the facts: throughout prewar Europe few city-dwellers owned firearms or kept them at home, and even fewer Jews did. The cult of the independent and pugnacious individual that so fires the American imagination is a useless construct when we are recreating events in Europe in the 1930s and 1940s. As students come up against the reality of the Holocaust, they encounter the staggering implications of German policies and the human response to those events. Wiesel records the anguished cry in *Night:* "Where is God?"[14]

The history reveals intricate levels of complexity and of cause and effect not usually found in the literary accounts. But, as we shall see, we are after more than mere catharsis that leaves the student terrified but unchanged. It is in the dynamic combination of literature and history that we have found the key to cognitive and perhaps even behavioral change. Nevertheless, we make every effort to avoid privileging one kind of text over the other—that is to say, "the truth" is not to be found strictly in one realm as opposed to the other. The effort is always toward complementarity and symbiosis. Indeed, one realm is impoverished without the other.

In actual practice, in our balance between a history lecture and discussion of literary texts, the students must respond to and employ at least two methodological approaches to the material on any given day. They are accordingly asked to "stretch" in their ability to regard the material. In the current course structure, we use Gilbert's *The Holocaust* as the primary historical source; formerly, we used Lucy Dawidowicz's *The War against the Jews.* The "literary" texts typically include Elie Wiesel's *Night,* Tadeusz Borowski's *This Way for the Gas, Ladies and Gentlemen,* and readings in Albert H. Friedlander's *Out of the Whirlwind,* among them pieces by Alexander Donat, Primo Levi, Chaim Kaplan, Ilse Aichinger, Eugene Heimler, Hans Jonas,

and Leon Wells. Recently, we have added selections from Richard
Rubenstein and John Roth's *Approaches to Auschwitz,* because of its
excellent treatment of the history of antisemitism, and added
Thomas Keneally's *Schindler's List* at the end of the course to give
some sense of how a righteous gentile operated sustained rescue
efforts.[15]

In every class we strive to have the students reach a stronger sense
of the moral center of the event. For us, teaching is a moral under-
taking, to the extent that its opposite—willful or unconscious ignorance—can be seen as having moral or ethical consequences. Furthermore, teaching does not take place in an ethical vacuum. Our
respect for the material, for the survivors who speak to our classes,
and for the pain students experience in a Holocaust course, rein-
forces for students the difficult tasks associated with such a course.
For it is a moral decision of sorts to decide to take a course on the
Holocaust (although they might be reluctant to admit that). So,
what is the "moral center of the event"? Each day, in both segments
of the class, we take pains to locate for students those moments when
a perpetrator, bystander, victim, or rescuer had a choice. We examine
that choice, the ethical and moral implications of both or all sides.
Frequently, a choice was made in an instant: "Naturally, come in,
come in," said Magda Trocmé to a refugee at her door.[16] Often, a
choice was made by an external agent, as in the story of the young
mother in Warsaw who left her room without her identity papers to
get milk for her baby: arrested, she was forced to leave her baby behind.[17] Christopher Browning, in his extraordinary book *Ordinary
Men,* explores the choices available to perpetrators, sharing his sadness that of nearly five hundred men in Reserve Police Battalion 101,
"a mere dozen men . . . had responded instinctively" to their com-
manding officer's offer to let them excuse themselves from shooting
Jews.[18]

For Holocaust educators, the agony students (and educators
themselves) feel when confronted by "choiceless choice" is one of the
greatest challenges. It is here, perhaps, more than at any other moment, that our course differs from others, for we have designed one
assignment that places our students squarely in the path of the moral
moment, that moment of choice. As we will explain later, this assignment is a fiction-writing exercise: to create a plausible scene and
plausible characters, and then place the characters in that moment

of choice. Prior to that assignment, which comes two-thirds of the way through the course, the literature and history students encounter will prepare them more fully for the challenge of the written assignment.

With regard to the literary texts, one of our chief interests is for the students to attend keenly to the details of an author's tone and point of view. One of the best contrasts of tone is between Wiesel's *Night* and Borowski's *This Way for the Gas, Ladies and Gentlemen.* Wiesel's book is permeated by his anger at both perpetrators and bystanders, the anguish and guilt in his difficult relationship with his father, and his accusatory stance toward the God of his childhood who appears to permit such atrocity. There is a certain cathartic effect, both within the book and within the lives of those who read it. The anger is justified. It has clearly identifiable targets, and it serves to register the degree of revulsion from the atrocity by its victims as well as those of us who do not have firsthand experience of it. *Night* contains pertinent scenes that our students return to time and again. For instance, male students typically find themselves deeply involved with the scene, the first at Auschwitz, when elders stop the young men who have knives from striking out against their tormentors. Female students are often drawn to the unbaked pie left behind by a family in the ghetto. Our students with strong Christian backgrounds must encounter the complex of incidents and conflicts that result in Eliezer's becoming the "accuser" of his God.[19] In these instances, our students have the opportunity to open up new lines of consciousness—not merely the Aristotelian release of pity and fear, but an enhanced receptivity to the victims' and survivors' experience. There is an implicit contrast to the values and experiences inculcated in our own country. Our students personally come to realize new and different ways of looking at the literature of atrocity, as free as possible of interferences conditioned in them in this culture. In a certain way, Wiesel's book facilitates a conscious awareness of the striking cultural, religious, and social differences between the victims and contemporary American readers.

Borowski's book, on the other hand, while it does contain flashes of anger (often directed at other prisoners or at the narrator's self), generally just reports events. When anger or calls for revenge are directed at the Germans, they often come from sources that are not part of a story's narrative voice and structure, and are thus distanced from the controlling viewpoint. In contrast to Wiesel, Borowski's controlling narrative consciousness is almost toneless, emotionless, yet filled with abundantly horrifying details. Students typically find this approach more disturbing than that in *Night,* where the emotional content provides readers a framework of sorts for dealing with their own emotions. Our students seem to expect, and experience, a degree of anger in *Night;* they are on more familiar ground there than in *This Way for the Gas.*

Frequently, confronting choice at the moral center of an event can be overwhelming. Students look for a way out, a rationalization, the silver lining. This is a delicate moment. Allowing students to find something "good," or some redeeming logic in a tragic event, is to fall into what George Steiner calls the "blackmail of transcendence." [20] Far more often than not, the choice confronting victims lacked moral alternatives. As Lawrence Langer has said, in Auschwitz "choice died," replaced by "choiceless choice": young mothers were chosen for life on the ramp in Birkenau but had to give up their children; women who gave birth were saved by inmate physicians who killed the newborn infant. At the heart of Langer's chapter "Auschwitz: The Death of Choice," he asks: "Does moral choice have any meaning here?" [21]

Anchoring the historical segment of the class, we have, as noted above, chosen Gilbert's tome *The Holocaust.* We have made a conscious choice for a victim-centered account. Gilbert's richly detailed portrayal is a heroic effort to put individual names on every possible victim and Holocaust site. The weight of Gilbert's text, building as it does relentlessly through some 828 pages, naturally begins to bear down on students. "There are so *many* names!" "These names are so, well, so *foreign!*" "How do you expect us to keep all these details straight for the final?" "I feel so overwhelmed!" In the same fashion that the literature draws students in on a personal level, Gilbert's wealth of detail, the fact that victims have names, personalizes the Holocaust for students. That they feel overwhelmed is exactly what we hope; the Holocaust *is* overwhelming. (As for having to remember all those names, our final is open-book.)

In the end, it is the power of Gilbert's book to move students, the impact of victims' experiences, and the force of their testimony on virtually every page that combine to work so well with the literature, enabling students to internalize the Holocaust and to feel that its lessons have meaning for them in their personal lives. We know this works, because of student evaluation comments that validate our approach: "I learned a lot about myself while learning about the Holocaust." "[This course] challenged me to think and seriously question everything that I took for granted as being gospel." "This has been the most difficult course I will ever take while in college. Very depressing material and I have been forced to rethink my relationship with God. I still have trouble answering the questions: Why did it happen? Will it happen again?" "This course opened my eyes. Provided me with my own testimony of the Holocaust. Influenced my attitude towards my fellow man. Taught me to count my blessings. Helped me grow closer to my family." "I have developed many new thoughts and interpretation[s] of our existence because of the discussions." "This is the first course that changed the way I look at things."

If Gilbert's book brings with it all the tragic richness of victims, it also brings a challenge: how do we then cover the perpetrators? This Professor Lee does during the first part of each morning. The history segment is more structured than the literature/discussion part. We begin with history from well before World War I, tracing the duality of Jewish life in Europe on the one hand and the roots of antisemitism on the other. Particularly challenging for many of today's students is the problem of Christian antisemitism. Here selections from Rubenstein and Roth's *Approaches to Auschwitz* are particularly effective in helping youthful students understand, among other things, the origins of antisemitism in the context of the birth of Christianity, the growth of the medieval Church, and the reawakening of antisemitism during the century following the Enlightenment.[22] As our survey moves into the twentieth century, through the First World War and Weimar Germany, it is crucial that students appreciate not only the generic nature of European antisemitism (tsarist pogroms, the Dreyfus affair) but also the function of science and pseudoscience (Darwinism and eugenics) in the creation of a new antisemitism: racial antisemitism. Germany's defeat in World War I, the collapse of the Weimar experiment, and the rise of Hitler set the stage for our entry into National Socialist Germany and the persecution of the Jews prior to World War II.

This brings us once again to the question of perpetrators. Our choice of Gilbert's victim-centered text means that in the lectures

Professor Lee must deal in some depth with the perpetrators. While almost all Holocaust literature is written from the victim's perspective, historians have for the most part concentrated on the perpetrators.[23] Thus, a wealth of historical material presents itself, from Raul Hilberg's classic *Destruction of the European Jews* to the tour de force of Browning's *Ordinary Men* to Daniel Goldhagen's controversial *Hitler's Willing Executioners: Ordinary Germans and the Holocaust.*[24] Perpetrator material works very well in the classroom, because we can explore at some length nuances of language and euphemism, as well as the problems of motivation and concealment. Students are stunned and angered by perpetrator behavior. Whereas early in the course their questions are aimed at the unfamiliar details of the nineteenth and early twentieth centuries and at establishing a clear sense of chronology, at this point they take on a certain gravitas: "How could the Nazis be so blunt, so matter-of-fact about what they were doing?" "Was anybody fooled by the language of concealment?" "Did the Germans distort language to fool others or to fool themselves?" "How could men with wives and children take such pride in killing Jews?" Our recent discussions have benefited from the appearance of several quite different works. On the one hand, perpetrator and bystander behavior is presented in terrifying clarity by Ernst Klee, Willi Dreesen, and Volker Riess in *"The Good Old Days": The Holocaust as Seen by Its Perpetrators and Bystanders.*[25] On the other hand, the contrast between perpetrator and rescuer behavior provokes very good thought and discussion as to motive, character, and human nature.[26] It is wise to allow students periodically to reestablish contact with human goodness, and the juxtaposition of rescuers and perpetrators offers such a chance.

There is a natural tension between perpetrators and rescuers, as there is between most perpetrator-centered historical accounts and victim-centered literature. For Holocaust educators this is creative tension. As they confront perpetrators, victims, and rescuers and struggle to grasp human behavior and human nature, our students inevitably reach the most delicate moment of the course.[27] Examining the behavior of those caught in the events of the Holocaust, students ask questions of themselves. At its best, study of the Holocaust becomes study of self. As the Lord of the Flies says to Simon in William Golding's novel: "Fancy thinking the Beast was something you could hunt and kill! . . . You knew, didn't you? I'm part of you. . . ."[28]

While we neither promote nor discourage creative tension, it is our belief that the greatest chance for both cognitive and affective learning comes from an emphasis on the *victim*. This victim-centered approach leads to a powerful encounter with one's own inner reality, often to a catharsis of sorts. This can be problematic, as Lawrence Langer reveals in his excellent work *Versions of Survival*. There Langer discusses the problems associated with "the collision between memory and truth" and "a dual vision" in which the narrator is "torn between how it really was and how, retrospectively, he would like to believe it had been"[29]—an interpretive act that amounts to wishful thinking.

Our audience is, statistically, almost completely Christian, usually from a rural or suburban background. If they have thought about their set of religious beliefs at all, they often tend toward fundamentalism and have usually never experienced serious challenges to their inherited belief system. This often leads to some wrenching, anguished efforts to, in the words of Owen Barfield, "save the appearances" of their comfortable, secure belief structure.[30] A telling example of this happened when an honors student wrote her term paper on "The Problem of Anne Frank." She evinced a clear understanding of the central issues of Anne's diary and executed her essay very well for the first five pages; but then came the sixth page. Here she unburdened herself by arguing that Anne's *real problem* was that she "had not accepted the Lord Jesus Christ as her Savior." Professor Steele's dismay over this assertion was surpassed only by our inability to understand how this student had arrived at that conclusion after completing the readings for such a course. Obviously, this passage presented a terrible problem for the professor who had to grade the paper. At the time unprepared for this kind of argument, Steele found that he could not at first grade the paper. In a subsequent interview with the student, he tried to explain that this was a form of "blaming the victim." The student could not see this. After further discussion, Steele graded the paper in recognition of what amounted to her "good faith" effort. She was basically ignorant of how her interpretation could be perceived by others who did not share her particular religious orientation and fervor. His anguish over this essay has since been replaced by a more coherent set of reactions and methods by which to handle viewpoints like this, largely sustained by direct classroom encounters with items such as Luther's "The

Jews and their Lies"[31] and analyses of antisemitism and the historical Christian teaching of contempt for Jews and Judaism.[32] The basic effort now is to make clear to students the historical, institutional roots of antisemitism, itself a closed hermeneutical system, that may underlie students' attitudes and interpretive maneuvers.

Such interpretive problems aside, the aforementioned creative effort is the centerpiece of the course. We have designed an assignment, as mentioned, that promotes the student's personal engagement with the moral crisis at the black heart of the Holocaust. By the end of the course, in addition to reading assigned readings and classroom material, students have watched *Night and Fog,* often segments from Claude Lanzmann's *Shoah* and the Simon Wiesenthal Center's documentary *Genocide,* and heard the personal testimonies of a survivor and a liberator. They are now prepared for their papers. Each student must develop a short (seven- to ten-page) fictional account of a *moral crisis* faced by either a victim, a perpetrator, a rescuer, or a bystander: for example, how does a parent choose to leave a child, or to remain with a loved one during a roundup? How does the *Einsatzkommando* rationalize his work, or the railroad worker his? What keeps a bystander from acting?

If, for instance, the paper is about the victim, we are really asking the student to conceive in his or her own words that "choiceless choice" that the Nazis often purposely forced on the victims. What we ask of students is that the papers have historical accuracy, and at the same time that their characters be given depth and a believable predicament. It is a powerful challenge to move students to a deeper understanding of time and place. They often produce very moving fiction, works that have drawn them into the vortex of the Holocaust by their act of creating characters, motivation, actions, and consequences, all centered on a historically believable moral crisis. There will always be a handful of students for whom this is an impossible exercise, but the vast majority surprise themselves with papers of remarkable quality.

Our students' creative efforts include, but are not limited to, the following eight approaches:

1. Efforts involving the protection of parents, the saving of children.

2. Portrayals of rescuers attempting to help strangers (with the underlying implication being a concern with what the author would have done).

3. Scenarios clearly involving a certain degree of escapism, that is, a focus that digresses from the task, leading to accounts that are at best tangential to the Holocaust (thus a direct gaze on the details of the Holocaust appears to have been difficult to maintain).

4. Attempts to work out frustrations with the material through cathartic depictions of both perpetrators and victims, occasionally revealing a certain measure of disgust with the victims or grudging consciousness of the difficulties facing the perpetrators.

5. Scenarios indicating a desire to rehabilitate the perpetrators, to make them seem less barbaric, revealing the traumatic nature of this material for Germanophiles or those with German relatives, experience, or connections.

6. Accounts showing an unrealistic sense of the prevailing conditions in the camps, for example, confusing the easy access to goods and materials today with the facts at the time (students often fail to realize the extreme problems encountered in locating, acquiring, and using the basic materials needed to give a victim a chance at escape or survival, materials such as paper, pens, ink, diaries, disguises, fake documents, and the like, not to mention weapons).

7. Portrayals of attempts to escape or go into hiding.

8. Accounts of decisions leading to suicide, occasionally rendered in baldly escapist terms, although when well done they are very powerful.

In more than a decade of our teaching this course together, we became convinced of the need to expose the dominant interpretive paradigm that most readers bring to the reading act (occasionally appearing as a factor in the creative effort, as outlined above). Concern here led to Steele's receiving a research grant that allowed him to investigate modes of interpreting Holocaust literature. The most crucial aspect of misinterpreting Holocaust literature or misrepresenting historical conditions by imposing a Christian orientation, he found, involved the students' unwitting use of transcendent expectations, inherited from Christian theology, that are almost completely incompatible with the revelations of the literature of atrocity. In particular, Steele's teaching and research has benefited greatly from Frank Kermode's fine book, *The Genesis of Secrecy,* and John Gager's interesting formulations on these paradigms in his *Origins of Anti-semitism.*[33]

Kermode dedicates his book to all "outsiders," those who are, by definition, unable to enter into the secrets of a text (in his work, largely the Bible, but this can be extended to other texts that are understood and interpreted only through a biblical interpretive fil-ter, as in the case of our student writing about Anne Frank). Insiders, by contrast, have "immediate access to the mystery." Furthermore, insiders affirm and must accept "the superiority of latent over mani-fest sense." Since these insiders already know the mysteries, only they "can discover what the story really means." In spite of this privilege, interpreters do not necessarily share the same history as the texts they interpret, nor do they have an "objective understanding" of their own historical stance, although this helps create "the complex of prejudices we bring to the task of discovering a sense" in a text. For Kermode, "individual acts of interpretation are rarely if ever per-formed in full consciousness of these meta-interpretive considera-tions." Insiders prefer "spiritual over carnal readings," using the par-adigm interpretive model formed when early Christians created from the Torah a new book, the so-called Old Testament, by "her-meneutical fiat."[34] Steele's own work in the realm of the relationships among Christianity, tragedy, and Christian-influenced literary de-mands for transcendence is ratified by Kermode's observations that there are "supraliterary forces, cultural pressures, which tend to make us seek narrative coherence," that "we are programmed to prefer ful-fillment to disappointment," that "we are in love with the idea of fulfillment, and our interpretations show it." Based on all this, Ker-mode concludes that "we resemble the writers of the New Testament and their immediate successors" in our interpretive acts of reading.[35]

Often, this complex of the "insider's" interpretive behaviors is brought by student readers to bear on a text. In their most radical use, such interpretive maneuvers can make a Jewish text from the Holocaust virtually disappear, to be replaced by or converted into a Christianized version, pleasing to the reader but having no founda-tion whatsoever in the original. We may quite justifiably ask whether any reading of such a text is adequate, or whether in this realm a hermeneutical categorical imperative operates that is absent where the stakes are not quite so high, where six million deaths do not weigh in the balance.

Princeton's John Gager, a theologian, has remarkably valuable insights into the function of a hermeneutical paradigm. He writes, in his *Origins of Anti-semitism*:

> At the unconscious level, it determines what we see in a text and what we fail to see; what we find meaningful, what we dismiss and what we overlook as peripheral; how we make connections between isolated objects in our intellectual landscape; how it is possible to ignore or devalue the significance of anomalies in the same landscape.
>
> Once we step outside a paradigm, once we question not specific issues or puzzles within the paradigm but the paradigm itself, all is lost. . . . The goal of criticism at this point is to bring the existence of the paradigm into conscious awareness and to demonstrate the extent to which it governs the interpretive process.[36]

With regard to the early Christians, in their relating Christ to Torah, Gager goes on to note, it "is apparent here that the beginning point has determined the final result"[37]—an observation that could be taken as a gloss on Kermode's sense of the "insiders" who operate at the interpretive level forearmed with all the necessary keys to a text's mysterious kingdom.

This is highly problematic, however, both as a general method and especially in the Holocaust kingdom. Readers there best not be too smug, too certain about the substantive worth of their preconceptions. In our classroom, an important goal is that our students understand why Holocaust literature is so difficult to read and fully understand. Part of the difficulty lies not in the text and its message but within the reader, whose set of interpretive tools is often not well designed to decode the messages from the Holocaust experience. We have encountered revealing examples of student interpretations that are grounded in a belief system not very consonant with Holocaust literature. Examples include the statements that the pit full of burning Jewish babies in *Night* is a possible overpopulation control device; that the Christian God does not need to reveal His reasons for the terrible things that happen on earth, as the divine plan will be revealed in all its majesty in due course; and that Jews should have used their time constructively in the death camps to convert to Christianity. Within the context of the Holocaust and its literature, such responses are ahistorical, although clearly rooted deep within Christian history. These students have executed precisely what their belief system stipulates with regard to the disconfirming other, Jews and Judaism. Indeed, perhaps these students are unreachable—a daunting, unnerving thought. (We note that fundamentalist Christian students are somewhat underrepresented in our class, compared to their presence in the general student body—about 15 percent at Pacific. This seems to indicate that fundamentalists prefer not to register for the course.)

Any Holocaust course that seeks to join history and literature must, at some point, enter theological terrain. One matter we try to help our students deal with is their desire for things to "turn out all right." Lawrence Langer has cautioned his readers against the temptation to find a moral or a meaning to the Holocaust, Steiner's "blackmail of transcendence." Indeed, we encourage our students, in light of the Holocaust, to question their own received beliefs of the nature of God. Originally we tried to postpone this question until the end of the course, as a kind of summary of affective learning. We no longer do that, preferring instead to ask students early in the term to consider the nature of a God who would allow such things to take place, and noting that this issue is implicit throughout the course's readings. As a point of focus, we have found the essay by Hans Jonas, "The Concept of God after Auschwitz," in Friedlander's *Out of the Whirlwind,* to be particularly thought-provoking. Wrestling with this proves to be a real journey of self-discovery for students, many of whom have a traditional view of an all-knowing, all-good, all-powerful God.

We have found it possible to reach students through their core values, and to provoke them to ask questions about those core values, during their experience in our course. This is challenging for both them and us. For this reason, if no other, we feel fortunate to approach our course as partners, for in our productive relationship we can support one another on this very personal journey through the history and literature of the Holocaust.

Reuven Hammer

Commemorations and the Holocaust

When the Temple was destroyed for the second time, large numbers in Israel became ascetics, binding themselves neither to eat nor to drink wine. Rabbi Joshua began a discussion with them and said to them, "My sons, why do you not eat meat nor drink wine?" They replied, "Shall we eat flesh which used to be brought as an offering on the altar, now that the altar is no more? Shall we drink wine which used to be poured as a libation on the altar, now that the altar is no more?" He said to them, "If that is so, we should not eat bread either because the meal offerings have ceased." They said, "That is so—we can manage with fruit." He said to them, "We should not eat fruit either because there is no longer an offering of first fruit . . . nor should we drink water because there is no longer the ceremony of the water libation." To this they could find no answer, so he said to them, "My sons, come and listen to me. Not to mourn at all is impossible because the blow has fallen. To mourn overmuch is also impossible. Therefore have the Sages ordained: A man may stucco his house, but he should leave a little unfinished. A man may prepare a full-course banquet, but he should leave off an item or two. A woman can put on her ornaments, but leave off one or two."

—Talmud Baba Batra 60b

MY PURPOSES IN THIS ESSAY ARE TWOFOLD: FIRST, TO DISCUSS THE WAYS in which the Holocaust is being commemorated in order to place this within a larger framework; and second, to suggest a possible role for the scholar and teacher of the Holocaust in this process of commemoration.

My own interest in this subject began in the 1960s when, as a rabbi and community leader, I became aware that the Holocaust was being commemorated, in the United States, basically by Holocaust survivors and their families. On some Sunday in the spring soon after Passover, near the twenty-seventh of Nissan, Holocaust Memorial Day, Yom Hashoah, groups of survivors would gather together for a community event with appropriate prayers, readings, and speeches. Unless that date happened to fall on a Sunday, the commemoration was seldom on Yom Hashoah itself. Few members of the general community attended, and although a purpose was served, it seemed that the real meaning and purpose of a memorial day was being missed and that the entire event might vanish in America when survivors themselves ceased to exist.

My attempt following that was to bring this commemoration into the liturgical calendar, to create congregational and individual forms of ritual commemoration—*mitzvot* (commandments) for Yom Hashoah (see this essay's appendix). I did this through a series of articles in magazines published by the Conservative movement,[1] and through two pamphlets issued by the Rabbinical Assembly of New York, "A Sample Yom HaShoah Service" and "Suggestions and Material for Yom Hashoah Vehagevurah." On a personal level, I carried out these suggestions in the congregation I served, and encouraged others to do the same in theirs.

In Israel, where I have lived since 1973 and where the commemoration of Yom Hashoah is extensive, my work has been somewhat different, although the aim is identical. There the problem is that public commemoration was not personal enough and that, again, a liturgical framework was not provided. The result was the issuing of a *Seder Tefilot L'yom Hashoah Vehagevurah,* a special service to be held in synagogues on Yom Hashoah.[2]

Today, as this approach is echoed by more and more individuals and groups, I am ever more confident that—to borrow words from the Book of Esther concerning the opposite event (Purim, the Holocaust with a happy end)—"these days [will be] recalled and observed in every generation by every family, every province, and every city. And these days . . . shall never cease among the Jews, and the memory of them shall never perish among their descendants" (Esther 9:28).

THE PURPOSES OF COMMEMORATION

Commemoration, including memorialization, is as old as human civilization. There are two types of memorialization: that of individuals and that of events.

It would require a psychological understanding of human nature for us to delve into the reasons for the memorialization of individuals. Undoubtedly they include the desire somehow to preserve the dead person who was important to those left behind. In some sense, one who is remembered has not died. In biblical tradition, children are a continuation of the life of a parent. This explains why the widow of a man who has died childless is to marry his brother, and the child of that union is to be called by the first husband's name: "The first son that she bears shall be accounted to the dead brother, that his name may not be blotted out in Israel" (Deut. 25:6).[3] This practice also explains the verse that contains the phrase chosen as the name of Israel's Holocaust center, Yad Vashem. About eunuchs who have joined the covenant with God, the prophet says: "I will give them, in My House and within My walls, *a monument and a name* (*yad vashem*) better than sons or daughters. I will give them an everlasting name which shall not perish" (Isa. 56:5). The Bible also mentions physical monuments erected in order to strengthen memories of the dead. "Deborah, Rebecca's nurse, died, and was buried under the oak below Bethel; so it was named Allon-bachut [the oak of weeping]"; "[o]ver [Rachel's] grave Jacob set up a pillar; it is the pillar at Rachel's grave to this day" (Gen. 35:8, 19–20). The Cave of Machpelah in Hebron served (and serves) not only as a burial place but as a memorial to the Patriarchs and Matriarchs (Gen. 49:29–32). And these simple memorials pale in comparison to the magnificent monuments erected to the Egyptian pharaohs and in other civilizations as well. Although the aim of the grand tombs was more to ensure eternal life to the dead nobles, surely remembrance played a role as well.

Later Judaism adopted many customs to keep the memory of individuals alive: the recitation of the Kaddish prayer, the erection of a monument, and the annual observance of the date of death as a day of mourning. The practice of reciting the Kaddish prayer has its origins in a story told in a late *midrash* in which Rabbi Akiba encounters a soul in torment in Gehenna who says he can be rescued from this if his son will recite the Kaddish. Although for most people that is hardly their reason for reciting this prayer, this reason does still function. It was somewhat startling to read in the newspaper *Ha'aretz* on July 2, 1992, that a group of ultraorthodox Jews, encouraged by Rabbi Haim Krizoit of Brussels, was planning to erect a yeshiva on the site of Auschwitz in order to study *mishnayot* (rabbinic laws) there since the study of these sections of Judaism's primary legal code is held to be efficacious for the "raising of the soul." As a matter of fact, this venture was announced at the culmination of an ultraorthodox campaign to study six million *mishnayot* in memory of the six million Jews who perished in the Holocaust. As if to emphasize the diversity of ways people find for memorializing, in August 1992 an Israeli rock singer whose parents were survivors announced that he planned to hold a memorial concert in Auschwitz in order to demonstrate that the Nazis had not succeeded in destroying the Jewish people, rather the spirit of Jewish life, joy, and music remained alive.

World literature, too, is replete with admonitions to remember, probably none more eloquent than Shakespeare's words:

HAMLET'S
GHOST: "Remember me . . ."

HAMLET   Remember thee?
(THE SON):   Ay—thou poor ghost, while memory holds a
                     seat
                     In this distracted globe. Remember thee?
                     Yea, from the table of my memory
                     I'll wipe away all trivial fond records . . .
                     And thy commandment all alone shall live
                     Within the book and volumn of my brain,
                     Unmix'd with baser matter: yes, by heaven!

This is then echoed by the dying son Hamlet, in his command to Horatio:

                     Report me and my cause aright
                     To the unsatisfied . . .
                     If thou didst ever hold me in thy heart,
                     Absent thee from felicity awhile,

> And in this harsh world draw thy breath in
> pain,
> To tell my story.

In both passages there is a purpose to the remembering and the telling: not only to keep the memory alive but to move one to action to right a wrong and to see to it that the story be known and told correctly. The reasons for memorializing the Holocaust are not very different.

If the desire to memorialize the *individual* (which is of course also the desire to be memorialized oneself one day) is one root of the impetus to commemorate the Holocaust, the other root, no less powerful, is the need to commemorate *events*. This, too, has ancient expressions both in Judaism and in every ancient civilization. A few examples will suffice.

On the positive side, triumphs are always commemorated. The Bible urges that we remember the Exodus and speak of it constantly. A holiday, Passover, is proclaimed to commemorate it. So, too, for the victory over the Persians remembered on Purim. When the Maccabees triumphed, they followed the normal Hellenistic custom of creating commemorative days for their successful battles, such as the Day of Nicanor, and the most famous, of course, was the Feast of Lights or, as it came to be known, Hanukkah, the Feast of Dedication. The ancient Egyptians erected the Mernephta Stele with a list of their own battle triumphs (ironically including, "Israel is laid waste, his seed is not," which scholars have explained in various ways, some taking it as a reference to the splitting of the sea as seen from the Egyptian point of view).[4] The Bible also commands us to remember the eventual defeat of Amalek who, "undeterred by fear of God, surprised you on the march, when you were famished and weary, and cut down all stragglers in the rear. Therefore . . . you shall blot out the memory of Amalek from under the heaven. Do not forget!" (Deut. 25:18–19). "Inscribe this in a document as a reminder, and read it aloud to Joshua: I will utterly blot out the memory of Amalek from under the heaven! . . . The Lord will be at war with Amalek throughout the generations" (Ex. 17:14–16). In this case "memory" probably means "remnants." Thus Amalek, the symbol of human evil, is never forgotten. It is no wonder that religious literature on the Holocaust often refers to the Nazis as "Amalek."

Commemorating defeats is less common, but in ancient Israel more than one memorial day was instituted when the First Temple was destroyed, in 586 B.C.E. That traumatic event was commemorated by no fewer than four different fast days representing various stages leading up to the destruction, the last one being the fast of Tisha B'Av (the ninth day of the month of Av). The purpose of these fasts was to perpetuate the memory of Jerusalem in the spirit of the verse from the Psalms, "If I forget you, O Jerusalem" (Ps. 137:5) and thus keep alive the hope of return and restoration. They are aimed not only at remembering but at achieving a goal. The postexilic prophet Zechariah envisioned their abolition once the goal had been attained and the people returned to their own land: then "the fast of the fourth month, the fast of the fifth month, the fast of the seventh month, and the fast of the tenth month shall become occasions of joy and gladness, happy festivals for the house of Judah" (Zech. 8:19). The mourning practices undertaken after the destruction of the Second Temple in the year 70 C.E. (referred to in the epigraph with which this essay begins) remains part of general Jewish practice to this day. Days of mourning were proclaimed during the Middle Ages when Jewish communities were destroyed by Crusaders or, later, in pogroms. These did not become general days of mourning for all Jewry, although a special prayer (*Av Harahamim,* Father of Mercy) composed for such a commemoration did become part of the general Sabbath service.

There is a major difference between acts of commemoration and academic studies of them. Scholars, historians, sociologists, and others investigate what happened, ascribing importance, cause and effect, to these events. Some historians also judge events by the criteria of their own values or those of the society in which they live. Actual commemoration, on the other hand, attempts to ascribe to events significance—even ultimate, cosmic significance—and to prod people to action as a result. It lifts events out of the realm of history into the realm of meaning. It makes events part of the consciousness and conscience of the group, part of the heritage of each member, binding the individual to the group's collective consciousness (or subconscious). A statement in the Passover Haggadah sums it up well: each person must view him/herself as if he/she had participated in the Exodus from Egypt. The specific facts of the Exodus are less important than the understanding of the Exodus as the divine work of redemption. Time and again God is identified in the Bible as "the Lord your God who brought you out of the land of Egypt, the house of bondage" (Ex. 20:2), this event being the proof of God's existence, God's power, and God's concern in establishing a particular relationship with Israel. Commemorating the Exodus, then, means reaffirming belief in this relationship. To be effective the commemoration must generate within the individual the feeling of being part of the event and not merely hearing about it. Through commemoration an event moves from the distant past into the continual present, from the realm of facts into the realm of values, from the world of ideas into the world of experience.

METHODS OF COMMEMORATION

There are four primary modes of commemoration, which also appear together in various combinations. The four are physical memorials, written memorials, memorials in time, and the creation of myths.

Physical Memorials

Physical memorials include commemorative markers over graves, pillars (such as the stela mentioned above) that depict events as the ruler wishes them to be remembered, and arches such as those in Rome erected as reminders of triumphs. This method of commemoration remains extremely popular. The Arch of Triumph in Paris, Nelson's Pillar in London, and in the U.S. capital the Washington, Lincoln, and Jefferson memorials and the Vietnam Wall all serve this purpose. Note how all of these go beyond simple markers to create experiential values, whether through the feelings of grandeur and transcendental, semidivine meaning conveyed in the Jefferson and Lincoln buildings, almost pantheons where one worships the spirit of these men, or through the stark simplicity and blackness of the more recent Vietnam memorial, which conveys the dark mood of that war. The Soviet Union was particularly proficient in erecting monuments to the heroism of the "Great Patriotic War" (World War II) and, before that, to the October Revolution, as well as heroic statues of leaders such as Lenin and Stalin, many of which eventually suffered the same fate as the ideology they represented.

Written Memorials

Any telling of events is, in a sense, a commemoration; but a written memorial goes beyond that in having as its intent not the recitation of facts but the commemoration of the event. An ancient example is the Book of Lamentations, a collection of dirges written in the lofty language of poetry, whose reading or chanting is intended to affect the reader or listener emotionally. During the Middle Ages similar chronicles and dirges were written by Jews concerning the massacres of the Crusades. The most cogent example in a positive vein in the Jewish tradition is the Haggadah, a liturgical composition for the beginning of Passover. Unlike most liturgy, however, this is not intended primarily for the ears of God but for the ears of human beings. (The very word *haggadah* means the "telling.") It is a unique creation, combining the written or spoken text with a ritual meal and a series of specific symbols. The effect is to make the individual feel as if he/she were participating in the Exodus and, through judicious interpretation of texts, to assign meaning and values to the event it recounts. In the years since the creation of the State of Israel, various attempts have been made (so far without success) to create a similar "Haggadah of Independence Day" to invest that occasion with greater meaning.

Memorials in Time

Tying specific holidays to a regular moment in the calendar creates memorials in time that can have at least as great an impact as physical memorials in space. The use of such commemorative dates is known to all peoples. The Jewish tradition is particularly rich in them. Some have already been mentioned above: Purim, Hannukah, Tisha B'Av, and of course Passover. In Judaism these are usually combined with written commemorations but go far beyond them in their experiential aspect. Judaism's offshoots, Christianity and Islam, follow this same pattern, each in its own way. So do secular states. May Day and the anniversary of the October Revolution served this purpose for the Soviet Union. Almost every nation has a date to commemorate what is significant to it: Bastille Day, the Fourth of July, Thanksgiving, and so on.

The Creation of Myths

Unlike the three methods discussed above, myths usually are not created by one person or group but develop gradually within the community. (The exception is the creation of official myths within totalitarian regimes by their ministries of propaganda.) I use the term "myth" to mean not a story in the life of the gods (as in Greek myths) but an interpretation of an event that then becomes the way in which that event is popularly perceived. Myths may be close to the true account or far from it, but once accepted they gain a life of their own that is independent of historical truth and become a force within their culture regardless of contradictory historical realities. Historians may "debunk" myths and trace their development, but history continues on one plane and myth on another. To explode a myth that has become part of a people's tradition is a fairly meaningless act unless the entire culture collapses. Historians have proven beyond any doubt that Jesus was not born on December 25, but that has not affected Christianity. Trumpeldor did not say, "It is good to die for our land," but that will never make a dent in Zionist ideology. American independence was proclaimed on July 2, not July 4, but no one intends to change Independence Day. When certain Bible critics began to question the historicity of Moses, the essayist Ahad Ha'am quite rightly contended that it made absolutely no difference if Moses ever existed or not: he would continue to hover over every Passover seder everywhere. Myths perish, if at all, only when the society which they sustained comes to an end. The Soviet myths, many of them deliberately fabricated, have now virtually ceased to exist, but in their time they were extremely powerful and instrumental in guiding the Soviet state toward its goals.

Myths usually simplify events so that they can be grasped easily. In this respect the historian is the very opposite of the myth-maker. The historian's goal is to investigate all the possible details, to strive for factual accuracy and comprehensiveness. Recognizing the impossibility of arriving at a truth that includes everything, the historian strives to achieve an interpretation encompassing the available evidence and marked by logical coherence. The historian recognizes the complexity of truth. Myth tends to ignore this. Such complexity is of little value in perpetuating and commemorating an event. When the Haggadah states that "whoever has not discussed three things has not fulfilled the obligations of the seder, and they are: the Passover lamb, unleavened bread, and bitter herbs," it is obviously teaching that the meaning of Passover can be condensed into these three main symbolic concepts. Rabbinic tradition states that the First Temple was destroyed because of three primary sins—idolatry, bloodshed, and sexual immorality—while the Second Temple was destroyed because of causeless hatred (Talmud Yoma 8a). What a historian would do with this, I can only imagine. Nevertheless, throughout Jewish history this formulation has served Jews as an indication of the lessons and the values attached to the destruction. Thus the myth simplifies and extracts the essence of desired meaning, often at the expense of the facts, and perpetuates the significance of the event as a creative, binding force for the people.

APPLICATION TO THE HOLOCAUST

If any event in Jewish history has ever demanded commemoration, it is surely the Holocaust. There is a need to remember the lives of those who perished and a need to place this tragic event within a meaningful context, if such is possible. The massive numbers, the anonymity of so many, the lack even of graves to visit, make this process even more urgent for the survivors—and who is not in some sense a survivor? This event looms so overwhelmingly, not only for Jews, but for all people, that it cries out for commemoration. The Holocaust calls into question so many basic assumptions of humanity, science, and religion that it is impossible to ignore. As Abraham Joshua Heschel remarked, "After the Holocaust, I can understand how we can still believe in God. But how can we still believe in man?" The urge to memorialize the Holocaust is both natural and spontaneous. It has expressed itself in all four forms of commemoration outlined above: the physical, the written, the calendrical, and the mythologizing.

Physical Memorials

In many cases the story of the erection of monuments is interesting in and of itself.[5] In areas under Soviet hegemony, there were great difficulties in erecting Holocaust memorials that would specifically mention Jews: the preferred term was "victims of fascism." (One exception that I have seen is the monument in Minsk over the mass grave of thousands of Jews slain with deliberate irony on Purim, March 2, 1942. Also unusually, that monument is inscribed in Yiddish.) In Riga the Soviet authorities opposed even the orderly collection of bones in the forest area of Rumbele where a slaughter similar to that of Babi Yar had taken place. Eventually the Jewish community succeeded in gathering the bones and creating mass graves that could be tended and cared for.

The famous Warsaw ghetto memorial is one of the best known and has been recreated at Jerusalem's Yad Vashem. Paris has more than one monument to deported Jews. New York now has a Holocaust museum, although on a smaller scale than that in Washington. Even in Berlin, after much debate and deadlocked efforts, ground should be broken for a Holocaust memorial in January 1999. Since the breakup of the Soviet Union a memorial has been erected in Riga, Latvia, on the site of the destroyed synagogue of the ghetto.

Within the Jewish community, almost every synagogue has some sort of Holocaust memorial. In Israel, Yad Vashem has several monuments in addition to its educational programs, the most prominent being the Valley of Destroyed Communities, which took ten years to complete and memorializes more than five thousand Jewish communities whose names are inscribed on its monumental rock walls. Kibbutz Yad Mordecai has, in addition to a museum, a monumental statue of Mordecai Anielewicz, the heroic martyr of the Warsaw ghetto. And many years before Yad Vashem, there existed a small memorial hall on Mount Zion.[6]

Written Memorials

It is difficult to separate specifically commemorative literature from the general literature that features or is set during the Holocaust, but one can safely say that writings of survivors certainly falls into that genre. Autobiographies, such as *On the Brink of Nowhere* by Meir Levenstein and fictionalized ones such as Elie Wiesel's *Night,* are permeated with an aura of commemoration. Wiesel constantly refers to his task as that of bearing witness. He feels compelled to tell the story over and over so that it shall not be forgotten.

During the Holocaust itself, some Jews wrote their stories and hid them so that a record would remain for posterity. Among the best-known examples are Emmanuel Ringelblum's *Notes from the Warsaw Ghetto* (immortalized by John Hersey's magnificent fictional account, *The Wall*) and Chaim Kaplan's *Scroll of Agony*. Victims also wrote poetry, poetry that expressed their emotions and recorded events, poetry with the feeling of the biblical Lamentations: such books as *I Never Saw Another Butterfly* and the collection of poetry entitled *Min Hametzar Karati* (Out of Despair I Called).[7] It is said that when the famous historian Simon Dubnow was murdered in the Riga ghetto at the age of eighty-one, his last words were: "Brothers, do not forget! Recount what you hear and see! Brothers, make a record of it all!"

There is also a body of liturgical literature that has grown as people have created prayers to recite and readings for Yom Hashoah. And although not "written," the many accounts recorded on audio and video tape and film are similar acts of commemoration: e.g., survivors' stories now being taped by various institutions and documentary movies such as *Night and Fog*. These continue where writing leaves off. If one is to judge by Steven Spielberg's explicit declarations, even his *Schindler's List,* the most widely known film on the Holocaust, was intended not as drama but as memorial.

Commemoration in Time

Three dates have become times of memorial commemoration for the Holocaust: the anniversary of *Kristallnacht,* November 9, to recall the night of smashed windowpanes, burnt shops and synagogues, and beaten Jews in 1938; the Tenth of Tevet, which the rabbinate of Israel declared as the memorial for those who perished and whose date of death is unknown; and the Twenty-seventh of Nissan, declared by the Knesset to be *Yom Hashoah Vehagevurah,* "Memorial Day for Martyrs and Heroes of the Holocaust." The first is more likely to have significance for German and Austrian survivors, for whom the memory of that night is still a living trauma. The Jewish community as a whole, however, finds it difficult to observe so many memorials and prefers to concentrate on the more official Yom Hashoah.

Judith Tydor Baumel's book *Kol-Bekhiyot* provides a full discussion of the Tenth of Tevet and Yom Hashoah; a few words of summary are in order here.[8] The date in the month of Tevet stems from religious authorities. It is observed mainly in synagogues, by survivors, and has little impact on the general community. It gives those who lost relatives in the Holocaust an opportunity to recite Kaddish in their memory. In recent years the ultraorthodox community in Israel, which has many reservations about Yom Hashoah—considering it not only secular but even an imitation of non-Jewish ways of mourning—has taken to observing the Tenth of Tevet in a more public fashion.

Yom Hashoah, when first proposed, evoked many psychological difficulties and was only hesitantly accepted. When finally implemented, however, it became a major day on the calendar of the Jewish state and, subsequently, throughout the world. In Israel it provides an excellent focus for teaching about the Holocaust in schools. Since radio and television devote themselves exclusively to the Holocaust on that date, it is all-pervasive. All public entertainment is prohibited, and sirens are sounded, bringing all activity to a halt. Recently the practice of reading lists of names of Holocaust victims has been added, under the slogan, "Each individual has a name." In the Diaspora, more and more organizations and synagogues are beginning to make Yom Hashoah a regular part of the Jewish year, and non-Jewish organizations have begun to commemorate it as well. Although legislated by a secular body, Yom Hashoah has taken on a religious nature as synagogues adopt it. Nevertheless, it can be observed by people of all orientations: religious and secular, Jewish and non-Jewish.

The basic elements in Yom Hashoah programs are usually special prayers, readings from primary and secondary sources, appropriate films or slides, personal testimony, and the recitation of names, as well as such symbolic actions as lighting memorial candles and a six-branched menorah and wearing remembrance pins or yellow stars.

Yom Hashoah functions as an individual and collective *"yartsayt"* for each of the six million victims. On this day we who remember see ourselves as if we somehow experienced the Holocaust. Yom Hashoah calls on humanity to remember what happened (just as the Bible enjoins us to remember Amalek), to make certain that antisemitism, genocide, and human evil cannot gain ascendancy again. It calls on us to discover how people can be educated to resist evil and not to capitulate to it.

One element of the Passover ritual is also helpful in planning for Yom Hashoah: the exhortation to tell the story according to the listener's capacity to understand. There is one way of telling it to the wise person and a different one for the simple person. Thus myth and ritual are opened to include questioning, discussion, and as much information as possible. This is an aspect in which historians and other Holocaust scholars can be particularly helpful and can provide the needed balance and corrective to myth. Especially now, during the formative period of this commemorative day, it is important that guidance be provided so that the commemoration not be confined to some rigid, narrow focus but explore as many avenues as possible. For some, a limited number of ideas may be sufficient. For others, the material should be widened and deepened.

Myths

Since myth by nature evolves slowly, it is too early to determine which myths will eventually accompany Yom Hashoah as appropriate commemorations. Some early Holocaust myths, such as the accusation that Jews went to their deaths like "sheep to the slaughter," have already been rejected. It is not accidental that the full name of Yom Hashoah is "Yom Hashoah Vehagevurah"—the Day of Holocaust and Heroism. Heroism has become an important part of the myth. Every opportunity is taken to emphasize the times when Jews rebelled, when they fought back, when they sought to escape, when they killed Nazis.

Other elements of myth (remember that the term "myth" here does not imply falsehood) that have emerged so far include civilization's capitulation to evil (the notion that culture does not prevent people from descending to barbarous conduct); the prevalence of antisemitism within the cultural and religious baggage of the Western world and the need to combat it; the silence of the world in the face of evil; and the heroism of the righteous gentiles whose saving of Jews brought light to a dark world.

THE ROLE OF THE HOLOCAUST SCHOLAR

The commemoration of the Holocaust is a legitimate part of Holocaust studies. As many of the books cited above demonstrate, the study of what was and is being done in commemoration yields much of interest. The study of the myths of the Holocaust—their origin and relation to fact, the purpose they serve, and the reasons for their creation—is another important part of Holocaust education.

Experience has demonstrated that although Holocaust courses are, and indeed should be, taught on the highest academic level, with the same measure of rigor and objectivity that any academic course demands,[9] almost invariably the subject becomes a matter of personal involvement for many, even most, of the students. When Yom Hashoah draws near, these students are frequently the instigators of special commemorative events or are drawn into the circle of those who plan and participate in such events. These commemorations need not be sectarian events. As A. Roy Eckardt has written:

> At issue in the Shoah is the moral credibility of a Christian faith that could contribute so powerfully and so culpably to the unparalleled suffering of a specific collectivity of human beings: the Jewish people. . . . The Shoah is a Christian event because of the church's participation in the reality of Israel. What happens to Jews happens to Christians. It is thus fitting that each year Yom Hashoah observances now take place in large numbers of American churches.[10]

Franklin Littell similarly emphasizes the importance of these commemorations for gentiles as well as Jews, since both groups "are just as deaf to the story and the lessons of the Holocaust."[11] The scholar may be called upon to assist or may be directly involved in planning and carrying out such a commemoration. He or she can provide material and knowledge for use in the ceremony, be they facts or access to pictorial or written material, primary or secondary, that can enrich the program.

Far beyond that, however, the scholar is invaluable in being able to assist in understanding the events of the Holocaust and placing them within the context of human history and society. The scholar can also help those who seek to learn from the past so it will not be repeated. This is not to say there are simple answers that can enable humanity to change so as to avoid the re-emergence of evil; but whatever can be done to better understand what has happened will surely have implications for human conduct. Such knowledge and understanding, taught as part of courses, will affect the student and be incorporated into the commemorations. Thus the Holocaust scholar's role, both directly and indirectly, is vital to the process of commemorating the Holocaust.

In recent years there has been criticism of the emphasis placed on the Holocaust in Jewish studies and in the priorities of Jewish life and consciousness. It was reported in 1992, for example, that Israel's then-minister of education and culture, Shulamit Aloni, questioned the sending of Israeli youth on trips to the European concentration camps, contending that it might create excessive feelings of nationalism.[12] The same report mentioned that Yehuda Elkana counseled some years ago that it would be healthier for Israel to forget the Holocaust, since remembering it can only lead to hatred and enmity. Others have felt that overemphasizing the Holocaust in Jewish education gives an incorrect and overly pessimistic picture of Jewish existence. There has also been criticism of those who exploit the emotion attached to the Holocaust for political purposes, for fund-raising, or for personal gain.

While some of this criticism may be justified, I believe that most of it is incorrect and even immoral in ignoring the fact that, when all is said and done, the Shoah indeed represents the greatest tragedy in Jewish history and is an event of staggering evil in the history of humankind. If Amalek must be remembered forever, if God has a perpetual war with Amalek, generation after generation, what must God think of the perpetrators of the Holocaust? Scholars cannot escape their human responsibility to remember and pay honor to the victims of evil and to study the Holocaust and commemorate it appropriately in all its uniqueness. In the words of Emil Fackenheim, Yom Hashoah "cannot be but another day of mourning. For us to lump the Holocaust with all the others would be to act as if nothing new had happened in the history of horror when the attempt was made to 'exterminate' the Jewish people."[13] The appropriate commemoration of the Holocaust is the only way we have of coming to terms with this overwhelming event.

APPENDIX: SUGGESTED RITUALS FOR
COMMEMORATING YOM HASHOAH

1. On the Sabbath before Yom Hashoah Isaiah 42 is read as a special Haftarah (prophetic reading).

2. Organizations and individuals refrain from meetings and joyous parties on Yom Hashoah.

3. Each synagogue holds a special commemoration the evening of Yom Hashoah.

4. Six candles or a special six-branched menorah are lit and remain burning throughout the day.

5. Psalm 94, 43, or 10 is inserted at the conclusion of all services that day, followed by the recitation of an extra Kaddish in memory of the six million.

6. The story is remembered and told through readings concerning the Holocaust and the resistance. This is a *mitzvah* (commandment).

7. A sign of remembrance such as a *zachor* pin is worn by each individual.

8. A candle is lit and a prayer recited mentioning the name of an individual who perished in the Holocaust.

9. *Tzedakah* (charity) is given to an organization devoted to the Holocaust.

Notes

Donald G. Schilling, "Introduction"

1. Percy Knauth, "Buchenwald," *Time,* April 30, 1945, pp. 40, 43, as quoted in Robert Abzug, *Inside the Vicious Heart* (New York: Oxford University Press, 1985), p. 45.

2. Arno Mayer, *Why Did the Heavens Not Darken? The "Final Solution" in History* (New York: Pantheon, 1990), p. xv.

3. As quoted in *Holocaust: Religious and Philosophical Implications,* ed. John K. Roth and Michael Berenbaum (New York: Paragon House, 1989), p. 3.

4. Elie Wiesel, "Twentieth Anniversary Keynote," in *What Have We Learned? Telling the Story and Teaching the Lessons of the Holocaust: Papers of the Twentieth Anniversary Scholars' Conference,* ed. Franklin H. Littell, Alan L. Berger, and Hubert G. Locke (Lewiston, Maine: Edward Mellon Press, 1993), pp. 7–8.

5. Philip Hallie, *Lest Innocent Blood Be Shed* (New York: Harper and Row, 1979), p. 2.

6. As quoted in the *New York Times,* April 12, 1995, p. B10.

7. Elie Wiesel, for example, argues that teaching the Holocaust enmeshes us in a paradox. He says, "I have never believed that this is a subject that can be taught systematically. But because it cannot be taught, you must teach it." See his "Twentieth Anniversary Keynote," pp. 11–12.

8. Peter Hayes, ed., *Lessons and Legacies: The Meaning of the Holocaust in a Changing World* (Evanston, Ill.: Northwestern University Press, 1991), pp. 1–6.

Michael R. Marrus, "Good History and Teaching the Holocaust"

1. Drago Arsenijevic, *Voluntary Hostages of the S.S.* (Geneva: Ferni, 1979).

2. Michael R. Marrus, *The Holocaust in History* (Hanover, N.H.: Brandeis University Press/University Press of New England, 1987). See also Marrus, "Reflections on the Historiography of the Holocaust," *Journal of Modern History* 66 (March 1994): 92–116.

3. Many are unhappy with the use of the term because of its original Greek meaning of "a sacrifice, consumed by fire." See Marrus, *The Holocaust in History*, pp. 3–4.

4. Quoted in Roger Gottlieb, "The Concept of Resistance: Jewish Resistance during the Holocaust," *Social Theory and Practice* 9 (1983): 37.

5. Raul Hilberg, *The Destruction of the European Jews*, 3 vols., rev. ed. (1961; New York: Holmes and Meier, 1985), 3:1030–31. For an extended, critical evaluation of Jewish responses, see David Biale, *Power and Powerlessness in Jewish History* (New York: Schocken, 1986), pp. 141–44 and passim.

6. Raul Hilberg, *Perpetrators, Victims, Bystanders: The Jewish Catastrophe, 1933–1945* (New York: Aaron Asher, 1992), ch. 16.

7. Ibid., p. 177.

8. Yehuda Bauer, *They Chose Life: Jewish Resistance in the Holocaust* (New York: American Jewish Committee, Institute of Human Relations, 1973).

9. In the testimony of the writer Jehoszua Perle, quoted in *Nazism 1919–1945*, vol. 3, ed. Jeremy Noakes and Geoffrey Pridham, *Foreign Policy, War, and Racial Extermination* (Exeter: University of Exeter Press, 1988), p. 1159.

10. Gottlieb, "The Concept of Resistance," p. 34.

11. The terms "intentionalist" and "functionalist" were first used in this connection by Tim Mason, "Intention and Explanation: A Current Controversy about the Interpretation of National Socialism," in *Der Führerstaat: Mythos und Realität*, ed. Gerhard Hirschfeld and Lothar Kettenacker (Stuttgart: Klett-Cotta, 1981), pp. 21–40. Christopher Browning was the first to apply these terms to the study of the Holocaust. For an excellent summary of his views, see *The Path to Genocide: Essays on the Launching of the Final Solution* (New York: Cambridge University Press, 1992), esp. chap. 5, "Beyond 'Intentionalism' and 'Functionalism': The Decision for the Final Solution Reconsidered," which supersedes his analysis in *Fateful Months: Essays on the Emergence of the Final Solution* (New York: Holmes and Meier, 1985), chap. 1.

12. Ian Kershaw, *The Nazi Dictatorship: Problems and Perspectives of Interpretation* (London and Baltimore: E. Arnold, 1985), p. 105.

13. Richard Breitman, *The Architect of Genocide: Himmler and the Final Solution* (New York: Knopf, 1991), p. 153.

14. Robert L. Koehl, *RKFVD: German Resettlement and Population Policy, 1939–1945* (Cambridge, Mass.: Harvard University Press, 1957); Martin Broszat, *Nationalsozialistische Polenpolitik, 1939–1945* (Stuttgart: Deutsche Verlags-Anstalt, 1961); Christopher Browning, "Nazi Resettlement Policy and the Search for the Final Solution to the Jewish Question, 1939–1941," *German Studies Review* 9 (1986): 497–519.

15. Andreas Hillgruber, "Die 'Endlösung' und das deutsche Ostimperium als Kernstück des rassenideologischen Programms des Nationalsozialismus," *Vierteljahrshefte für Zeitgeschichte* 20 (1972): 133–53; Hillgruber, "Die ideologisch-dogmatische Grundlage der Nationalsozialistischen Politik der Ausrottung der Juden in den besetzten Gebieten der Sowjetunion und ihre Durchführung, 1941–1944," *German Studies Review* 2 (1979): 263–96; Jürgen Förster, "The Wehrmacht and the War of Extermination against the Soviet Union," *Yad Vashem Studies* 14 (1981): 413–47; Förster, *Das Deutsche Reich und der Zweite Weltkrieg,* vol. 4, *Der Angriff auf der Sowjetunion* (Stuttgart, 1983), pp. 413–47, 1030–78.

16. Helmut Krausnick and Hans-Heinrich Wilhelm, *Die Truppe des Weltanschauungskrieges: Die Einsatzgruppen der Sicherheitspolizei und des SD 1938–1941* (Stuttgart: Deutsche Verlags-Anstalt, 1981); Yehoshua Büchler, "Komandostab Reichsführer-SS: Himmler's Personal Murder Brigades in 1941," *Holocaust and Genocide Studies* 1 (1986): 11–25; Alfred Streim, *Die Behandlung sowjetischer Kriegsgefangenen im "Fall Barbarossa"* (Heidelberg and Karlsruhe: Muller, Juristischer Verlag, 1981), 74–93; Christian Streit, *Keine Kamaraden: Die Wehrmacht und die sowjetischen Kriegsgefangenen* (Stuttgart: Deutsche Verlags-Anstalt, 1978).

17. Michael Burleigh and Wolfgang Wippermann, *The Racial State: Germany, 1933–1945* (Cambridge and New York: Cambridge University Press, 1991).

18. I have discussed the question of uniqueness in *The Holocaust in History,* pp. 18–25.

19. See Daniel Jonah Goldhagen, "The Evil of Banality," *The New Republic,* July 13 and 20, 1992, p. 52. For another work in the same vein, drawing heavily on intellectual history, see Paul L. Rose, *Revolutionary Antisemitism in Germany, from Kant to Wagner* (Princeton, N.J.: Princeton University Press, 1990).

20. The outstanding background survey for the entire region is Ezra Mendelsohn, *The Jews of East Central Europe between the Wars* (Bloomington: Indiana University Press, 1983). On Poland, see the edited volume

by Yisrael Gutman, Ezra Mendelsohn, Jehuda Reinharz, and Chone Shmeruk, *The Jews of Poland between Two World Wars* (Hanover, N.H.: University Press of New England, 1989).

21. George Mosse, *Toward the Final Solution: A History of European Racism* (New York: Harper and Row, 1978), p. 150.

22. See Antony Kushner, "Ambivalence or Antisemitism: Christian Attitudes and Responses in Britain to the Crisis of European Jewry during the Second World War," *Holocaust and Genocide Studies* 5 (1990): 175–89. U.S. polling data is summarized in David S. Wyman, *The Abandonment of the Jews: America and the Holocaust, 1941–1945* (New York: Pantheon, 1984), pp. 14–15. On Canada, see Irving Abella and Harold Troper, *None Is Too Many: Canada and the Jews of Europe, 1933–1948* (New York: Random House, 1983).

23. I have tried to do this myself in "The Theory and Practice of Anti-Semitism," *Commentary* 74 (August 1982): 38–42.

24. Lucjan Dobroszycki, "Jewish Elites under German Rule," in *The Holocaust: Ideology, Bureaucracy and Genocide: The San José Papers,* ed. Henry Friedlander and Sybil Milton (Millwood, N.Y.: Kraus International, 1980), pp. 221–30.

25. István Deák, "Could the Hungarian Jews Have Been Saved?" *New York Review of Books,* February 4, 1982. See also the exchange between Deák and Helen Fein, Albert Benton, and William McCagg, Jr., "Genocide in Hungary: An Exchange," *New York Review of Books,* May 27, 1982.

26. Helen Fein, *Accounting for Genocide: National Responses and Jewish Victimization during the Holocaust* (New York: Free Press, 1979).

27. Walter Laqueur, *The Terrible Secret: Suppression of the Truth about Hitler's "Final Solution"* (Boston: Little, Brown, 1980); Martin Gilbert, *Auschwitz and the Allies* (New York: Holt, Rinehart, and Winston, 1981); Deborah Lipstadt, *Beyond Belief: The American Press and the Coming of the Holocaust, 1933–1945* (New York: Free Press, 1986); Yehuda Bauer, "When Did They Know?" *Midstream* (April 1968): 51–58; Alex Grobman, "What Did They Know? The American Jewish Press and the Holocaust," *American Jewish History* 68 (1979): 327–52; Hans-Heinrich Wilhelm, "The Holocaust in National Socialist Rhetoric and Writings— Some Evidence against the Thesis that before 1945 Nothing Was Known about the 'Final Solution,'" *Yad Vashem Studies* 16 (1984): 95–127; David Bankier, "The Germans and the Holocaust: What Did They Know?" *Yad Vashem Studies* 20 (1990): 69–98.

28. See Menachem Friedman, "The Haredim and the Holocaust," *Jerusalem Quarterly* 53 (1990): 86–114.

29. The phrase "a vast and murky cult of victimhood" is that of Bart

Testa, "Fiddling with Our Neuroses while Rome Burns," *Globe and Mail,* July 24, 1992.

Gerhard L. Weinberg, "The Holocaust and World War II: A Dilemma in Teaching"

1. H. P. Willmott, *The Great Crusade: A New Complete History of the Second World War* (New York: Free Press, 1990).
2. Sebastian Haffner, *The Meaning of Hitler* (New York: Macmillan, 1979); Arno J. Mayer, *Why Did the Heavens Not Darken? The "Final Solution" in History* (New York: Pantheon, 1988).
3. Compare the speech of January 30, 1941, in *Hitler: Reden und proklamationen, 1932–1945,* ed. Max Domarus, 2 vols. (Neustadt a.d. Aisch: Schmidt, 1962), 2:1663, with *Der Grossdeutsche Freiheitskampf,* ed. Philipp Bouhler, vol. 2 (Munich: Eher, 1941), p. 222; and the speech of January 30, 1942, in Domarus, 2:1829, with Bouhler, vol. 3 (Munich: Eher, 1944), p. 197.
4. The list may be found in *Akten zur deutschen auswärtigen Politik 1918–1945,* ser. E, vol. 1 (Göttingen: Vandenhoeck und Ruprecht, 1969), no. 150.
5. The most recent examination of this question in relation to the *Einsatzgruppen* is in Ronald Headland, *Messages of Murder: A Study of the Reports of the Einsatzgruppen of the Security Police and the Security Service, 1941–1943* (Rutherford, N.J.: Fairleigh Dickinson University Press, 1992).
6. Helmut Krausnick and Hans-Heinrich Wilhelm, *Die Truppe des Weltanschauungskrieger: Die Einsatzgruppen der Sicherheitspolizei und des SD, 1938–1942* (Stuttgart: Deutsche Verlags-Anstalt, 1981); Horst Boog et al., *Der Angriff auf die Sowjetunion,* 2 vols. (Stuttgart: Deutsche Verlags-Anstalt, 1983).
7. *Akten zur deutschen auswärtigen Politik,* ser. D, vol. 13, no. 515.
8. *Akten zur deutschen auswärtigen Politik,* ser. D, vol. 13, no. 516.
9. Ronald W. Zweig, "British Plans for the Evacuation of Palestine in 1941–1942," *Studies in Zionism* 8 (Autumn 1983): 291–303.
10. I. S. O. Playfair, *The Mediterranean and Middle East,* vol. 1, *The Early Successes against Italy* (London: HMSO, 1954), p. 442.
11. Winston S. Churchill, *The Second World War,* vol. 4, *The Hinge of Fate* (Boston: Houghton Mifflin, 1950), pp. 382–83. See also *The Papers of George Catlett Marshall,* ed. Larry I. Bland (Baltimore: Johns Hopkins University Press, 1991), 3:250.
12. Sri Nandan Prased, *Expansion of the Armed Forces and Defence Organisation, 1939–45,* Official History of the Indian Armed Forces in the

Second World War, 1939–1945 (Combined Interservices Historical Section India and Pakistan, 1956), appendices 13 and 16.

13. Byron Farwell, *Armies of the Raj: From the Mutiny to Independence, 1858–1947* (New York: Norton, 1989), 310.

14. Andreas Hillgruber, "Die 'Endlösung' und das deutsche Ostimperium als Kernstück des rassenideologischen Programms des Nationalsozialismus," *Vierteljahrshefte für Zeitgeschichte* 22 (1972): 133–53; reprinted in updated form in his *Deutsche Großmacht-und Weltpolitik im 19. und 20. Jahrhundert* (Düsseldorf: Droste, 1977), pp. 252–75.

15. Eberhard Jäckel, *Hitler's World View: A Blueprint for Power,* 2d ed. (Cambridge, Mass.: Harvard University Press, 1981); and Jäckel, *Hitler's Herrschaft: Vollzug einer Weltanschauung* (Stuttgart: Deutsche Verlags-Anstalt, 1986).

16. Many examples are found in the files of the Reichskommissar für die Festigung deutschen Volkstums. An especially fascinating one is that concerning General Heinz Guderian, RDV 40 in Bundesarchiv Koblenz, R 49.

17. Raul Hilberg, *The Destruction of the European Jews* (New York: Holmes and Meier, 1985), pp. 954, 957.

18. On this topic, see Jonathan Steinberg, *All or Nothing: The Axis and the Holocaust, 1941–1943* (London: Routledge, 1990).

19. *Kriegstagebuch des Oberkommandos der Wehrmacht, 1940–1945* (Frankfurt: Bernard und Graefe, 1961), 4:179 ff.

20. See Gerhard L. Weinberg, "The 'Final Solution' and the War in 1943," in *Fifty Years Ago: Revolt amid the Darkness,* Planning Guide for Commemorative Programs (Washington, D.C.: United States Holocaust Memorial Museum, 1993), p. 13.

Christopher R. Browning, "Ordinary Germans or Ordinary Men? Another Look at the Perpetrators"

1. Daniel Jonah Goldhagen, "The Evil of Banality," *The New Republic,* July 13–20, 1992, pp. 49–52.

2. Lucy S. Dawidowicz, *The War against the Jews, 1933–1945* (New York: Holt, Rinehart, and Winston, 1975), pp. 220–21.

3. Marlis Steinert, *Hitler's War and the Germans: Public Mood and Attitude during the Second World War,* ed. and trans. Thomas E. J. de Witt (Athens: Ohio University Press, 1977); Walter Laqueur, *The Terrible Secret: Suppression of the Truth about Hitler's "Final Solution"* (Boston: Little, Brown, 1981); Lawrence Stokes, "The German People and the Destruction of the European Jews," *Central European History* 6:2 (1973): 167–91; Sarah

Gordon, *Hitler, Germans, and the "Jewish Question"* (Princeton, N.J.: Princeton University Press, 1984); Robert Gellately, *The Gestapo and German Society: Enforcing Racial Policy, 1933–1945* (Oxford: Clarendon Press, 1990). In contrast, however, see Michael Kater, "Everyday Anti-Semitism in Prewar Nazi Germany," *Yad Vashem Studies* 16 (1984): 129–59.

4. Ian Kershaw, "The Persecution of the Jews and German Public Opinion in the Third Reich," *Leo Baeck Yearbook* 26 (1981): 261–89; *Popular Opinion and Political Dissent in the Third Reich: Bavaria 1933–1945* (Oxford: Clarendon Press, 1983); *The "Hitler Myth": Image and Reality in the Third Reich* (Oxford: Clarendon Press, 1987); and "German Popular Opinion and the 'Jewish Question,' 1939–1943: Some Further Reflections," in *Die Juden im Nationalsozialistischen Deutschland: 1933–1943/ The Jews in Nazi Germany 1933–1943,* ed. Arnold Paucker (Tübingen: J. C. B. Mohr, 1986), pp. 365–85. Otto Dov Kulka, "'Public Opinion' in Nazi Germany and the 'Jewish Question,'" *Jerusalem Quarterly* 25 (Fall 1982): 121–44, and 26 (Winter 1983): 34–45; Otto Dov Kulka and Aaron Rodrigue, "The German Population and the Jews in the Third Reich: Recent Publications and Trends in Research on German Society and the 'Jewish Question,'" *Yad Vashem Studies* 16 (1984): 421–35. David Bankier, "The Germans and the Holocaust: What Did They Know?" *Yad Vashem Studies* 20 (1990): 69–98; and *The Germans and the Final Solution: Public Opinion under Nazism* (Oxford and Cambridge, Mass.: Basil Blackwell, 1992).

5. Peter H. Merkl, *Political Violence under the Swastika: 581 Early Nazis* (Princeton, N.J.: Princeton University Press, 1975).

6. Kershaw, *The "Hitler Myth,"* pp. 232–39.

7. Kershaw, "The Persecution of the Jews," p. 264.

8. Ibid., p. 279.

9. Ibid., pp. 280–81; Bankier, *The Germans and the Final Solution,* pp. 72, 84.

10. Kulka, "'Public Opinion' in Nazi Germany," p. 36; Bankier, *The Germans and the Final Solution,* pp. 101–15.

11. Bankier, *The Germans and the Final Solution,* p. 117; Kershaw, "German Popular Opinion," p. 373.

12. Kulka and Rodrigue, "The German Population and the Jews," pp. 430–35.

13. Bankier, *The Germans and the Final Solution,* pp. 114–15, 137, 140, 146, 151–52.

14. Kershaw, "The Persecution of the Jews," pp. 281, 288.

15. Kershaw, *Popular Opinion and Political Dissent,* p. 277.

16. Kulka, "'Public Opinion' in Nazi Germany," pp. 43–44.

17. Kulka and Rodrigue, "The German Population and the Jews," p. 435.

18. Bankier, *The Germans and the Final Solution,* pp. 155–56, 151–52.

19. For a brief overview of the "non-German volunteers," see Raul Hilberg, *Perpetrators, Victims, Bystanders: The Jewish Catastrophe, 1933–1945* (New York: Aaron Asher, 1992), pp. 87–102.

20. International Military Tribunal (hereafter IMT), vol. 38, pp. 86–94 (221-L, conference of July 16, 1941).

21. Bundesarchiv-Militärarchiv Freiburg (hereafter BA-MA), RW 41/4, Daluege to HSSPF, July 31, 1941.

22. Ereignismeldung no. 48, August 10, 1941, in *The Einsatzgruppen Reports,* ed. Yitzhak Arad, Shmuel Krakowski, and Shmuel Spector (New York: Holocaust Library, 1989), p. 82.

23. BA-MA, 16407/4, "Special orders for the treatment of the Ukrainian question," Rückw. H. Geb. 103, July 11, 1941.

24. BA-MA, 16407/8, Rückw. H. Geb. Süd, November 14, 1941.

25. BA-MA, RH 26-45/121, 45th Infantry Division, July 22, 1941; Special Archives Moscow (hereafter SM), 1275-3-662, pp. 6–13, FK 675 to Security Division 444 via FK (*Feldkommandanturen*) 675, August 11, 1941; and pp. 14–16, FK 183 to Security Division 444, August 13, 1941.

26. SM 11 B/1275-3-662, pp. 38–40, Ortskommandantur II/575 to FK 676, September 25, 1941.

27. Bundesarchiv Koblenz (hereafter BA), R 94/6, Security Division 454, special order concerning Ukrainian auxiliary police, August 18, 1941.

28. BA-MA, 16407/4, Rückw. H. Geb. 103, special orders for the treatment of the Ukrainian question, July 11, 1941; 16407/8, Rückw. H. Geb. Süd, November 14, 1941.

29. SM, 125-3-661, FK 676 situation report, Pervomaysk, September 9, 1941.

30. BA, R 94/6, Security Division 454, special order concerning Ukrainian auxiliary police, August 18, 1941.

31. SM, 1275-3-662, pp. 17–19, FK 675 to FK 675, August 14, 1941.

32. SM, 1275-3-662, pp. 30–32, FK 675 to SD 444, August 31, 1941; pp. 38–40, OK II/575 to FK 676, September 25, 1941; 1275-3-665, pp. 12–22, OK I/253 to FK 246, October 15, 1941.

33. BA-MA, 16407/4, Rück. H. Geb. 103, special orders for the treatment of the Ukrainian question, July 11, 1941; SM, 1275-3-662, pp. 5–8, Oberfeldkommandantur Winniza (FK 675) to SD 444, August 1, 1941; BA, R 94/6, SD 454, special order concerning the Ukrainian auxiliary police, August 18, 1941.

34. SM, 1275-3-662, pp. 38–40, OK II/575 to FK 676, September 25, 1941.

35. SM, 1275-3-666, pp. 13–18, FK 240 monthly report, October 19, 1941.

36. SM, 1275-3-661, pp. 39–47, FK 676 to SD 444, October 21, 1941.

37. SM, 1275-3-665, pp. 12–22, FK I/253 to FK 246, October 15, 1941.

38. Dr. Otto Rasch of *Einsatzgruppe* C reported that it was not easy to incite pogroms in the Ukraine. It was "deemed important to have men from the militia (Ukrainian auxiliary police force) participate in the execution of Jews." EM no. 81, September 12, 1941. Six days earlier in Radomshyl *Sonderkommando* 4b shot 1,107 adult Jews, while the Ukrainian militia shot 561 Jewish children. EM no. 88, September 19, 1941. But the *Einsatzgruppen* in the south do not report the kind of regular participation of local auxiliaries reported by Jäger and Lange in the Baltic.

39. SM, 1275-3-662, pp. 5–8, Oberfeldkommandantur Winniza to SD 444, August 1, 1941; pp. 14–16, FK 183 to SD 444, August 13, 1941.

40. BA-MA, 16407/8, Rück. H. Geb. Süd, "Auxiliary manpower from the native population," November 14, 1941.

41. Zhitomir Archive, 1182-1-2, Generalkommissar Zhitomir to Stadts/Gebietskommissare, December 15, 1941; Nikolayev Archive, 1432-1-1, FK 193 order no. 34, January 13, 1942.

42. Nürnberg Document NO-286: Daluege report of January 1943.

43. BA, R 19/122, SSPF (SS and *Polizeiführer*) Ukraine to RFSS (Reichsführer SS), November 25, 1942.

44. BA, R 19/464, RFSS to BdO (*Befehlshaber der Ordnungspolizei*) Prague and others, November 17, 1941; R 19/121, RFSS note, November 8, 1941.

45. BA, R 94/7, Gendarmerie-Gebietsführer Brest-Litovsk, monthly report, December 5, 1942.

46. Zhitomir Archive, 1151-1-21, Generalkommissar Zhitomir, February 24, 1942, to Gebiets- and Stadtskommissare.

47. Zhitomir Archive, 1182-1-35, KdO (*Kommandeur der Ordnungspolizei*) Zhitomir, May 24, 1943.

48. BA, R 94/7, Gendarmerie-Gebietsführer Brest-Litovsk, monthly report, November 8, 1942.

49. Ibid., December 5, 1942.

50. Minsk Archive, 658-1-1, KdG (*Kommandeur der Gendarmerie*) Zhitomir to Gendarmerie-Posten, June 6, 1942.

51. Zhitomir Archive, 1182-1-35, KdG Zhitomir "special order," August 4, 1942.

52. Zhitomir Archive, 1182-1-17, pp. 113–18, BdO Ukraine, June 29, 1943, memo on training the *Schutzmannschaft.*

53. Zhitomir Archive, 1151-1-147a, RFSS guidelines on "politische Betreuung" ("political nurturing"), June 24, 1942.

54. Zhitomir Archive, 1172-1-17, guidelines for six-week training of *Schutzmänner* in BdO Ukraine, n.d. See also Zhitomir Archive, 1151-1-147a, BdO Ukraine Polizeischulungsleiter, August 22, 1942, instructions for "politische Betreuung der Schutzmannschaften."

55. BA, R94/7, Gendarmerie-Gebietsführer Brest-Litovsk, monthly report, October 6, 1942.

56. Ibid., November 8, 1942.

57. Ibid., December 5, 1942.

58. Brest Archive, 995-1-7, Gend. Post Mir to Gend. Gebietsführer Baranoviche, August 20, 1942.

59. Brest Archive, 995-1-7, Gend.-Hauptmannschaft Baranoviche to KdG Belorussia (Minsk), September 29, 1942.

60. Brest Archive, 995-1-4, Gend. Post Mir to Gend. Gebietsführer Baranoviche, October 1, 1942.

61. Ibid., November 15, 1942.

62. Staatsanwaltschaft Hamburg, 141 Js 1957/62, testimony of E., pp. 2167, 2169, 2172, 3351.

63. Christopher R. Browning, *Ordinary Men: Reserve Police Battalion 101 and the Final Solution in Poland* (New York: HarperCollins, 1992), p. 151.

Allan Fenigstein, "Reconceptualizing the Behavior of the Perpetrators"

1. Eric Zilmer, Molly Harrower, Barry Ritzler, and Robert Archer, *The Quest for the Nazi Personality: A Psychological Investigation of Nazi War Criminals* (Hillsdale, N.J.: Erlbaum, 1995).

2. Theodor W. Adorno, Else Frenkel-Brunswik, D. J. Levinson, and R. N. Sanford, *The Authoritarian Personality* (New York: Harper, 1950).

3. Stanley Milgram, "Obedience to Criminal Orders: The Compulsion to Do Evil," *Patterns of Prejudice* 1 (1967): 3–7; and *Obedience to Authority: An Experimental View* (New York: Harper and Row, 1974).

4. Michael Selzer, "Psychohistorical Approaches to the Study of Nazism," *Journal of Psychohistory* 4 (1976): 215–24.

5. See Roger Brown, *Social Psychology* (New York: Macmillan, 1965); *Studies in the Scope and Method of "The Authoritarian Personality,"* ed. Richard Christie and Marie Janoda (Glencoe, Ill.: Free Press, 1954).

6. Work along these lines includes Henry V. Dicks, *Licensed Mass Murder: A Sociopsychological Study of Some SS Killers* (New York: Basic

Books, 1972); Gustave M. Gilbert, "The Mentality of SS Murderous Robots," *Yad Vashem Studies* 5 (1963): 35–41; Molly Harrower, "Rorschach Records of the Nazi War Criminals: An Experimental Study after Thirty Years," *Journal of Personality Assessment* 40 (1976): 341–51; Douglas Kelley, "Preliminary Studies of the Rorschach Records of the Nazi War Criminals," *Rorschach Exchange* 10 (1946): 45–48; Barry Ritzler, "The Nuremberg Mind Revisited: A Quantitative Approach to Nazi Rorschachs," *Journal of Personality Assessment* 42 (1978): 344–53.

7. Robert Jay Lifton, *The Nazi Doctors: Medical Killing and the Psychology of Genocide* (New York: Basic Books, 1986).

8. Raul Hilberg, "The Nature of the Process," in *Survivors, Victims, and Perpetrators: Essays on the Nazi Holocaust,* ed. Joel E. Dimsdale (Washington, D.C.: Hemisphere, 1980); John Sabini and Maury Silver, "Destroying the Innocent with a Clear Conscience: A Sociopsychology of the Holocaust," in *Survivors, Victims, and Perpetrators.*

9. Otto Dov Kulka, "'Public opinion' in Nazi Germany and the Jewish Question," *Jerusalem Quarterly* 26 (Winter 1983): 38.

10. Mark Resnick and Vincent Nunno, "The Nuremberg Mind Redeemed: A Comprehensive Analysis of the Rorschachs of Nazi War Criminals," *Journal of Personality Assessment* 57 (1991): 19–29.

11. Sarah Gordon, *Hitler, Germans, and the "Jewish Question"* (Princeton, N.J.: Princeton University Press, 1984).

12. See Thomas F. Pettigrew, "Personality and Sociocultural Factors in Intergroup Attitudes: A Cross-national Comparison," *Journal of Conflict Resolution* 2 (1958): 29–42; and "Prejudice," in *Harvard Encyclopedia of American Ethnic Groups,* ed. Stephen Thernstrom (Cambridge, Mass.: Harvard University Press, 1980).

13. Milgram, "Obedience to Criminal Orders," pp. 5–6. For publication details of Arendt's seminal book, see n. 15 below.

14. See Ervin Staub, *The Roots of Evil: The Origins of Genocide and Other Group Violence* (New York: Cambridge University Press, 1989).

15. Hannah Arendt, *Eichmann in Jerusalem: A Report on the Banality of Evil* (New York: Viking, 1963).

16. Hilberg, "The Nature of the Process."

17. Christopher R. Browning, *Ordinary Men: Reserve Police Battalion 101 and the Final Solution in Poland* (New York: HarperCollins, 1992), p. 174.

18. Arendt, *Eichmann in Jerusalem.*

19. Browning, *Ordinary Men,* p. 162.

20. Ibid., pp. 171, 173–74.

21. Milgram, *Obedience to Authority,* p. 13.

22. Ibid., p. 41.

23. Browning, *Ordinary Men,* p. 74.

24. Daniel J. Goldhagen, "The Evil of Banality," *The New Republic,* July 13–20, 1992, pp. 49–52.

25. Browning, *Ordinary Men,* p. 74.

26. Ibid., p. 65.

27. Ibid., p. 69.

28. Ibid., p. 74.

29. Yehuda Bauer, *A History of the Holocaust* (New York: Franklin Watts, 1982); Jacob Robinson, *And the Crooked Shall Be Made Straight: The Eichmann Trial, the Jewish Catastrophe, and Hannah Arendt's Narrative* (New York: Macmillan, 1965).

30. Hannah Arendt, introduction to Berndt Naumann, *Auschwitz* (New York: Praeger, 1966).

31. Raul Hilberg, "The Significance of the Holocaust," in *The Holocaust: Ideology, Bureaucracy, and Genocide,* ed. Henry Friedlander and Sybil Milton (Millwood, N.Y.: Kraus, 1980).

32. Browning, *Ordinary Men;* and Daniel Goldhagen, "The Cowardly Executioner: On Disobedience in the SS," *Patterns of Prejudice* 19 (1985): 19–32.

33. Browning, *Ordinary Men;* Daniel J. Goldhagen, *Hitler's Willing Executioners: Ordinary Germans and the Holocaust* (New York: Knopf, 1996).

34. Browning, *Ordinary Men,* p. 65.

35. Goldhagen, "The Cowardly Executioner."

36. Ibid.

37. Milgram, *Obedience to Authority,* p. 188.

38. David Mark Mantell, and R. Panzarella, "Obedience and Responsibility," *British Journal of Social and Clinical Psychology* 15 (1976): 239–45; Harvey A. Tilker, "Socially Responsible Behavior as a Function of Observer Responsibility and Victim Feedback," *Journal of Personality and Social Psychology* 14 (1970): 95–100.

39. Henri Tajfel, *Human Groups and Social Categories: Studies in Social Psychology* (Cambridge: Cambridge University Press, 1981).

40. H. Tajfel et al., "Social Categorization and Intergroup Behavior," *European Journal of Social Psychology* 1 (1971): 149–78; H. Tajfel and John C. Turner, "An Integrative Theory of Intergroup Conflict," in *The Social Psychology of Intergroup Relations,* ed. William G. Austin and Stephen Worchel (Monterey, Calif.: Brooks/Cole, 1979).

41. See, for example, Willem Doise et al., "An Experimental Investigation into the Formation of Intergroup Representations," *European Journal of Social Psychology* 2 (1972): 202–4; Charles Ferguson, and Harold Kelley, "Significant Factors in Overevaluation of Own Group's Product,"

Journal of Abnormal and Social Psychology 69 (1964): 223–28; James Howard and Myron Rothbart, "Social Categorization and Memory for Ingroup and Outgroup Behavior," *Journal of Personality and Social Psychology* 38 (1980): 301–10; H. Tajfel et al., "Social Categorization and Intergroup Behavior."

42. See Lucy S. Dawidowicz, *The War against the Jews* (New York: Holt, Rinehart, and Winston, 1975).

43. Tajfel and Turner, "An Integrative Theory of Intergroup Conflict."

44. John Turner, "Towards a Cognitive Redefinition of the Social Group," in *Social Identity and Intergroup Relations,* ed. Henri Tajfel (Cambridge: Cambridge University Press, 1982).

45. Dawidowicz, *The War against the Jews;* Gordon, *Hitler, Germans, and the "Jewish Question."*

46. Claudia Koonz, "Genocide and Eugenics: The Language of Power," in *Lessons and Legacies: The Meaning of the Holocaust in a Changing World,* ed. Peter Hayes (Evanston, Ill.: Northwestern University Press, 1991).

47. Norman Cohn, *Warrant for Genocide: The Myth of the Jewish World Conspiracy and the "Protocols of the Elders of Zion"* (London: Eyre and Spottiswood, 1967).

48. Jürgen Hagemann, *Die Presselenkung im Dritten Reich* (Bonn: Bouvier, 1970).

49. Thomas Keneally, *Schindler's List* (New York: Simon and Schuster, 1982), p. 350.

50. For example, Dawidowicz, *The War against the Jews;* Goldhagen, *Hitler's Willing Executioners;* Hans Mommsen, "The Reaction of the German Population to the Anti-Jewish Persecution and the Holocaust," in Hayes, *Lessons and Legacies,* pp. 141–54.

51. Browning, *Ordinary Men,* pp. 183, 178.

52. Ibid., p. 178.

53. Ibid., p. 181.

54. Ibid., p. 183.

55. Cohn, *Warrant for Genocide;* Gordon, *Hitler, Germans, and the "Jewish Question."*

56. Browning, *Ordinary Men,* p. 182.

57. Ibid., p. 184.

58. Ibid., p. 186.

59. Ibid., p. 184.

60. Goldhagen, "The Evil of Banality," p. 52.

61. Staub, *The Roots of Evil.*

62. Dawidowicz, *The War against the Jews,* p. 19.

63. Gordon, *Hitler, Germans, and the "Jewish Question."*

64. Bauer, *A History of the Holocaust;* Gordon, *Hitler, Germans, and the "Jewish Question."*

65. John C. Turner, *Rediscovering the Social Group: A Self-Categorization Theory* (Oxford: Basil Blackwell, 1987).

66. For example, Gustav LeBon, *The Crowd: A Study of the Popular Mind* (London: Unwin, 1896).

67. See, for example, Alfons Heck, *A Child of Hitler* (Frederick, Colo.: Renaissance House, 1985).

68. Philip Zimbardo, "The Human Choice: Individuation, Reason, and Order versus Deindividuation, Impulse, and Chaos," in *Nebraska Symposium on Motivation,* vol. 17, ed. William J. Arnold and David Levine (Lincoln: University of Nebraska Press, 1969).

69. Robert D. Johnson and Leslie I. Downing, "Deindividuation and Valence of Cues: Effects on Prosocial and Antisocial Behavior," *Journal of Personality and Social Psychology* 37 (1979): 1532–38.

70. Stephen D. Reicher, "The St. Paul's Riot: An Explanation of the Limits of Crowd Action in Terms of a Social Identity Model," *European Journal of Social Psychology* 14 (1984): 1–21.

71. George Kren and Leon Rappaport, *The Holocaust and the Crisis of Human Behavior* (New York: Holmes and Meier, 1980).

72. Mika Haritos-Fatouros, "The Official Torturer: A Learning Model for Obedience to the Authority of Violence," *Journal of Applied Social Psychology* 18 (1988): 1107–20.

73. Staub, *The Roots of Evil.*

Dina Porat, "Jewish Decision-Making during the Holocaust"

1. For the main arguments of the two historiographical schools, see *Yad Vashem Studies* 19 (1988); for the historians' dispute, see *Ist der Nationalsozialismus Geschichte? Zu Historisierung und Historikerstreit,* ed. Dan Diner (Frankfurt: Fischer Taschenbuch Verlag, 1987); Richard J. Evans, *In Hitler's Shadow: West German Historians and the Attempt to Escape from the Nazi Past* (New York: Pantheon, 1989).

2. On these concepts and the controversy they caused, see Richard Z. Cohen, "On the Responsibility of the Jews in the Process of Their Destruction in the Writings of and the Polemics on Bruno Bettelheim, Raul Hilberg, and Hannah Arendt" [Hebrew] (M.A. thesis, Hebrew University, 1972).

3. See the works of historians Jacob Robinson, Israel Gutman, Yehuda Bauer, Aharon Weiss, Yitzhak Arad, Shmuel Krakowski, Shmuel Spector, Shalom Cholawski, Dov Levin, and others.

4. Avraham Tory, *Surviving the Holocaust: The Kovno Ghetto Diary*, ed. and with an introduction by Martin Gilbert, textual and historical notes by Dina Porat (Cambridge, Mass.: Harvard University Press, 1990), pp. 43–45.

5. See Leon (Leib) Garfunkel, *Jewish Kovno at the Time of the Destruction* [Hebrew] (Jerusalem: Yad Vashem, 1959).

6. Tory, *Surviving the Holocaust*, p. 44.

7. Ibid., pp. 37–39 (October 4, 1941); Garfunkel, *Jewish Kovno*, pp. 64–67.

8. Tory, *Surviving the Holocaust*, p. 45.

9. Regarding the fortress, see Dina Porat, "Jews from the Third Reich in the Ninth Fort near Kovno, 1941–1942, *Tel Aviver Jahrbuch für Deutsche Geschichte* (1991): 339–62; and Alter Feitelson, "The Ninth Fort" [Hebrew], in *Lithuanian Jewry* (Tel Aviv: The Association of the Lithuanian Jews in Israel, 1981), 4:151–58.

10. Tory, *Surviving the Holocaust*, pp. 46–47.

11. For the number of victims, see Leon Garfunkel, "The Most Important Events in the Ghetto's Life," *Lithuanian Jewry*, 4:63–72. All sources give a more or less identical description of the rabbi's ruling and the October 28 *Aktion*.

12. On "dying rather than crossing," see Maimonides' ruling in Hilchot Yesodei Hatora, chap. 5, Halacha 5; and the Mishnah: Trumot, chap. 8, Mishnah 12.

13. For opposing opinions on traditional Jewish patterns of leadership and their effect during the Holocaust, compare Raul Hilberg, *The Destruction of the European Jews* (New York: Holmes and Meier, 1985), pp. 1–17, and Isaiah Trunk, *Judenrat: The Jewish Councils in Eastern Europe under Nazi Occupation* (New York: Macmillan, 1972), chaps. 2, 11, and 16.

14. The first Jewish underground in a ghetto actually started operating in the ghetto of Minsk in July 1941. Yet the decision made there was to fight *outside* the ghetto, in the nearby forests.

15. Abba Kovner's *Proclamation by Jewish Pioneer Youth Group in Vilna, Calling for Resistance*, "Let us not go like sheep to the slaughter!" read on January 1, 1942, in Vilna. The full text is published in *Documents on the Holocaust* (Jerusalem: Yad Vashem, 1981), pp. 433–34.

16. For a description of Vilna on the eve of the war, see Israel Kausner, *Vilna, "Jerusalem of Lithuania"* [Hebrew] (Haifa: Ghetto Fighters' House, 1983).

17. See Chaika Grossman, "The Rebellion Was Born Out of the Certainty of Extermination" [Hebrew], *Yalkut Moreshet* 47 (November 1989).

18. Abba Kovner, "Flames in Ashes," in *The Ghettos Wars Book* [He-

brew], ed. Yitzhak Zukerman and Moshe Basok (Ein Harod: Kibbutz Hameuchad, 1956), pp. 411–13.

19. For the number of victims, see Yitzhak Arad, *Ghetto in Flames: The Struggle and Destruction of the Jews of Vilna in the Holocaust* (Jerusalem: Yad Vashem; New York: Anti-Defamation League/B'nai Brith, 1980), p. 186; and Ruza Korczak, *Flames in Ash* (Merhavia: Sifriyat Poalim, 1964), pp. 65–66.

20. For the history of the rescue committee, see Dina Porat, "The Rescue Committee," in *The Blue and Yellow Stars of David: The Zionist Leadership in Palestine and the Holocaust, 1939–1945* (Cambridge, Mass.: Harvard University Press, 1990).

21. Ibid.

22. Ibid.

23. Ibid.

24. Stephen S. Wise, *Challenging Years: The Autobiography of Stephen S. Wise* (New York: Putnam's Sons, 1949), p. 274.

25. Ibid., p. 275.

26. Ibid., p. 276.

27. Stephen S. Wise, *Servant of the People: Selected Letters,* ed. C. H. Voss (Philadelphia: Jewish Publication Society, 1969), p. 251; and David S. Wyman, *The Abandonment of the Jews: America and the Holocaust, 1941–1945* (New York: Pantheon, 1984), pp. 45–47.

28. Wise, *Servant of the People,* p. 248.

29. Wyman, *The Abandonment of the Jews,* pp. 45–48.

30. Ibid., p. 46.

31. Wise, *Servant of the People,* 251.

32. Wyman, *The Abandonment of the Jews,* p. 45.

33. Wise, *Challenging Years,* pp. 219, 224, 228, 229, 232.

34. Wise, *Servant of the People,* p. 249.

Judith Tydor Baumel, "Gender and Family Studies of the Holocaust: A Historiographical Overview"

I wish to thank Menachem Kaufmann, Eli Tzur, and Dan Michman for their valuable comments and assistance regarding this essay, which was written as part of a project on women during the Holocaust sponsored by the Institute of Holocaust Research at Bar-Ilan University.

1. Millions of copies of Anne Frank's diary were eventually published, in a total of thirty-six countries as of this writing (Netherlands, West Germany, France, Britain, the United States, East Germany, Switzerland, Italy, Denmark, Sweden, Norway, Finland, Iceland, Spain, Argentina, Mexico, Uruguay, Portugal, Brazil, Greece, Turkey, Hungary, Poland, Romania, the

Soviet Union, Czechoslovakia, Yugoslavia, Japan, Israel, India, South Korea, Thailand, Republic of China, South Africa, Indonesia, and Bulgaria). For the history of her diary and its various editions, see the complete annotated edition, first published in 1986: *De Dagboeken van Anne Frank*, with introduction by Harry Paape, Gerhard van der Stroom, and David Barnouw (Staatsuitgeverij, 's Gravenhage 1986/Uitgeverij Bert Bakker 1986); now available in English as *The Diary of a Young Girl: The Definitive Edition*, ed. Otto Frank and Mirjam Pressler, trans. Susan Massotty (New York: Doubleday, 1995).

2. On similar integration of these and related topics, see Kathryn Kish Sklar, "A Call for Comparisons," *American Historical Review* 95:4 (October 1990): 1114.

3. For the history of the term "Holocaust," see Gerd Korman, "The Holocaust in American Historical Writing," *Societas* 2 (Summer 1972): 251–70. For a development of this theory, see Yehuda Bauer, "Against Mystification: The Holocaust as a Historical Phenomenon," *The Holocaust in Historical Perspective* (Seattle: University of Washington Press, 1978), pp. 30–31.

4. Long before women's history took root as a field in the mid- to late 1970s, German scholars were exploring gender- and family-related issues within the political, social, economic, and military contexts of the Third Reich. See, for example, Gabriele Bremme, *Die politische Rolle der Frau in Deutschland* (Göttingen: Van den Hoeck and Rüprecht, 1956); Maria Kubasec, *Sterne über dem Abgrund: Aus dem Leben der Antifascisten Dr. Maria Grollmuss* (Bautzen: VEB, Domowina, 1961); Ursula von Gersdorff, *Frauen im Kriegsdienst, 1914–1945* (Stuttgart: Deutsche Verlags-Anstalt, 1969). Later studies included Gerda Zorn and Gertrud Meyer, *Frauen gegen Hitler: Berichte aus dem Widerstand, 1933–1945* (Frankfurt: Roderberg-Verlag, 1974); Angelika Reuter and Barbara Poneleit, *Seit 1848: Frauen im Widerstand und im Faschismus* (Münster: Verlag Frauenpolitik, 1977); and Dörte Winkler, *Frauenarbeit im "Dritten Reich"* (Hamburg: Hoffmann und Campe, 1977).

Such volumes were later augmented by studies such as those of Barbara Beuys, *Familienleben in Deutschland: Neue Bilder aus der deutschen Vergangenheit* (Reinbeck bei Hamburg: Rowohlt, 1980); Hanna Elling, *Frauen in deutschen Widerstand: 1933–1945* (Frankfurt: Röderberg-Verlag, 1981); Frauengruppe Faschismus Forschung, ed., *Mutterkreuz und Arbeitsbuch* (Frankfurt: Fischer, 1981); Dorothee Klinksiek, *Die Frau im NS-Staat* (Stuttgart: Deutsche Verlag-Anstalt, 1982); Annette Kuhn and Valentine Rothe, *Frauen im deutschen Faschismus* (Düsseldorf: Schwann, 1982); Maruta Schmidt and Gabi Dietz, eds., *Frauen unterm Hakenkreuz: Eine Dokumentation* (Berlin: DTV, 1983); Georg Tidl, *Die Frau im Nationalsozialis-*

mus (Vienna: Europa Verlag, 1984); Renate Wiggershaus, *Frauen unterm Nationalsozialismus* (Wuppertal: P. Hammer, 1984); and Marianne Lehker, *Frauen im Nationalsozialismus* (Frankfurt: Materialis Verlag, 1984). Similar research projects have been conducted outside of Germany, some of which have their roots in wartime and even prewar studies; for example, Clifford Kirkpatrick, *Nazi Germany: Its Women and Its Family Life* (New York and Indianapolis: Bobbs-Merrill, 1938); Katherine Thomas, *Women in Nazi Germany* (London: V. Gollancz, 1943); Jill Stephenson, *Women in Nazi Society* (London: Croom Helm, 1967); Richard Evans, "German Women and the Triumph of Hitler," *Journal of Modern History* 48, supp. (March 1976): 123–64; Jacques R. Pauwkes, *Women, Nazis, and Universities: Female University Students in the Third Reich* (Westport, Conn.: Greenwood Press, 1984); Rita Thalmann, ed., *Femmes et Fascismes* (Paris: Tierce, 1986).

5. If an essay did refer to Jewish women and children, it usually mentioned them in passing and confined itself to those living in Germany. Later research projects on German family and feminism during the Weimar and Nazi periods—particularly those projects conducted during the 1980s—began to include more serious references to the lives and fate of Jewish women and children. Again, however, they were confined geographically to Germany, thus excluding close to 95 percent of European Jewry from their scope. See, for example, Renate Bridenthal, Atina Grossmann, and Marion Kaplan, eds., *When Biology Became Destiny: Women in Weimar and Nazi Germany* (New York: Monthly Review Press, 1984); and Claudia Koonz, *Mothers in the Fatherland: Women, the Family, and Nazi Politics* (New York: St. Martin's Press, 1987).

6. Kiryl Sosnowski, *The Tragedy of Children under Nazi Rule* (New York: Howard Fertig, 1983).

7. Many of these studies originated in a desire to refute accusations of wartime collaboration. See, for example, Helen Astrup and B. L. Jacot, *Oslo Intrigue: A Woman's Memoirs of the Norwegian Resistance* (New York: McGraw-Hill, 1954); Nicole Chatel, ed., *Des Femmes dans la Résistance* (Paris: Julliard, 1972); Ania Francos, *Il Était des Femmes dans la Résistance* (Paris: Stock, 1978); Benedicta Maria Kempner, *Nonnen unter dem Hakenkreuz* (Würzburg: Naumann, 1979); Kevin Sim, *Women at War: Five Heroines Who Defied the Nazis and Survived* (New York: Morrow, 1982); Antonia Hunt, *Little Resistance: A Teenage English Girl's Adventures in Occupied France* (London: Secker and Warburg, 1982); Vera Laska, ed., *Women in the Resistance and in the Holocaust: The Voices of Eyewitnesses* (Westport, Conn.: Greenwood Press, 1983); Margaret L. Rossiter, *Women in the Resistance* (New York: Praeger, 1986); Lore Cowan, *Children of the Resistance:*

The Young Ones who Defied the Nazi Terror (New York: Meredith Press, 1969).

8. On the history of the "Oneg Shabbat" archives, see *Notes from the Warsaw Ghetto: The Journal of Emmanuel Ringelblum,* ed. and trans. Jacob Sloan (New York: Schocken, 1974), pp. ix–xxvii. The portions of the archive that were found after the war are now in the Yad Vashem archives in Jerusalem, microfilm collection MJ.

9. Denise Dufurnier, *Ravensbrück, The Women's Camp of Death* (London: Allen and Unwin, 1948).

10. Ruzhka Korchzak, *Flames in the Ashes* [Hebrew] (Tel Aviv, 1946); Zivia Lubetkin, *The Last on the Wall* [Hebrew] (Ein Harod: Kibbutz Hameuchad, 1947); Olga Lengyel, *Five Chimneys: The Story of Auschwitz* (Chicago: Ziff-Davis, 1947); Gisella Perl, *I Was a Doctor in Auschwitz* (New York: International University Press, 1948); Kitty Hart, *I Am Alive* (New York: Coward-McCann, 1960); Mary Berg, *The Diary of Mary Berg* (New York: L. B. Fischer, 1945); Gusta Draenger, *Pamietnik Justyny* (Kraków, 1946). On Anne Frank, see n. 1 above.

11. The phrase appeared in Abba Kovner's famous January 1, 1942, proclamation in the Vilna ghetto calling for revolt. The full text appears in *Documents on the Holocaust: Selected Sources on the Destruction of the Jews of Germany and Austria, Poland, and the Soviet Union,* ed. Yitzhak Arad, Yisrael Gutman, and Abraham Margaliot (Jerusalem: Yad Vashem, 1981), p. 433. On the attitude toward survivors in the newly established State of Israel, see Chana Torok Yablonka, "The Absorption of Holocaust Survivors in the Emerging State of Israel and the Problems of Their Integration in Israeli Society" (Ph.D. diss., Hebrew University, 1989), pp. 292–315.

12. On the history of this day and its national and religious significance, see my book *A Voice of Lament: The Holocaust and Prayer* [Hebrew] (Ramat Gan: Bar-Ilan University, 1992), pp. 65–69.

13. See, for example, Dina Porat, "'In Forgiveness and Kindness': The Meeting between Ruzhka Korchzak and the Yishuv and Its Leaders" [Hebrew], *Yalkut Moreshet* 52 (1992): 9–33.

14. See, for example, my "Social Interaction among Jewish Women in Crisis: A Case Study," *Gender and History* 7:1 (1995): 64–84.

15. Two that did appear during this period were actually diaries of young women: Mary Berg and Anne Frank.

16. Hanka H. [*sic*], *W ghetcie i obozie, Pamietnik dwunastoletniej dziewczyny* (Kraków, 1946).

17. Ernst Papanek Collection, Manuscripts Division, New York Public Library.

18. For example, Mark Dworzecky, *Medical Notes* [Hebrew], special edition (September 1946); *The Jewish Frontier* (November 1946); and *Notebooks* [Hebrew] (October 1946).

19. Raul Hilberg, *The Destruction of the European Jews* (New York: Octagon, 1961).

20. Kathryn Close, *Transplanted Children* (New York, 1953); Norman Bentwich, *They Found Refuge: An Account of British Jewry's Work for Victims of Nazi Oppression* (London: Cresset Press, 1956); Recha Freier, *Let the Children Come: The Early History of Youth Aliyah* (London: Weidenfeld and Nicolson, 1961). Other books of the period are Donald Lowrie, *The Hunted Children* (New York: Norton, 1963); Jacqueline Bernard, *The Children You Gave Us* (New York: Jewish Child Care Association of New York, 1973); and Perez Leshem, *Strasse zur Rettung 1933–1939: Aus Deutschland vertrieben—Bereitet sich Jüdische Jugend auf Palästina vor* (Tel Aviv: Verband der Freunde der Histadrut, 1973).

21. Women's and children's memoirs of this period include Rachel Auerbach, *In the Streets of Warsaw, 1939–1945* [Hebrew] (Tel Aviv: Am Oved, 1954); Batya Berman-Temkin, *An Underground Diary* [Hebrew] (Tel Aviv, 1957); Grete Salus, *Eine Frau Erzählt* (Bonn: Bundeszentrale für Heimatdienst, 1958); Chaika Klinger, *From a Ghetto Diary* [Hebrew] (Merhavia, 1959); Helena Sharshevsky, *Between the Cross and the Mezuzah* [Hebrew] (Merhavia, 1959); Marga Minco, *Bitter Herbs: A Little Chronicle*, trans. Roy Edwards (New York: Oxford University Press, 1960); Gemma LaGuardia Gluck, *My Story* (New York: D. McKay Co., 1961); Reska Weiss, *Journey through Hell* (London, 1961); Fredka Mazia, *Comrades in the Storm* [Hebrew] (Jerusalem, 1964); David Rubinowicz, *Diary of David Rubinowicz*, trans. Derek Bowman (Edmonds, Wash.: USA Creative Options, 1982); Moshe Flinker, *Young Moshe's Diary: The Spiritual Torment of a Jewish Boy in Nazi Europe* [Hebrew] (Jerusalem: Yad Vashem, 1965); Halina Birnbaum, *Nadzieja umiera ostatnia* (Warsaw, 1967); and Elisabeth Singer, *Children of the Apocalypse* (London: Hodder and Stoughton, 1967). The trend continued into the next decade, with Judith Strick Dribben, *A Girl Called Judith Strick* (New York: Cowles, 1970); Donia Rosen, *The Forest, My Friend* (New York: Bergen Belsen Memorial Press, 1971); Vladka Meed, *On Both Sides of the Wall: Memoirs from the Warsaw Ghetto*, trans. Steven Meed (New York: Holocaust Library, 1979); and Yitzhak Rudashevsky, *Diary of a Boy from Vilna* (Tel Aviv: Ghetto Fighters' House, 1973).

22. *We Came as Children: A Collective Autobiography*, ed. Karen Gershon (London: Victor Gollancz, 1956); Inge Deutschkron, *. . . denn ihrer war die Hölle: Kinder in Gettos und Lagern* (Cologne: Verlag Wissenschaft und Politik, 1965).

23. Lena Kuchler-Zilberman, *My Hundred Children* (New York, 1957).

24. On the emotional rehabilitation of survivors in the United States, see William B. Helmreich, *Against All Odds: Holocaust Survivors and the Successful Lives They Made in America* (New York: Simon and Schuster, 1992).

25. Individual memoirs of Jewish women and children include the following: Eva Heyman, *The Diary of Eva Heyman* (Jerusalem: Yad Vashem, 1974); Joseph Joffo, *A Bag Full of Marbles* (Boston: Houghton Mifflin, 1974); Corrie Ten Boom, *The Hiding Place* (Boston: G. K. Hall, 1973); Germaine Tillion, *Ravensbrück,* trans. Gerald Satterwhite (Garden City, N.Y.: Anchor, 1975); Byrna Bar Oni, *The Vapor* (Chicago, 1976); Fania Fenelon, *Playing for Time* (New York: Atheneum, 1977); Ilse Koehn, *Mischling, Second Degree: My Childhood in Nazi Germany* (New York: Greenwillow Books, 1977); Isabella Leitner, *Fragments of Isabella: A Memoir of Auschwitz* (New York: Crowell, 1978); Charlotte Delbo, *None of Us Will Return: Auschwitz and After* (Boston: Beacon, 1978); Sandra Brand, *I Dared to Live* (New York: Shengold Publishers, 1978); Leesha Rose, *The Tulips Are Red* (South Brunswick, N.J.: A. S. Barnes, 1978); Johanna Reiss, *The Upstairs Room* (New York: Crowell, 1979); Liliana Zuker-Bujanowska, *Liliana's Journal: Warsaw 1939–1945* (New York: Dial, 1980); Bertha Ferderber-Salz, *And the Sun Kept Shining* (New York: Holocaust Library, 1980); Jack Kuper, *Child of the Holocaust* (Garden City, N.Y.: Doubleday, 1968); Livia E. Jackson, *Elli: Coming of Age in the Holocaust* (New York: Time Books, 1980); Georgia M. Gabor, *My Destiny: Survivor of the Holocaust* (Arcadia, Calif.: Amen Publishing, 1981); Frida Michelson, *I Survived Rumbuli* (New York: Holocaust Publications, 1979); Aranka Siegel, *Upon the Head of a Goat: A Childhood in Hungary* (New York: New American Library, 1981); Sara Zyskind, *Stolen Years* (Minneapolis: Lerner Publications, 1981); Gerda S. Haas, *These I Do Remember: Fragments from the Holocaust* (Freeport, Me.: Cumberland Press, 1982); Kitty Hart, *Return to Auschwitz* (New York: Atheneum, 1982); Agnes Sassoon, *Agnes: How My Spirit Survived* (Edgeware, Eng., 1983); Judith Kerr, *When Hitler Stole Pink Rabbit* (London: Collins, 1971); Nechama Tec, *Dry Tears: The Story of a Lost Childhood* (New York: Oxford University Press, 1984); Aranka Siegal, *Grace in the Wilderness* (New York: Farrar, Straus, Giroux, 1985); Clara Asscher-Pinkhof, *Star Children,* trans. Therese Edelstein and Inez Smidt (Detroit: Wayne State University Press, 1986); Inge Auerbacher, *I Am a Star-Child of the Holocaust* (New York: Prentice-Hall, 1986); Frida Scheps Weinstein, *A Hidden Childhood* (New York: Hill and Wang, 1985); Joseph Ziemian, *The Cigarette Sellers of Three Crosses Square* (Minneapolis: Lerner Publications, 1975); Thomas Geve, *Guns and Barbed Wire: A*

Child Survives the Holocaust (Chicago: Academy Chicago, 1987); Zila Rosenberg-Amit, *Not To Lose the Human Face* [Hebrew] (Tel Aviv: Bet lohameha-getaot, ha-kibuts ha-meuhad, 1990); Alicia Appleman-Jurman, *Alicia: My Story* (New York: Bantam, 1988); Bela Ya'ari-Hazan, *Bronislawa Was My Name* [Hebrew] (Tel Aviv: Bet lohame ha-getaot, ha-kibuts ha-meuhad, 1991); and Lili Thao, *I Remained Myself: A Story of a Teenager from Lvov* [Hebrew] (Tel Aviv: Bet lohame ha-getaot, ha-kibuts ha-meuhad, 1991).

26. One early exception is *Women's Resistance* [Hebrew] (Tel Aviv: Allgemeine Elektricitäts-Gesellschaft [General Electric Company], 1979), the collected memoirs of Jewish women prisoners in the A.E.G. camp in Germany.

27. Lore Shelley, ed. and trans., *Secretaries of Death: Accounts by Former Prisoners Who Worked in the Gestapo of Auschwitz* (New York: Svengold, 1986); Judith Tydor Baumel, ed., *Voices from the Canada Commando* [Hebrew] (Jerusalem, 1989); and Azriel Eisenberg, ed., *The Lost Generation: Children in the Holocaust* (New York: Pilgrim Press, 1982).

Other books in this category are Vera Laska, ed., *Women in the Resistance and in the Holocaust: The Voices of Eyewitnesses* (Westport, Conn.: Greenwood Press, 1983); Ruth Schwertfeger, *Women of Theresienstadt: Voices from a Concentration Camp* (Oxford: Berg, 1989); Karin Berger, Elisabeth Holzinger, Lotte Podgornik, and Lisbeth N. Trallor, *Ich geb Dir einen Mantel, daß Du ihn noch in Freiheit tragen kannst: Widerstehen im KZ Österreichische Frauen erzählen* (Vienna: Promedia, 1987); Claudine Vegh, *I Didn't Say Goodbye: Interviews with Children of the Holocaust* (New York: Dutton, 1984); Senta Radax-Ziegler, *Sie kamen durch: Das Schicksal zehn jüdischer Kinder und Jugendlicher, die 1938/39 aus Österreich Flüchten mußten* (Vienna, 1988).

28. Joseph Walk, *The Education of the Jewish Child in Nazi Germany: The Law and Its Application* [Hebrew] (Jerusalem: Yad Vashem, 1975); Chaim Schatzker, "Reality and Imagination—Perceptions of the Organized Jewish Youth during the Holocaust," in *Comprehending the Holocaust: Historical and Literary Research,* ed. Asher Cohen, Joav Gelber, and Charlotte Wardi (Frankfurt and New York: P. Lang, 1988), pp. 215–23; "Maccabi Hatzair: The Last Jewish Youth Group in Germany" [Hebrew], in *Tnuot Hanoar Haziyoniyot Bashoah* (Haifa, 1989), pp. 81–103; "The Jewish Youth Movement in Germany in the Holocaust Period," *Leo Baeck Institute Year Book* 32 (1987): 157–81; ibid., 33 (1988): 301–25; Esther Judith Baumel, "The Jewish Refugee Children in Great Britain 1938–1945" (M.A. thesis, Bar-Ilan University, 1979); Judith Tydor Baumel, *Unfulfilled Promise: The Rescue and Resettlement of Jewish Refugee Children in the United States, 1934–1945* (Juneau, Ak.: Denali Press, 1991); Deborah

Dwork, *Children with a Star: Jewish Youth in Nazi Europe* (New Haven, Conn.: Yale University Press, 1991).

Other studies falling into this category are Judith Hemmendinger, *Survivors: Children of the Holocaust* (Bethesda, Md.: National Press, 1986); Lotte Adolphs, *Kinder in Ketten: Kinderschicksale in Ghettos und Konzentrationslagern* (Duisburg: W. Braun, 1984); Sarah Moskovitz, *Love Despite Hate: Child Survivors of the Holocaust and Their Adult Lives* (New York: Schocken, 1983); George Eisen, *Children and Play in the Holocaust: Games among the Shadows* (Amherst: University of Massachusetts Press, 1988); Ernst Papanek with Edward Linn, *Out of the Fire* (New York: Morrow, 1975); and Sybil Milton, ed., *The Art of Jewish Children, Germany, 1936–1941: Innocence and Persecution* (New York: Philosophical Library, 1989).

29. Marion A. Kaplan, *The Making of the Jewish Middle Class: Women, Family, and Identity in Imperial Germany* (New York: Oxford University Press, 1991); Kaplan, *The Jewish Feminist Movement in Germany: The Campaigns of the Jüdischer Frauenbund, 1904–1938* (Westport, Conn.: Greenwood Press, 1979); Andreas Lixi-Purcell, ed., *Women of Exile: German-Jewish Autobiographies since 1933* (New York: Greenwood Press, 1988); Gabriele Kreis, *Frauen im Exil: Dichtung und Wirklichkeit* (Düsseldorf: Claassen, 1984); Joan S. Ringelheim, "Women and the Holocaust: A Reconsideration of Research," *Signs* 10 (1985): 741–61; "The Unethical and the Unspeakable: Women and the Holocaust," *Simon Wiesenthal Center Annual* 1 (1984): 69–87; Judith Tydor Baumel, "Die 'Zehnerschaft' als Beispiel für weibliche Selbsthilfe unter dem NS-Regime," *Tel Aviver Jahrbuch für Deutsche Geschichte* (1992): 271–88.

More recent research includes Miriam Gillis-Karlebach's examination of the lives of German-Jewish rabbis' wives, "The German-Jewish Rebbetzin under Hitler" [Hebrew], and the late Joseph Karniel's study, "Jewish Women in Austria after the Anschluss" [Hebrew], both in *Ot 3* (1996), special edition about women during the Holocaust. Also see Rita Thalmann, "Jüdische Frauen nach dem Pogrom 1938," and Claudia Koonz, "Courage and Choice among German Jewish Women and Men," both in *The Jews in Nazi Germany 1933–1945*, ed. Arnold Paucker, Sylvia Gilchrist, and Barbara Suchin (Tübingen: J. C. B. Mohr, 1986), pp. 183–303.

30. See, for example, Barrie Throne with Marilyn Yalom, eds., *Rethinking the Family: Some Feminist Questions* (New York: Longman, 1982); Hunter College Women's Studies Collective, *Women's Realities, Women's Choices: An Introduction to Women's Studies* (New York: Oxford University Press, 1983); Ellen C. DuBois et al., *Feminist Scholarship: Kindling in the Groves of Academe* (Urbana: University of Illinois Press, 1985).

31. On the catalysts for historical Holocaust research in various coun-

tries and fields, see Yisrael Gutman and Gideon Greif, eds., *The Historiography of the Holocaust Period* (Jerusalem: Yad Vashem, 1988).

32. See Dwork, *Children with a Star,* introduction.

33. The work on women as leaders is taking place as part of the biography project sponsored by Yad Ya'ari, Givat Haviva, Israel.

34. Research on women's religious lives is sponsored by the Arnold and Leona Finkler Institute of Holocaust Research, Bar-Ilan University, Ramat Gan.

35. Work on motherhood has been encouraged by Touro College master's program, Jerusalem branch.

36. See Dwork, *Children with a Star,* introduction.

Dan Laor, "The Legacy of the Survivors: Holocaust Literature in Israel"

1. The English version of this text is included in Simon Halkin, *Modern Hebrew Literature* (New York: Schocken, 1970), pp. 137–38.

2. This accusation was recently repeated by journalist Avi Katzman in a critical essay published in *Ephes Shetavim* 2 (Winter 1993): 97–105.

3. See Shoshana Felman and Dori Laub, *Testimony: Crises of Witnessing in Literature, Psychoanalysis, and History* (New York: Routledge, 1992), p. 5. For the references to Elie Wiesel, see pp. 3, 113–14.

4. The list of writer-survivors not discussed in this paper is long and includes names such as Uri Orlev, Shamai GoIn, Itamar Yaoz-Kest, K. A. Bertini, Yaakov Besser, Meir Bossak, Benzion Tomer, and others.

5. Quoted from Stephen Spender's introduction to Abba Kovner and Nelly Sachs, *Selected Poems* (Harmonsworth: Penguin, 1971), p. 9.

6. In Israeli literature, this genre is practiced by writer-survivors such as Meir Bossak, Itamar Yaoz-Kest, Yaakov Besser, and others.

7. Abba Kovner, *Ad Lo Or* (Merhavia: Sifriyat Poalim, 1947).

8. Abba Kovner, *Mi-kol ha-ahavot* ("From All the Loves") (Tel Aviv: Sifriyat Poalim, 1965), 127–78.

9. *My Little Sister and Selected Poems, 1965–1985,* trans. Shirley Kaufman and Nurit Orchan (Oberlin, Ohio: Oberlin College, 1986), pp. 21–75.

10. Edward Alexander, "Abba Kovner: Poet of Holocaust and Rebirth," *Midstream* 22:8 (October 1977): 52.

11. It seems that Kovner's major source of influence is the liturgical poem "Ahot Ketana" ("Little Sister"), by the thirteenth-century poet Avraham he-Hazan Gerundi, traditionally recited on the eve of Rosh Hashana. The little sister—symbol of the Israeli nation—is described in that poem as enduring great troubles yet remaining loyal to her heavenly lover. See

Hayim Shirman, *Hashira haivrit besefarad uveperovans* ("Hebrew Poetry in Spain and Provence") (Jerusalem, 1961), 1:291–94.

12. *Panim el Panim* ("Face to Face"), 2 vols.(Merhavia: Sifriyat Poalim, 1953–55).

13. For an analysis of this concept, see Saul Friedlander, "The *Shoah* between Memory and History," *Jerusalem Quarterly* 53 (Winter 1990): 118–30.

14. Abba Kovner, *A Canopy in the Desert: Selected Poems,* trans. Shirley Kaufman with Ruth Adler and Nurit Orchan (Pittsburgh: University of Pittsburgh Press, 1971), pp. 93–205. See also comments on this poem by Edward Alexander in *A Canopy in the Desert,* pp. 56–58.

15. Ka.Tzetnik, *Sunrise over Hell,* trans. Nina Dinur (London: W. H. Allen, 1977). The pen name "Ka.Tzetnik" is often printed in Dinur's novels together with the writer's personal number in Auschwitz: 135633. As Tom Segev explains in *The Seventh Million,* trans. Haim Watzman (New York: Hill and Wang, 1983), p. 4: "The name comes from the German acronym KZ (Ka Tzet) for *Konzentrationslager*—concentration camp. The inmates were referred to as Ka-Tzetniks, by number: Dinur had been Ka-Tzetnik 135633, and this was how he signed his works." Later he omitted the number.

16. Quoted by Gideon Hausner, *Justice in Jerusalem* (New York: Harper and Row, 1966), p. 171.

17. Interview by Raphael Bashan, *Ma'ariv,* April 6, 1961.

18. Hana Yaos, *Siporet ha-shoah be-ivrit* ("The Holocaust Literature in Hebrew") (Tel Aviv: Eked, 1980), pp. 72–76.

19. Dinur combined all his works (including the recent one) under this heading to suggest that his oeuvre is one continuous book that illuminates the destiny of an archetypal Jewish family in our time. Strictly speaking, the ties between the books are marginal, though the semiautobiographical character Harry Preleshnik is present in all of them. Preleshnik shifts from the position of a *Mussulmann* in Auschwitz to that of a free man in the State of Israel, though constantly haunted by his past in *Phoenix over the Galilee* (New York: Harper and Row, 1966).

20. *House of Dolls,* trans. Moshe M. Kohn (New York: Simon and Schuster, 1955); *Piepel* (London: A. Blond, 1961). A *Piepel* was a boy selected by the block chiefs of Auschwitz for their sexual orgies. A revised edition of *Piepel* was published under the title *Atrocity* (New York: Lyle Stuart, 1963).

21. Gideon Talpaz, "Salamandra—Ba-sheniya," *Ma'ariv,* September 24, 1971.

22. K. A. Bertini, "Beit ha-bubot," *Gilyonot* (1953): 289.

23. Interview by Bashan, *Ma'ariv.*

24. Appelfeld's first book, a collection of short stories entitled *Ashan* ("Smoke"), came out in Tel Aviv in 1962; it was reissued in Jerusalem in 1982.

25. Israel Gutman, ed., *Encyclopedia of the Holocaust* (New York: Macmillan, 1990), 4:1473–76.

26. Aharon Appelfeld, *Mesilat ha-Barzel* (Jerusalem: Keter, 1991).

27. Aharon Appelfeld, "1946," *Jerusalem Quarterly* 7 (Spring 1978): 104–44.

28. Aharon Appelfeld, *The Immortal Bartfus,* trans. Jeffrey M. Green (London: Weidenfeld and Nicolson, 1987). Originally published in Hebrew, 1983.

29. Aharon Appelfeld, *Baddenheim, 1939,* trans. Dalya Bilu (Boston: Godine, 1980). Original in Hebrew, 1975.

30. Aharon Appelfeld, *The Age of Wonders,* trans. Dalya Bilu (Boston: Godine, 1980). Original in Hebrew, 1978.

31. Aharon Appelfeld, *The Healer,* trans. Jeffrey M. Green (New York: Grove Weidenfeld, 1990). Original in Hebrew, 1985.

32. Philip Roth, "Walking the Way of the Survivor: A Talk with Aharon Appelfeld," *New York Times Book Review,* February 28, 1988, p. 28.

33. Interview with Avraham Balaban, *Yediot Ahronot,* June 27, 1980.

34. The interview was broadcast in English on December 24, 1984, and printed after Pagis's death in *Hadoar,* November 14, 1986, p. 15. The connection between that insight and Pagis's poetry is made by Sidra Dekoven Ezrahi, "Dan Pagis—Out of Line: A Poetics of Decomposition," *Prooftexts* 10 (1990): 339. In a previous interview Pagis speaks insightfully on this same matter. See *Iton 77* 38 (February 1983): 32–33.

35. This point is clearly made by Naomy Sokoloff in her excellent analysis "Transformations: Holocaust Poems in Dan Pagis's *Gilgul,*" *Hebrew Annual Review* 8 (1984): 215–93.

36. *Variable Directions: The Selected Poetry of Dan Pagis,* trans. Stephen Mitchell (San Francisco: North Point Press, 1989), p. 29.

37. Theodor Adorno, *Prismen* (Frankfurt: Suhrkamp, 1955), p. 31.

Lawrence Baron, "Teaching about the New Psychosocial Research on Rescuers in Holocaust Courses"

This essay is a revised version of my article "Integrating the New Psycho-social Research about Rescuers of Jews into the Teaching of Holocaust Courses," *Shofar* 10:2 (Winter 1992): 97–107.

1. For example, see Margot Stern Strom and William S. Parsons, *Fac-*

ing History and Ourselves: Holocaust and Human Behavior (Watertown, Mass.: International Educations, 1982), pp. 147–57, 228–29.

2. Ibid., pp. 285–90; Yehuda Bauer, *A History of the Holocaust* (New York: Franklin Watts, 1982), pp. 289–95; and Richard L. Rubenstein and John K. Roth, *Approaches to Auschwitz: The Holocaust and Its Legacy* (Atlanta: John Knox, 1987), pp. 216–23. Much more extensive comparison of national rescue experiences can be found in Leni Yahil, *The Holocaust: The Fate of European Jewry, 1932–1945* (New York: Oxford University Press, 1990), pp. 573–652.

3. Strom and Parsons, *Facing History and Ourselves,* pp. 290–92; Sidney M. Bolkosky, Betty Rotberg Ellias, and David Harris, *Life Unworthy of Life: A Holocaust Curriculum* (Farmington Hills, Mich.: Center for the Study of the Child, 1987), pp. 123–36; Bauer, *A History of the Holocaust,* pp. 286–89, 324–25; and Rubenstein and Roth, *Approaches to Auschwitz,* pp. 223–28. Two popular books that exemplify the narrative approaches to rescuers are Philip Friedman, *Their Brothers' Keepers* (New York: Holocaust Library, 1978), and Peter Hellman, *Avenue of the Righteous* (New York: Bantam, 1981).

4. For an early review article on this problem, see Lawrence Baron, "The Holocaust and Human Decency: A Review of Research on the Rescue of Jews in Nazi-Occupied Europe," *Humboldt Journal of Social Relations* 13:1/2 (1986): 237–51.

5. Phillip Hallie, *Lest Innocent Blood Be Shed: The Story of Le Chambon and How Goodness Happened There* (New York: Harper and Row, 1979).

6. Perry London, "The Rescuers: Motivational Hypotheses about Christians Who Saved Jews from the Nazis," in *Altruism and Helping Behavior,* ed. J. Macaulay and L. Berkowitz (New York: Academic Press, 1970), pp. 241–50. For the first study of rescuers based on survey data, see Manfred Wolfson, "Zum Widerstand gegen Hitler: Umriß eines Gruppenporträts deutscher Retter von Juden," *Tradition und Neubeginn* (Munich: Heymann, 1975), pp. 391–407.

7. For recent review articles on the literature covered in this paper, see Lawrence Baron, "The Moral Minority: Psycho-social Research on the Righteous Gentiles," in *What Have We Learned? Telling the Story and Teaching the Lessons of the Holocaust,* ed. Franklin H. Littell, Alan L. Berger, and Hubert G. Locke (Lewiston, Maine: Edwin Mellen, 1993), pp. 119–40; David P. Gushee, "Many Paths to Righteousness: An Assessment of Research on Why Righteous Gentiles Helped Jews," *Holocaust and Genocide Studies* 7:3 (Winter 1993): 372–401.

8. Samuel P. Oliner and Pearl M. Oliner, *The Altruistic Personality: Rescuers of Jews in Nazi Europe* (New York: Free Press, 1988), pp. 261–72; Nechama Tec, *When Light Pierced the Darkness: Christian Rescue of Jews*

in Nazi-Occupied Europe (New York: Oxford University Press, 1986), pp. 87–98. Tec found that people who helped Jews for ulterior reasons such as monetary gain differed significantly from the rescuers who sought to help with no expectation of personal gain. A study with much smaller pools of interviewed rescuers and controls is Kristen R. Monroe, Michael C. Barton, and Ute Klingemann, "Altruism and the Theory of Rational Action: Rescuers of Jews in Nazi Europe," *Ethics* 101:1 (October 1990): 103–22.

9. Tec, *When Light Pierced the Darkness,* p. 183.

10. Oliner and Oliner, *The Altruistic Personality,* p. 222.

11. Eva Fogelman, *Conscience and Courage: Rescuers of Jews during the Holocaust* (New York: Anchor, 1994), p. 6.

12. Mordecai Paldiel, "Hesed and the Holocaust," *Journal of Ecumenical Studies* 23:1 (Winter 1986): 106; also see Monroe, Barton, and Klingemann, "Altruism," pp. 119–22, for a similar conclusion. Although the latter dispute most motivational theories about rescuers, they view the decision to help Jews as a natural extension of the rescuer's core identity.

13. Lawrence Baron, "Teaching about the Rescuers of Jews," in *Methodology in the Academic Teaching of the Holocaust,* ed. Zev Garber, Alan Berger, and Richard Libowitz (Lanham, Pa.: University Press of America, 1988), pp. 144–45.

14. Tom Tugend, "Hollywood's Time to Tell," *Jerusalem Post,* December 25, 1993, p. 12. In this interview Steven Spielberg says he deliberately avoided trying to explain why Oskar Schindler rescued Jews: "I felt it was less important to really define it, that it should remain personal, perhaps it should remain a mystery."

15. Eva Fogelman, "The Rescuers: A Sociopsychological Study of Altruistic Behavior during the Nazi Era" (Ph.D. diss., City University of New York, 1987), p. 198.

16. Oliner and Oliner, *The Altruistic Personality,* p. 272.

17. London, "The Rescuers" pp. 247–49.

18. Tec, *When Light Pierced the Darkness,* pp. 152–60.

19. Lawrence Baron, "The Dutchness of Dutch Rescuers: The National Dimension of Altruism," in *Embracing the Other: Philosophical, Psychological, and Historical Perspectives on Altruism,* ed. Pearl M. Oliner et al. (New York: New York University Press, 1992), p. 322; Lawrence Baron, "The Dynamics of Dutch Decency during the Holocaust," *Holocaust Studies Annual: 1990 General Essays,* ed. Jack Fischel and Sanford Pinsker (New York: Garland, 1990), pp. 103–4.

20. Hallie, *Lest Innocent Blood Be Shed,* pp. 24–25, 132–33, 166–68.

21. Fogelman, *Conscience and Courage,* pp. 329–30; Oliner and Oliner, *The Altruistic Personality,* pp. 176–77, 306, 377–78.

22. Fogelman, *Conscience and Courage,* pp. 253–70.

23. Oliner and Oliner, *The Altruistic Personality,* pp. 176–86.

24. Ibid., pp. 253–57.

25. Ibid., pp. 199–222. For a thoughtful critique of the Oliners' tendency to distinguish too sharply between normative and principled orientations, particularly related to religious morality, see James W. Fowler, "The Psychology of Altruism," *First Things* 4 (June/July 1990): 43–49.

26. Douglas K. Huneke, *In the Darkness . . . Glimpses of Light: A Study of Nazi-Era Rescuers: A Report to the Oregon Committee for the Humanities* (1980), pp. 24–28, 31–33; Huneke, "A Study of Christians Who Rescued Jews during the Holocaust," *Humboldt Journal of Social Relations* 9:1 (Fall/Winter 1981/82): 144–49. For a study illustrating that the material assistance, intelligence, and peer support provided by rescue networks played an important role in influencing many individuals to rescue Jews, see Michael L. Gross, "Jewish Rescue in Holland and France during the Second World War: Moral Cognition and Collective Action," *Social Forces* 73:2 (December 1994): 463–96.

27. Fogelman, *Conscience and Courage,* pp. 161–80, 193–235.

28. David P. Gushee, *The Righteous Gentiles of the Holocaust: A Christian Interpretation* (Minneapolis: Fortress Press, 1994).

29. Fogelman, *Conscience and Courage,* p. 336; Oliner and Oliner, *The Altruistic Personality,* pp. 114–15, 184–85, 275, 312, 320.

30. Douglas K. Huneke, *The Moses of Rovno* (New York: Dodd, Mead, 1985), pp. 180–83; Fogelman, *Conscience and Courage,* pp. 209–11.

31. Frances G. Grossman, "A Psychological Study of Gentiles Who Saved the Lives of Jews during the Holocaust," in *Toward the Understanding and Prevention of Genocide,* ed. Israel W. Charny (Boulder, Colo.: Westview, 1984), pp. 202–16.

32. Oliner and Oliner, *The Altruistic Personality,* pp. 173–76, 188–99.

33. Eva Fogelman and Valerie Lewis Wiener, "The Few, the Brave, the Noble," *Psychology Today* 19:8 (August 1985): 62. A brief report on the results of this pilot study also can be found in Stephen P. Cohen, Eva Fogelman, and Valerie L. Wiener, "Rescuers: Why Righteous Gentiles Risked Their Lives to Save Jews," *Jewish Monthly* (January 1985): 16–19.

34. Fogelman, *Conscience and Courage,* pp. 237–51.

35. Mary Gruber, Pearl M. Oliner, and Samuel P. Oliner, "Extensivity and Altruism: A Conceptual Elaboration and Its Relationship to Gender," paper presented at the Conference on Theoretical and Social Implications of Rescuing People in Extreme Situations, Warsaw, June 1989.

36. Eva Fleischner, "Can the Few Become the Many? Some Catholics in France Who Saved Jews during the Holocaust," *Remembering for the*

Future, ed. Yehuda Bauer et al., vol. 1 (Oxford: Pergamon, 1990), pp. 241–42.

37. Andre Stein, *Quiet Heroes: True Stories of the Rescue of Jews in Nazi-Occupied Holland* (New York: New York University Press, 1988), p. 305. For a more extended discounting of psychosocial theories explaining the rescuers' behavior, see Andre Stein, "For the Love of Life: Making Sense of Dutch Rescuers of Jews," manuscript, 1987.

38. Eric Silver, *The Book of the Just: The Unsung Heroes Who Rescued Jews from Hitler* (New York: Grove, 1992), pp. 163–64. Hilberg dismisses any commonalities among rescuers, too. See Raul Hilberg, *Perpetrators, Victims, Bystanders: The Jewish Catastrophe 1933–1945* (New York: HarperCollins, 1992), p. 213.

39. Monroe, Barton, and Klingemann, "Altruism," pp. 121–22; Kristen R. Monroe, "A Different Way of Seeing Things: What We Can Learn from the Rescuers of Jews," *Dimensions: A Journal of Holocaust Studies* 7:1 (1993): 12–14.

40. Paldiel, "Hesed and the Holocaust," pp. 90–106; Mordecai Paldiel, "The Altruism of Righteous Gentiles," *Holocaust and Genocide Studies* 3:2 (1988): 190–93; Paldiel, "Sparks of Light," in *Faith and Freedom: A Tribute to Franklin H. Littell* (Oxford: Pergamon, 1987), pp. 45–69.

41. Mordecai Paldiel, *The Path of the Righteous: Gentile Rescuers of Jews during the Holocaust* (Hoboken, N.J.: Ktav, 1993), pp. 376–81.

42. Silver, *The Book of the Just.*

43. The paperback editions of Tec's, the Oliners', and Fogelman's books appeared in 1986, 1992, and 1995, respectively.

44. Gushee, *The Righteous Gentiles,* pp. 117–75.

45. Milton Meltzer, *Rescue: The Story of How Gentiles Saved Jews in the Holocaust* (New York: HarperCollins, 1988).

46. Pearl M. Oliner and Samuel P. Oliner, *The Roots of Altruism* (New York: American Jewish Committee, 1989); *Dimensions: A Journal of Holocaust Studies* 1:2 (Fall 1985), 3:3 (1988), 5:3 (1990), and 7:1 (1993). See part 5, "Helping as Historical Action," of the *Humboldt Journal of Social Relations,* special issue on altruism and prosocial behavior, 13:1/2 (1986): 237–373. See the "Book World" section devoted to the Oliners' *Altruistic Personality* in *The World and I: A Chronicle of Our Changing Era* 3:7 (July 1988): 346–401. Holocaust teachers should consult the following when preparing the unit on rescuers: Pearl M. Oliner and Samuel P. Oliner, "Righteous People in the Holocaust," *Genocide: A Critical Bibliographic Review,* vol. 2, ed. Israel W. Charny (New York: Facts on File, 1991). See the articles by Fleischner, Huneke, Sarah Moskovitz, the Oliners, Paldiel, and Tec in *Remembering for the Future,* vol. 1. A useful anthology for advanced college students is *Embracing the Other: Philosophical, Psychological,*

and Historical Perspectives on Altruism, ed. Pearl M. Oliner et al. (New York: New York University Press, 1992).

47. Miep Gies with Alison Leslie Gold, *Anne Frank Remembered: The Story of the Woman Who Helped to Hide the Frank Family* (New York: Simon and Schuster, 1987). Other useful rescuer biographies are Janet Keit, *A Friend among Enemies: The Incredible Story of Arie van Mansum in the Holocaust* (Richmond Hill, Ont.: Fitzhenry and Whiteside, 1991); and Diet Eman with James Schaap, *Things We Couldn't Say* (Grand Rapids, Mich.: William B. Eerdmans, 1994).

48. Dienke Hondius, "A New Perspective on Helpers of Jews during the Holocaust: The Case of Miep and Jan Gies," in *Anne Frank in Historical Perspective: A Teaching Guide for Secondary Schools,* ed. Alex Grobman and Joel Fishman (Los Angeles: Martyrs Memorial and Museum of the Holocaust, 1995), pp. 33–47.

49. Gay Block and Malka Drucker, *Rescuers: Portraits of Moral Courage in the Holocaust* (New York and London: Holmes and Meier, 1992). See n. 51 below for Rittner and Myers.

50. Fogelman, *Conscience and Courage,* pp. 355–59. For more on movies about rescuers of Jews, see Annette Insdorf, "A Conspiracy of Goodness: An Overview of Recent Films," *Dimensions* 3:3 (1988): 26–29.

51. Students should read Hallie's *Lest Innocent Blood Be Shed* after viewing *The Weapons of Spirit.* For *The Courage to Care,* they can consult Hallie, too, as well as the companion volume *The Courage to Care: Rescuers of the Jews during the Holocaust,* ed. Carol Rittner and Sondra Myers (New York: New York University Press, 1986). Also see "A *Moment* Interview with Marion Pritchard," *Moment* 9:1 (December 1983): 26–33; "Interview with Marion Pritchard," *Sh'ma* 14 (April 27, 1984): 97; and Marion Pritchard, "Circles of Caring: An Insider's View," *Dimensions* 5:3 (1990): 12–15. For more information on Irene Opdyke, who is featured in "The Courage to Care," see Eva Fogelman, "Psychological Origins of Rescue," *Dimensions* 3:3 (1988): 9–12; and Irene Gut Opdyke, *Into the Flames* (San Bernardino, Calif.: Borgo, 1992).

52. Lawrence A. Blum, *Moral Perception and Particularity* (New York: Cambridge University Press, 1994), pp. 65–97; Fogelman, *Conscience and Courage,* pp. 42–43, 53–54, 181–82; Luitgard N. Wundheiler, "Oskar Schindler's Moral Development during the Holocaust," *Humboldt Journal of Social Relations* 13:1/2 (1986): 333–56; Luitgard N. Wundheiler, "The Case of Oskar Schindler," *Dimensions* 3:3 (1988): 14–15; Elinor J. Brecher, *Schindler's Legacy: True Stories of the Last Survivors* (New York: Plume, 1994).

53. For background material on the experience of Jews in different European countries during the Holocaust, see Lawrence Baron, "The His-

torical Context of Rescue," in Oliner and Oliner, *The Altruistic Personality*, pp. 13–48; Yisrael Gutman and Chaim Schatzker, *The Holocaust and Its Significance* (Jerusalem: Zalman Schazar Center, 1984), pp. 169–82; Michael R. Marrus and Robert O. Paxton, "Western Europeans and the Jews," in *The Holocaust: Problems and Perspectives of Interpretation*, ed. Donald L. Niewyk, 2d ed. (Boston and New York: Houghton Mifflin, 1997), pp. 241–51.

54. Gushee, "Many Paths to Righteousness," p. 302.

Judith E. Doneson, "Why Film?"

1. Carol Angier, "Edgar Reitz," *Sight and Sound* (Winter 1990/91): 38.

2. See Anton Kaes's *From Hitler to Heimat: The Return of History as Film* (Cambridge, Mass: Harvard University Press, 1989). Refer to the published proceedings of the conference held at UCLA in 1990, *Probing the Limits of Representation*, ed. Saul Friedlander (Cambridge, Mass.: Harvard University Press, 1992); and Edgar Reitz's film *Heimat* (1984).

3. *The Black Book: The Nazi Crime against the Jewish People* (New York: Duell, Sloan and Pearce, 1946), p. 466.

4. Anton Kaes, "Holocaust and the End of History: Postmodern Historiography in Cinema," in *Probing the Limits of Representation*, pp. 207–8.

5. For a general view of the much-discussed effects of NBC's *Holocaust* throughout the United States and Western Europe, see Kaes, *From Hitler to Heimat;* Siegfried Zielinski, "History as Entertainment and Provocation: The TV Series 'Holocaust' in West Germany," in *Germans and Jews since the Holocaust*, ed. Anson Rabinbach and Jack Zipes (New York: Holmes and Meier, 1986); and Judith E. Doneson, *The Holocaust in American Film* (Philadelphia: Jewish Publication Society, 1987).

6. Kaes, "Holocaust and the End of History," p. 208.

7. Ibid., pp. 208–9.

8. John Rockwell, "An Elusive German Director Re-emerges in Edinburgh," *New York Times*, September 2, 1992.

9. I discuss the making of *Holocaust* in *The Holocaust in American Film*, in the chapter "Television and the Effects of *Holocaust*," pp. 143–96.

10. See Doneson, *The Holocaust in American Film*, p. 189.

11. *A Current Affair*, ABC TV, May 25, 1991. This segment of this tabloid news program dealt with a meeting of Holocaust survivors in New York. During the show many survivors were interviewed.

12. *Unsolved Mysteries*, NBC TV, [date unknown].

13. Perry Anderson, "Emplotment: Two Kinds of Ruin," in *Probing the Limits of Representation*, p. 64.

14. A Dutch survivor by the name of Pollack, connected with the Anne Frank House in New York, has been seeking a publisher for his manuscript of love letters.

15. Christopher Browning, "German Memory, Judicial Interpretation, Historical Reconstruction," in *Probing the Limits of Representation*, p. 33.

16. Carl L. Becker, "What Is Evidence? The Relativist View—'Everyman His Own Historian,'" in *The Historian as Detective*, ed. Robin W. Winks (New York: Harper Colophon, 1970), p. 20.

17. Gore Vidal, *Screening History* (Cambridge, Mass.: Harvard University Press, 1992), p. 2.

18. Quoted in Judy Stone, "Europa, America," *Jerusalem Report*, September 23, 1993.

19. Geoffrey Hartman, "Learning from Survivors: Notes on the Video Archive at Yale," in *Remembering for the Future: The Impact of the Holocaust on the Contemporary World*, vol. 2 (Oxford: Pergamon, 1989), p. 1713.

20. Solomon Perel spoke at a screening of *Europa, Europa* at the Jerusalem Film Festival in 1991. He indicated that while he was not in total agreement with all aspects of the film—he did not specify which—nonetheless he was satisfied with the final product. This, along with his participation in the film, allows the viewer to question the veracity of the tale from a historical perspective.

21. Pierre Sorlin, *The Film in History: Restaging the Past* (Totowa, N.J.: Barnes and Noble, 1980), p. 71.

22. John Kotre, *White Gloves: How We Create Ourselves through Memory* (New York: Free Press, 1995), p. 136.

23. Sander Gilman, *The Jew's Body* (New York: Routledge, 1991), p. 155.

24. István Deák, "Strategies of Hell," *New York Review of Books*, October 8, 1992.

25. Gilman, *The Jew's Body*, p. 173.

26. Ibid., p. 193. Unless otherwise noted, references to images and stereotypes associated with Jews in Europe, as well as the source of these stereotypes, are culled from Gilman, *The Jew's Body*.

27. Ibid., p. 99.

28. Ibid., p. 24.

29. See Judith E. Doneson, "The Use of Film in Teaching about the Holocaust," in *The Holocaust in University Teaching*, ed. Gideon Shimoni (Oxford: Pergamon, 1991).

30. Jack Kugelmass and Jonathan Boyarin, eds., *From a Ruined Garden: The Memorial Books of Polish Jewry* (New York: Schocken, 1983), p. 1.

Marshall Lee and Michael Steele, "The Affective Approach in the Interdisciplinary Holocaust Classroom"

1. The students will usually read six books (for example, those by Martin Gilbert, Carol Rittner and John K. Roth, Elie Wiesel, Tadeusz Borowski, Thomas Keneally, and Deborah Lipstadt), write one reflective essay, complete one "creative" work (described in this essay), and take a two-part final exam. They will also see two videos, listen to two or three personal accounts by guest speakers, including a survivor, view slides of the camps, and have access to a wide variety of materials and artifacts at the Oregon Holocaust Resource Center, located on campus in Portland.

2. On most campuses a Holocaust course is an elective; therefore, students who register for one are a self-selected sample. With that caveat in mind, we find that the makeup of our class in particular reveals what one would expect to find at many rural liberal arts colleges throughout the nation. Our course is a lower-division elective that can be taken for either literature or history credit. Roughly half of the students enrolled are freshmen, one-quarter sophomores, and the remaining quarter juniors and seniors. While females make up 56 percent of the student body at Pacific, between 60 and 65 percent of our students are female. Pacific University enrolls a significant number of students from urban high schools, but the average student comes from a smaller, suburban high school or from rural unified high schools of fewer than one thousand students. The majority of our students come from the Pacific Northwest (including Montana), California, Alaska, and Hawaii. Roughly two-thirds are first-generation college students; they are 85 percent white, and 95 percent label themselves Christian. Occasionally defensive of their Christian heritage, Pacific students are, by and large, very tolerant of other lifestyles—witness the broad-based campus support for gay and lesbian groups and opposition to recent ballot measures in Oregon aimed at restricting gay and lesbian rights—but are infrequently personally involved in social or political causes.

3. This was a laudable endeavor, we felt, but we did not enjoy the full support and understanding of our dean at the time. It was his view that the Holocaust was "just another slaughter," and thus not worthy of special classroom focus any more than, say, Rome's pillaging of Carthage. Without the dean's rudimentary support for a team-taught course, we simply asked the university registrar to list two separate courses—Holocaust History with Lee and Holocaust Literature with Steele—scheduled at the same time and assigned to the same lecture hall, one large enough to hold nearly one hundred students. Since then we have taught the class together every other year. It is always overenrolled, compared to other courses offered in

the College of Arts and Sciences. From all accounts, the students find it thoroughly interesting, challenging, and often disturbing.

4. Thomas Keneally, *Schindler's List* (New York: Simon and Schuster, 1982); and Janusz Korczak, *The Warsaw Ghetto Memoirs of Janusz Korczak* (Washington, D.C.: University Press of America, 1979).

5. Jerzy Kosinski, *The Painted Bird* (New York: Pocket Books, 1966).

6. Bruno Bettelheim, *The Informed Heart* (New York: Free Press, 1960).

7. Emmanuel Ringelblum, *Notes from the Warsaw Ghetto: The Journal of Emmanuel Ringelblum* (New York: McGraw-Hill, 1958).

8. Raul Hilberg, *The Destruction of the European Jews* (New York: Harper, 1961); and Leni Yahil, *The Holocaust: The Fate of European Jewry* (Oxford: Oxford University Press, 1991).

9. Martin Gilbert, *The Holocaust: A History of the Jews of Europe during the Second World War* (New York: Henry Holt, 1985).

10. Lucy Dawidowicz, *The War against the Jews, 1933–1945* (New York: Holt, Rinehart, and Winston, 1975); Deborah Dwork, *Children with a Star: Jewish Youth in Nazi Europe* (New Haven, Conn.: Yale University Press, 1991).

11. Gitta Sereny, *Into That Darkness: An Examination of Conscience* (New York: McGraw-Hill, 1974).

12. Vera Laska, *Women in the Resistance and in the Holocaust: The Voices of Eyewitnesses* (Westport, Conn.: Greenwood, 1983); and Claudia Koonz, *Mothers in the Fatherland: Women, the Family, and Nazi Politics* (New York: St. Martin's, 1987). See also in particular, on the question of life-giver/nurturer and the necessity of infanticide in Auschwitz, Gisella Perl, *I Was a Doctor in Auschwitz* (Salem, N.H.: Ayer, 1984); and Sara Nomberg-Przytyk, *Auschwitz: True Tales from a Grotesque Land* (Chapel Hill: University of North Carolina Press, 1985). No less shocking are the accounts of male doctors in Auschwitz: Miklos Nyiszli, *Auschwitz: A Doctor's Eyewitness Account* (New York: Fawcett Crest, 1960); and Robert Jay Lifton, *The Nazi Doctors: Medical Killing and the Psychology of Genocide* (New York: Basic Books, 1986).

13. Holocaust educators are fortunate to have the help of Carol Rittner and John K. Roth, whose recent work, *Different Voices: Women and the Holocaust* (New York: Paragon House, 1993), a marvelous collection of eyewitness accounts and analytical essays, has enriched our understanding of the unique experience of women in the Holocaust. Another important addition to the rapidly growing body of work by and about women during the Holocaust and the Nazi period is Alison Owings, *Frauen: German Women Recall the Third Reich* (New Brunswick, N.J.: Rutgers University Press, 1994).

14. Elie Wiesel, *Night,* trans. Stella Rodway (New York: Avon, 1966), p. 76.

15. Tadeusz Borowski, *This Way for the Gas, Ladies and Gentlemen* (New York: Penguin, 1976); Albert H. Friedlander, *Out of the Whirlwind* (New York: Schocken, 1976); Richard Rubenstein and John K. Roth, *Approaches to Auschwitz* (Atlanta: John Knox, 1987); and Keneally, *Schindler's List.*

16. Phillip Hallie, *Lest Innocent Blood Be Shed: The Story of the Village of Le Chambon and How Goodness Happened There* (New York: Harper and Row, 1979), p. 120.

17. Alexander Donat, *The Holocaust Kingdom* (New York: Schocken, 1965), pp. 62–63.

18. Christopher Browning, *Ordinary Men: Reserve Police Battalion 101 and the Final Solution in Poland* (New York: HarperCollins, 1992), p. 71.

19. Wiesel, *Night,* pp. 30, 40, 79.

20. George Steiner, *In Bluebeard's Castle: Some Notes towards the Redefinition of Culture* (New Haven, Conn.: Yale University Press, 1971), pp. 44–45.

21. Lawrence Langer, *Versions of Survival* (Albany: State University of New York Press, 1982), p. 72.

22. Rubenstein and Roth, *Approaches to Auschwitz,* esp. chap. 2.

23. Working as they did from documents, the first two postwar generations of historians gravitated toward the major source of documents: those captured from the Germans or developed by Allied and postwar governments as they sought to try German war criminals. It has taken much more painstaking work to assemble and analyze the documentary evidence left by victims and survivors. Indeed, historians have expanded their definition of documents to include graffiti, children's art, oral history, architectural drawings, and suitcases left on the Birkenau ramp.

24. Daniel Goldhagen, *Hitler's Willing Executioners: Ordinary Germans and The Holocaust* (New York: Knopf, 1996).

25. Ernst Klee, Willi Dreesen, and Volker Reiss, eds., *"The Good Old Days": The Holocaust as Seen by Its Perpetrators and Bystanders* (New York: Free Press, 1988). This is among the most graphic and disturbing books available on the Holocaust, a work made up entirely of field reports, letters, photographs, and diary entries by German soldiers, from enlisted men through senior officers. "This is a horrible book to read," says Lord Dacre of Glanton (Hugh Trevor-Roper) in the introduction. Excerpts will do; in its entirety, this book would surely provoke many students to drop the course.

26. The attention paid by scholars to perpetrators far outweighs that

paid to rescuers. In 1974, Yad Vashem sponsored an international conference on rescue, whose proceedings were published: Yisrael Gutman and Efraim Zuroff, eds., *Rescue Attempts during the Holocaust: Proceedings of the Second Yad Vashem International Historical Conference, April 1974* (Jerusalem: Yad Vashem, 1977). A number of the earliest works on rescuers remain classics: Hallie's *Lest Innocent Blood Be Shed*, Keneally's *Schindler's List*, along with Douglas K. Huneke, *The Moses of Rovno* (New York: Dodd, Mead, 1985); and Carol Rittner and Sondra Meyers, eds., *The Courage to Care: Rescuers of Jews in the Holocaust* (New York: New York University Press, 1986). More recently, scholars have turned with increasing interest to the question of rescue. Of these recent efforts, three stand out: Eric Silver, *The Book of the Just: The Unsung Heroes Who Rescued Jews from Hitler* (New York: Grove, 1992); Gay Block and Malka Ducker, eds., *Rescuers: Portraits of Moral Courage in the Holocaust* (New York: Holmes and Meier, 1992); and Eva Fogelman, *Conscience and Courage: Rescuers of Jews during the Holocaust* (New York: Anchor, 1994). For additional information on rescuers, see the essay by Lawrence Baron in this volume.

27. Particularly useful in developing the contrast between perpetrators, victims, bystanders, and to a degree rescuers is Raul Hilberg, *Perpetrators, Victims, Bystanders: The Jewish Catastrophe, 1933–1945* (New York: HarperCollins, 1992).

28. William Golding, *Lord of the Flies* (New York: Putnam, 1954).

29. Langer, *Versions of Survival*, pp. xi and 19.

30. Owen Barfield, *Saving the Appearances: A Study in Idolatry* (New York: Harcourt, Brace, 1965).

31. Morton Irving Seiden, *The Paradox of Hate* (South Brunswick, N.J.: Thomas Yoseloff, 1967), pp. 166–69.

32. For instance, see chap. 2 in Rubenstein and Roth's *Approaches to Auschwitz*.

33. Frank Kermode, *The Genesis of Secrecy: On the Interpretation of Narrative* (Cambridge, Mass.: Harvard University Press, 1979); and John G. Gager, *The Origins of Anti-semitism* (New York: Oxford University Press, 1983).

34. Kermode, *The Genesis of Secrecy*, p. xi, 2, 4, 18.

35. Ibid., pp. 64–65.

36. Gager, *The Origins of Anti-semitism*, pp. 198–99.

37. Ibid., p. 205.

Reuven Hammer, "Commemorations and the Holocaust"

1. Reuven Hammer, "Lessons of the Six Million," *The Torch* (Spring 1964): 5–7; "Not to Mourn Is Impossible," *Conservative Judaism* (Summer

1971): 46–50; and "Yom Hashoah: A New Holy Day," *United Synagogue Review* (Spring 1973): 8–9.

2. Rabbinical Assembly of Israel, *Seder Tefilot L'yom Hashoah Vehagevurah* ("Service for Holocaust Memorial Day"), (Jerusalem: The Masorti Movement, 1990).

3. See also Gen. 38:6–30 and Ruth 4:13–17.

4. Nathan M. Sarna, *Exploring Exodus: The Heritage of Biblical Israel* (New York: Schocken, 1986).

5. See, for example, Edward T. Linenthal, *Preserving Memory: The Struggle to Create America's Holocaust Museum* (New York: Viking, 1995).

6. For further information on these memorials, see such works as Sybil Milton, *In Fitting Memory: The Art and Politics of Holocaust Memorials* (Detroit: Wayne State University Press, 1991); James E. Young, *The Texture of Memory: Holocaust Memorials and Meaning* (New Haven, Conn.: Yale University Press, 1993); James E. Young, ed., *The Art of Memory: Holocaust Memorials in History* (New York: Prestel, 1994); and Geoffrey Hartman, ed., *Holocaust Remembrance: The Shapes of Memory* (Oxford: Blackwell, 1994).

7. Elie Wiesel, *Night* (New York: Hill and Wang, 1960); Emmanuel Ringelblum, *Notes from the Warsaw Ghetto* (New York: McGraw-Hill, 1958); John Hersey, *The Wall* (New York: Knopf, 1950); Chaim A. Kaplan, *Scroll of Agony: The Warsaw Diary of Chaim A. Kaplan* (New York: Macmillan, 1965); Hana Volavkova, ed., *I Never Saw Another Butterfly*, 2d ed. (New York: Schocken, 1978); M. Preger, ed., *Min Hametzar karati* (Jerusalem, 1954).

8. *Kol-Bekhiyot: Ha-Shoah Veha-tifilan* [Hebrew] (Ramat Gan: Bar-Ilan University, 1992).

9. See the essays by Michael R. Marrus, "Good History and Teaching the Holocaust," and Marshall Lee and Michael Steele, "The Affective Approach to the Interdisciplinary Holocaust Classroom," in this volume.

10. A. Roy Eckardt, *For Righteousness' Sake* (Bloomington: Indiana University Press, 1987), p. 216.

11. Franklin Littell, "The Future of Anti-Semitism," *Judaism* (Fall 1991): 511–20.

12. *Ha'aretz*, September 16, 1992.

13. Emil L. Fackenheim, *What Is Judaism?* (New York: Summit, 1987), p. 37.

Notes on Contributors

LAWRENCE BARON (Ph.D., University of Wisconsin) is the director of the Lipinsky Institute for Judaic Studies at San Diego State University. He is the co-editor of *Embracing the Other: Philosophical, Psychological, and Historical Perspectives on Altruism, Martin Buber and the Human Sciences,* and the author of numerous studies of rescuers in scholarly journals and edited volumes.

JUDITH TYDOR BAUMEL (Ph.D., Bar-Ilan University) teaches modern Jewish history at the University of Haifa and coordinates Holocaust studies at the Open University of Israel. The English edition of her latest book, *Kibbutz Buchenwald,* was published in 1997 by Rutgers University Press.

CHRISTOPHER R. BROWNING (Ph.D., University of Wisconsin) is professor of history at Pacific Lutheran University. Author of numerous important articles and books, including his seminal *Ordinary Men* (1992) and the incisive series of essays *The Path to Genocide* (1992), he is currently preparing *The Final Solution,* a volume in the Yad Vashem comprehensive history of the Holocaust.

JUDITH E. DONESON (Ph.D., Hebrew University) has taught courses on the Holocaust in film at Tel Aviv University and Washington University, St. Louis, as well as having worked on a filmed course of the contemporary Jewish world for the Institute of Contemporary Jewry at the Hebrew University. She has been a fellow at the Annenberg Institute for Jewish Research at the University of Pennsylvania. Doneson is the author of *The Holocaust in American Film* (1987), along with articles on the Holocaust in film and stereotypes of Jews in film appearing in such journals as *Holocaust and Genocide Studies* and *Studies in Contemporary Jewry.*

ALLAN FENIGSTEIN (Ph.D., University of Texas), is professor of psychology at Kenyon College, where he teaches an interdisciplinary course on the Holocaust. He is the author of a number of articles on self-consciousness appearing in such journals as the *Journal of Experimental Social Psychology, Journal of Personality and Social Psychology,* and *Journal of Personality.*

REUVEN HAMMER (Ph.D., Northwestern), the former dean of the Jerusalem branch of the Jewish Theological Seminary of America, is now on the faculty of the Seminary of Judaic Studies and the Hebrew University. His books include *Entering Jewish Prayer* (1994), *The Classic Midrash* (1995), and, as editor, *The Jerusalem Anthology: A Literary Guide* (1995).

DAN LAOR (Ph.D., Berkeley) is chairman of the Department of Hebrew Literature at Tel Aviv University. He has written and edited several books and numerous articles in the field of modern Hebrew literature. In recent years he has been involved in writing, teaching, and lecturing on Israeli Holocaust literature, for which he won the 1993 Buchman Prize awarded by Yad Vashem. His new book *The Life of S. Y. Agnon* was published in 1997 by Schocken Books in Israel.

MARSHALL LEE (Ph.D., University of Wisconsin) is professor and chair of history at Pacific University, where he has been teaching the the Holocaust since his arrival in 1974. He is the editor, with Wolfgang Michalka, of *Gustav Stresemann* (1982), and coauthor, with Michalka, of *German Foreign Policy, 1917–1933* (1987).

MICHAEL R. MARRUS (Ph.D., Berkeley) is professor of history at the University of Toronto. He has written extensively on the French-Jewish community and the Holocaust, including *Vichy France and the Jews* (with Robert Paxton, 1981), *The Unwanted: European Refugees in the Twentieth Century* (1985), and *The Holocaust in History* (1987).

DINA PORAT (Ph.D., Tel Aviv University) teaches in the Department of Jewish History and heads the Project for the Study of Antisemitism at Tel Aviv University. She is a member of the Yad Vashem Scientific Advisory Board and of its International Center for Holocaust Studies. Author of numerous articles on the Holocaust and antisemitism, she has also written *The Blue and the Yellow Stars of David* (1991) and edited the original Hebrew version of Avraham Tory's *Surviving the Holocaust: The Kovno Ghetto Diary* (1988) and provided the historical and textual notes for the English version (1991).

DONALD G. SCHILLING (Ph.D., University of Wisconsin) is professor of history at Denison University, where he regularly teaches a seminar on the Holocaust. His article "The Dead End of Demonizing: Dealing with the Perpetrators in Teaching the Holocaust" appears in *New Perspectives on the Holocaust* (1996). He is currently exploring the representation of the Holocaust in general histories of World War II.

MICHAEL STEELE (Ph.D., Michigan State University) is a Distinguished University Professor at Pacific University, where he has taught since 1975. Formerly president of the Oregon Holocaust Research Center, Steele published his book *Christianity, Tragedy, and Holocaust Literature* in 1995.

GERHARD L. WEINBERG (Ph.D., University of Chicago) is the William Rand Kenan, Jr. Professor of History at the University of North Carolina, Chapel Hill. Winner of numerous fellowships and awards, his many books and articles include the definitive study *The Foreign Policy of Hitler's Germany* (1970, 1980), the prizewinning *A World at Arms* (1994), and *Germany, Hitler, and World War II* (1995).